GW00357548

*This book is
part of the story of*

_____

JOSH SPERO has been the editor of *Spear's* magazine since 2010, covering everything from finance and philanthropy to art and luxury. He is also *Tatler's* art critic.

Before Spear's, he was at the *Independent* and has written for publications including *The Guardian*, *The Times*, *The Sunday Times* and the *Economist*. Before he was a journalist, he read Classics at Oxford.

SECOND-HAND
STORIES

☞

Josh Spero

For Owen,
The other half of
Team OJ (the less
murderous half).

Josh.

unbound

This edition first published in 2015

Unbound
4–7 Manchester Street, Marylebone, London W1U 2AE
www.unbound.co.uk

All rights reserved © Josh Spero, 2015

The right of Josh Spero to be identified as the author of this work
has been asserted in accordance with Section 77 of the Copyright,
Designs and Patents Act 1988. No part of this publication may be
copied, reproduced, stored in a retrieval system, or transmitted,
in any form or by any means without the prior permission of the
publisher, nor be otherwise circulated in any form of binding
or cover other than that in which it is published and without a
similar condition being imposed on the subsequent purchaser.

We are grateful to Anvil Press for permission to reproduce
extracts from Peter Levi's poetry and to his family for permission
to reproduce extracts from private correspondence

Typeset by Lindsay Nash
Art direction by Mecob

A CIP record for this book
is available from the British Library

ISBN 978-1-78352-124-1 (trade hbk)
ISBN 978-1-78352-168-5 (ebook)
ISBN 978-1-78352-125-8 (limited edition)

Printed in Great Britain

For my parents

Dear Reader,

The book you are holding came about in a rather different way to most others. It was funded directly by readers through a new website: Unbound.

Unbound is the creation of three writers. We started the company because we believed there had to be a better deal for both writers and readers. On the Unbound website, authors share the ideas for the books they want to write directly with readers. If enough of you support the book by pledging for it in advance, we produce a beautifully bound special subscribers' edition and distribute a regular edition and e-book wherever books are sold, in shops and online.

This new way of publishing is actually a very old idea (Samuel Johnson funded his dictionary this way). We're just using the internet to build each writer a network of patrons. Here, at the back of this book, you'll find the names of all the people who made it happen.

Publishing in this way means readers are no longer just passive consumers of the books they buy, and authors are free to write the books they really want. They get a much fairer return too – half the profits their books generate, rather than a tiny percentage of the cover price.

If you're not yet a subscriber, we hope that you'll want to join our publishing revolution and have your name listed in one of our books in the future. To get you started, here is a £5 discount on your first pledge. Just visit unbound.com, make your pledge and type Stories in the promo code box when you check out.

Thank you for your support,

Dan, Justin and John
Founders, Unbound

CONTENTS

Introduction   1

1. *Four Greek Authors*
   Rosh Pinah and University College School (1993–4)   9
   Leo Stevens (born 1981)   16

2. *Latin Prose Composition*
   University College School (2000–2)   29
   Sebastian Fernandez-Armesto (born 1982)   37

3. *Homer: Poet of the Iliad*
   Mods (2004)   55
   Emilie Vleminckx (born 1982)   59

4. Virgil: *Aeneid VIII*
   University Challenge (2003–4)   75
   Michael Brown (born 1942)   81

5. *The Latin Love Poets*
   Cherwell (2004–6)   101
   Mark Richards (born 1959)   106

6. *Introduction to Greek Verse Composition*
   Prose and Verse Composition (2002–4)   121
   Donald Russell (born 1920)   128

7. *The Odes of Pindar*
   Pindar (2004–6) and *The Times* (2004)   149
   Peter Levi (1931–2000)   154

8. *Thucydides*
   Thucydides (2004–6) and Dalston (2011)   207
   David Rundle (born 1929)   213

9. *A Commentary on Herodotus*
   Herodotus (2004–6) and Europe (2005)   221
   Tom Dunbabin (1911–55)   226

10. *Via Dell'Impero*
    Tutoring (2006–12)   265
    Belinda Dennis (1915–2003)   270

11. *Euthyphro/Apology of Socrates/Crito*
    James Naylor (1985–2009)   299

   Acknowledgements   311
   Notes on Research   313
   Notes   317
   Supporters   322

INTRODUCTION

*The history of countless places and objects which
themselves have no power of memory is never heard,
never described or passed on.*
W. G. SEBALD, *Austerlitz*

The concept of provenance, wondering where something
had been before it got to where it is, first struck me
when I started hanging around auction houses. The *Guardian* had accepted my pitch to report from behind the scenes
at Sotheby's during their June sales week in 2007, and the
experience was dazzling: champagne brunches populated
by overt millionaires and covert billionaires; suites of rooms
repainted overnight, ready for the next hang; and all that *art*,
multimillion-pound paintings that seemed to be unfinished,
canvases slashed through, cabinets of hand-painted cast-bronze pills sitting on razor-blade shelves. The head of the
press department loaded me down with catalogues which
described, evaluated and illustrated the art with commentaries
as erudite as academic articles and reproductions as hungry as
pornographic photo-shoots.

A key component of the account of each artwork was a
history of its ownership, which for Impressionist and Modern
pieces is vital: no auction house wants to be caught with looted
paintings, so they have to track them each step of the way.
This sculpture was given by the artist to a friend, whose heirs

sold it to a gallery, which sold it on to a well-known New York collector, who is now selling it so he can acquire more (subtext: expensive divorce). That ugly painting was uncovered in the cellar of a chateau, wrapped in brown paper and wholly unseen, a gift from the artist. And that work? Andy Warhol once glanced at it and made a catty comment. Not only did each step validate the work, it could also make it more valuable: to have a piece kept by the artist and then owned by several famous collectors would enhance its story.

It later occurred to me that while they might not be as expensive as paintings, books could also have a provenance – and I do not just mean those auctionable books, First Folios and Audubon's *Birds of America* and the like. Even the cheap paperbacks forgotten in crevices in second-hand bookstores must have had previous owners, and the books themselves often provide you with the owner's name (or owners' names), unlike paintings. The point was not that a book might have been owned by someone famous, but that it had a story of its own and the hands through which it had passed were themselves deserving of study.

That drove me to my bookshelves, in particular the greatest stock of second-hand books I had – my classics books from university and from the years I spent afterwards tutoring Latin and Greek, ancient texts of Plato and schoolboy guides to Homer – to see if anyone had inscribed their ownership. Off the shelves they all came, a few hundred of them surrounding me on my bedroom floor in crooked, uneven piles, until I wound up with a corpus of around fifty with individuals' or schools' names in them. This book, then, is the story of eleven of those books and the lives of the people who owned them before me.

In writing this book I decided to link these lives with my own, a stem of memoir for the petals and thorns of biography.

Some of the connections are made through the books – how its subject bore on my life, or how the book came into my possession or was (mis)used by me – and others through a rhyming, strong or faint, between my life and the owner's. The links are not all meant to be iron; nevertheless, I hope it seems as if both lives have glanced at and shed some illumination on one another.

When I started writing, the first Kindle had not been released. You could access out-of-copyright books on websites like Project Gutenberg and – of particular use to classicists – Perseus, with its texts in the original and their verbose Victorian translations. If you wanted a portable copy, you could print off the entire text, but at this point it was easier just to buy the real thing, and so we came back to books.

Until today, we had always come back to books and their antecedents, the physical objects. These books or scrolls or codices have survived generations, sometimes through care, sometimes through neglect. The ancient citizens of Oxyrhynchus in Egypt dumped their papyri in the communal rubbish tip and the local climate prevented them from mouldering away. Oxford classicists staged a nineteenth-century raid on the tip, and now twenty-first-century technology is allowing us to gaze on the lost works of antique writers. These books have *tales*. This is not to privilege the ancient and obscure, however; every book has a tale through its prolonged or peremptory association with its owner.

A good book in electronic format will still compel a reader, of course, but something is lost when we dematerialise the text – the human connection with the thing itself. This is sentiment, one can object. Yes, it is sentiment, but it is more than

that, too – it is making space for the book in your life, appreci-
ating the aesthetic and tactile qualities of print and paper and
binding, a physical experience in a number of dimensions. This
is not the argument of a fuddy-duddy classicist – as anyone
who has seen the alacrity with which I have taken to Twitter
would dolefully concede.

Sentiment should not be dismissed as an argument, either.
In the first place, people prize all kinds of objects that have
emotive connotations. Even the most inane knick-knack that
a parent has bought or a lover has given may be kept for far
longer than the purchaser intended. What value do we really
place on something that doesn't exist, where back-up copies
can be downloaded on to a new instantiation? If you are
reading this on an e-reader, please do not think I denigrate
the medium. Just consider whether this book will be possible
in a hundred years.

A nd so this book has several aims. One is to commemorate
and celebrate very specifically the lives of those who have
owned my books, from war heroes and poet-priests to actors,
teachers and students. The second is to make a stand for the
physical object – however tattered or smart, finely produced
or cheap – in the era of the digital. You can't sign your name
on your Kindle's copy of *Wuthering Heights*, and even if you
can pass it on, all you will leave is a digital vestige. My final
purpose, which is impossibly broad, is to make the reader pause
and consider their own books and objects and the lives of *their*
previous owners – to make them realise that even the lowliest
second-hand item carries with it the life and story of another,
and that our ownership of it makes us part of that life and story.

Josh Spero
April 2015

FOUR
GREEK AUTHORS

EXTRACTS FROM
HOMER, ANTIPHON, EURIPIDES
AND THUCYDIDES

EDITED WITH INTRODUCTION,
NOTES AND VOCABULARY BY
E. C. KENNEDY

Josh Spero
March 2008

4 00

FOUR GREEK AUTHORS

1565

Leo Stevens
5.1 MG

HIGHGATE SCHOOL

ROSH PINAH
and
UNIVERSITY COLLEGE SCHOOL
(1993–4)

In 1993, I was nine and attending Rosh Pinah, the local Jewish state primary in Edgware, north-west London, a small blue *kippah* skullcap clipped by requirement into my burgeoning Jewfro. Rosh Pinah provided both the benefits and the detriments of a religious education. Set against the deadly lessons in modern Hebrew, Zionist history and Bible stories were the feasts and festivals that occur with great frequency in Judaism. There were Purim parties, commemorating the saving of the Jews as told in the Book of Esther, which everyone attended in costume. I once went with a silver-foil axe and Cornflakes and Weetabix boxes stuck on to an apron, but my mother got told off because, apparently, coming as a serial killer was inappropriate. Hanukkah had the lighting of the nine-branched menorah to celebrate the rededication of the Temple in Jerusalem after the Maccabean Revolt. Pesach had the Seder, a long meal with a series of symbolic foodstuffs to tell the story of Exodus – horseradish for the bitterness of the Egyptian bondage, *charoset*, a paste of grated apple, chopped nuts, cinnamon and red wine, for the mortar the Jews used to build Pharaoh's treasuries. One festival – don't ask me which – involved joyous dancing in circles and trains in the hall to klezmery tunes and Levantine hullabaloo. At a ceremony

9

where parents presented their children with prayer books, then gravely shook their hands, my father high-fived me.

The lessons *were* deadly, full of fairy stories about biblical heroes. The non-religious classes weren't hard enough to distract me, which meant I was always acting up for attention. In English, a girl and I were allowed to slide through the graded readers to encounter more difficult stories of less familiar places. (Where on earth was 'Connecticut'? How did you even say it?) And though I certainly couldn't vocalise it like this, I could see that most of my school mates were already on the conveyor belt to the Jews' Free School, the nearest religious state secondary, and nothing beyond that that I wanted.

With time on my hands and glasses on my nose, I found challenge, or at least change, in books. (This is perhaps the appropriate moment to confess to my parents that I did not actually read *The Lord of the Rings* in a week at the age of seven.) At weekends I would go to Edgware's second-hand bookshop, a musty hole in the wall down the road from the salt-beef bar. Fruit-trays of paperbacks sat on trestle tables outside and I would search out half a dozen Hardy Boys books or *Alfred Hitchcock Mysteries*, tales of three boys who set up a detective agency in a junkyard. I knew Hitchcock as a kids' author (never mind that he never wrote the books) before I had ever seen one of his movies. The Hardy Boys appealed to me because of their adroit deductive skills and dashing abilities and distant Americanness, and because even back then I think I was a little in love with the preppy type of boy.

Whether it was because of my frustrated acting-out – I didn't burn the school down or anything – or because the teachers suggested it as a preventative measure, my parents

started looking for a private school for me so I could leave
Rosh Pinah a year early. We visited several schools that would
accept boys at ten, including the Junior Branch of University
College School in Hampstead and City of London School in
Blackfriars. What sticks in my mind most from those tours
are the ham sandwiches (*treif* – unkosher!) for tea in City's
refectory and deciding, following my mother's example, that I
liked two sugars in my coffee, even though I wasn't sure I liked
coffee. It felt...grown-up.

I sat the entrance exam for UCS in autumn 1993, refusing to wear my Casio calculator watch in case I was suspected
of cheating. One of my essays which was about a murderous
clown ended 'And then I woke up' – and I'm fairly sure that
in the general knowledge paper I wrote that Edmund Hillary
had brought potatoes to Britain. Nevertheless, they called me
for interview, and while my mother and I were walking down
the gleaming parquet corridor to the headmaster's office she
tripped up and landed with a thud. Cue the kindly headmaster,
Mr Hubbard, running out of his office. 'Mrs Spero, you must
take more water with it,' he said as he helped her up.

The day I got in, my mother stopped smoking. It wasn't
from shock but from necessity: the school fees would cost
my parents every spare pound and many thousands of un-spare
pounds over the next decade, and so my mother's tobacco habit
went. One thing that is not obvious about my mother, who is
funny and easy-going in society, is her iron will, kept for the
most private things – a juggernaut of her own spirit, biological
addiction to nicotine be damned, the cigarettes had to go. She
put out her desire in a second, as if extinguishing the flame of
a guilty match with one sharp breath.

The cigarettes were a symbol, albeit a financially insufficient one, so my mother went out to work. She had worked in retail administration in her twenties and had set up an au pair agency in her thirties, but I don't think she expected to have to take up work again, and certainly not for school fees. First was a job stacking light bulbs in the department store Fenwick's at Brent Cross. Brent Cross used to enchant me, with its vigorous central fountain under a high golden dome inlaid with a spiralling rainbow of glass, as if one of the architects of the shopping centre had been a Turkish sultan who wanted to bestow a touch of the Orient on Hendon. By the time I worked there at John Lewis, the ornate dome had been replaced by one of white metal and clear glass, beloved of the architecture of modern capitalism.

After Fenwick's, mum worked at an NHS doctors' surgery in Mill Hill for eight years under the tyranny of public-sector personalities, and then in 2005 moved to a private GP's practice, which has an elegance and quietness about it. The peace there is occasionally ruffled by the sound of money coughing.

University College School was founded as the feeder school to Jeremy Bentham's University College London, both on Gower Street in Bloomsbury, and it retained his strong free-thinking streak, while UCL retained his body (or, more correctly, his skeleton and clothes, padded out). As well as his utilitarian interests, Bentham was an enthusiast for the decriminalisation of homosexuality, which legacy was just as important to UCS as that of his liberalism. The liberalism saw UCS, which moved to Hampstead in 1907, become the first non-denominational school in the country – the godless college of Gower Street – and allowed a distinctively back-chatty streak to develop in the boys.

The Junior Branch, a later division, is hidden away on Holly Hill in Hampstead. Anyone who has visited what used to be called the Everyman cinema will have caught a glance of the long red-brick building, but otherwise it is unobtrusive, or at least forcibly discreet, behind high walls. Its corridors smelled of porridge and shoe polish and its classrooms were large and cold, sprung from an imposing late Edwardian architecture at odds with Rosh Pinah's suburban housing-estate feel. Break-times were concluded by the ringing of a hand-held bell rather than an electronic buzzer, and the boys played conkers and marbles, which would sound almost too twee to be true, had they not also played pogs, where you attacked small gaudy cardboard discs with a plastic slammer and got to keep those that landed face-up. A break-time occupation for me at Rosh Pinah had been playing kick-chase with the girls – kiss-chase being far too unchaste, and unappealing. There was no kiss-chase at UCS either.

It was almost as soon as I started at UCS, in September 1994, that I think I acquired my accent. 'Posh Josh' had been my nickname at Rosh Pinah, and I can believe at that age that I was a snob, even if culture for me was an insatiable diet of those mystery books. During lunch breaks, I had hung around with the dinner ladies, discussing current affairs (*had* Robert Maxwell thrown himself off his yacht?), a camp ersatz-adult – and not just because I wasn't interested in playing football with the boys and the girls wouldn't always have me. It was the company of grown-ups I sought, as my parents reminded me during an argument many years later – I wanted to sit with the grown-ups at dinner parties and offer whatever flitting opinion I could muster, rather than waste time with the children, who were not interested in how clever I thought I was and the range of topics I attempted to sound off about. (So what's changed, some would say.)

The Junior Branch proved more challenging in class. The lessons were harder and more interesting. There was French instead of Hebrew and dissections in the science lab instead of discussions about how many animals were on the Ark. My art teacher was a Hampstead Garden Suburb hippy who didn't mind us singing slightly naughty songs while we learned about complementary colours, and I had an abrasive Australian saxophone teacher who used to demand I practised my embouchure, a pursing of the lips around the mouthpiece – an expression that has served me well in moments of pique ever since.

But outside class, the challenge was all of the wrong kind. My un-humble attitude to my own academic achievements was hardly enchanting, and I still wanted to talk about the grown-up things I hadn't been able to at Rosh Pinah. It turns out ten-year-olds at private school aren't that interested in the Exchange Rate Mechanism, either. And I felt socially inferior, in two senses. First, I was outside the commune of boys who had been at UCS for several years already, boys tied by their history – a history of school plays, departed teachers, rugby matches – into a net, tauter the more one pushed at it. I was an arriviste, along with the three other new boys, who were respectively mousey, prickly and oily, and who seemed to find it as difficult to integrate as I did. The second sense was a mild embarrassment at my origins, hardly unique among schoolboys advanced beyond their parents' means, a slight if not negligible consequence of social mobility. I was from a semi in Edgware, a dismal and distant place, whereas the other boys seemed to occupy the golden plots of Hampstead Garden Suburb, where basketball hoops hung over flagstone terraces and a maternal Range Rover lined up next to a paternal Mercedes in the driveway. My dad drove a black cab, which from time to time would be covered in a gaudy livery – the numberless boxes of plasticky muffins that came with the Fabulous Bakin' Boys livery take some forgetting. While I was proud of him for being different from all the lawyerly fathers, he was a curio for my friends.

My isolation drove me to invert the social situation and within weeks I had acquired the Received Pronunciation notes that still slip out as I meet someone for the first time and graciously intone, like a dowager duchess, 'How do you do?' As a defence mechanism, it certainly worked. Added to my unlovable airs, it repelled all the other boys quite successfully for most of the rest of my school career. That isolation is something Leo Stevens entirely understood.

LEO STEVENS
(BORN 1981)

In 1981, in Finchley, a north-west London suburb that encompasses the detached in their detached houses as well as smaller, less prosperous ethnic communities, Leo Stevens was born to a Malay-Chinese nurse and an English physiotherapist. With a higher Chinese population than most parts of London, this was hardly unusual. Still, Leo felt uncomfortable: 'I think being Chinese mixed-race is different from being black mixed-race. Chinese people are almost invisible in a way.' Despite this alienation, or perhaps because of the comfort and familiarity of such alienation, it seems to me that Leo's life has been spent in pursuit of invisibility.

Leo first made himself unwillingly visible when he applied to two top private schools for entry at the age of eleven. He was at Summerside, a local state primary, but had never thought about going to Highgate or UCS until a teacher suggested he apply for scholarships there: 'Obviously I wouldn't be able to afford to go otherwise.' He says 'obviously', as if assuming that I assumed he was from a poor family. This defensiveness edging on brusqueness seems typical of him. There is a justifiable degree of reserve; after all, when a stranger calls and says he has one of your books and would like to talk to you, wariness is natural. But Leo is different: he is not occasionally wary, but generally reticent.

The UCS interview was far from a success, as Leo tells it: 'I never got in. Maybe it was the fact that I wore trainers to the interview and talked of my love for WWF wrestling that did it. I just didn't know what to expect, I hadn't been told.' He was caught in the paradox of anyone wanting to change their scene. There are codes and conventions one has to learn to win entrance to a new scene, yet they cannot be learned until one has entrance, or at least is told by people who have. The lack of the 'right' manners prevents one from ever discovering what the right manners are. Even so, still the defensiveness.

Leo got into Highgate, but never slotted in: 'I wasn't a middle-class person like the rest of them, I didn't fit into the Hampstead–Highgate boys. I wasn't very sporty, I liked listening to what I thought was good music, compared with the general rubbish. I didn't live in Hampstead Garden Suburb. Nobody else's parents were divorced at my school. I did feel like I had a lot less money.' When I asked him by email whether he interacted with UCS boys, who were theoretically – if agnostically – Highgate's local rivals, Leo is emphatic: 'No – I tried not to interact with people at my *own* school to be honest, and could never be bothered with UCS. A load of posh boys pretending to have some sort of rivalry over who had the worst uniform never bothered me.' If this sounds Bunterishly trivial, it reveals quite how shallow Leo thought his classmates were. But I don't think he ever confronted this, only confirmed it.

F*our Greek Authors*, a stubby orange paperback with crisp, thick white pages and freshly laid-out Greek text, came into Leo's possession when he was doing Greek GCSE (1995–7). The section he had to study from it was the contest of the bow from *Odyssey* XXI. Odysseus, by now the sole, ragged survivor of his storm-crashed wanderings, has been shown *xeinia* (hospitality) by the mysterious Phaeacians, who dine and entertain him, then convey him back to Ithaca, the island where he was king. In his two-decade-long absence – ten years at Troy, several more dodging the race of the Cyclopes and alluring, semi-divine females – a circle of suitors have been demanding that Odysseus' perspicacious wife Penelope marry them. Her dowry, naturally, is the kingdom. To escape notice, Odysseus in rags hides out with his swineherd and they pass the nights with meta-literature, telling *Odyssey*-like stories. Eventually he returns to the palace, still in rags, where the suitors mock and mistreat him, displaying a clear lack of the *xeinia* due to any guest, let alone the host whose substance they have consumed.

Penelope, her mind directed by the goddess Athene, challenges the suitors: whoever can string Odysseus' bow and fire it clean past twelve axes shall marry her. The suitors fail to string it and mock the beggar for even trying, but when he does it with proprietorial ease, they sense disaster. He shoots the arrow clean past the axes and the chapter ends with the murder of the suitors imminent.

Leo's book had to be returned at the end of his course, but it had captured him: the adventure; the human flavour of the epic drama; the unique language of 'Homer', a name associated with the wandering bards who forged the *Odyssey* over centuries, handing down versions to each other in an oral tradition. He enjoyed reading the original text rather than an abridged or simplified version, and his enthusiasm was stoked by his teacher, Mr Fotheringham, who guided him through the archaic infelicities of the language. At some point after Leo left, the book was sold by Highgate (or perhaps a student who failed to return it) to the Hellenic Bookservice in north London, a shop where unloved classics books look for new owners, like Battersea Dogs Home without the yapping.

Leo nearly didn't do his A-levels at Highgate. So little did he enjoy being there that he wanted to switch to nearby Woodhouse sixth-form college. Woodhouse, although academically successful, is a world away from Highgate School – perhaps a world closer to what Leo was comfortable with. Half of its students are from ethnic minorities, and it has a thousand students across the two years of A-levels (Highgate has two hundred). It does not date back four centuries, nor is it steeped in the skin-deep mystique of middle-class London. Everything that Leo ostensibly revolted against at Highgate would have been obviated at Woodhouse. But it was Latin, maths, physics and chemistry at Highgate instead.

His mother talked him out of leaving, just as, he says, she persuaded him to study law at university in 1999. At the time, he was unsure. Now, with a certain regret, he says he could have pursued classics or classical civilisations beyond school, and talks of re-reading his school set texts. It was 'the old Chinese thing' of entering a profession that motivated his mother, and there can be few children of immigrants who have not felt the same pressure. Why emigrate if not for your children to have a better – read, richer – life than you did?

He didn't enjoy his course at university either – in fact, he hated it – but people who read law frequently don't. 'It was all very academic, very theoretical. The theory of buying a house is very different from buying a house – then you do it.' Sheffield was another place Leo didn't feel he fitted in, although this time for the opposite reason: 'They thought I was posh!' He was a Londoner among those from the Midlands, and despite his private school background being unwanted, it still served to isolate him.

Leo completed his *de facto* rebellion by not taking the postgraduate course necessary to become a lawyer. Instead, he went into local government in October 2002, unchallenging and stable. Well, not always stable. 'I started off working in the housing benefits department. It wasn't very taxing but the people I worked with were fun. The first summer I was there we went out on strike for four weeks and the union paid our wages. It was four weeks of not going to work and pissing about.' A daily hour on the picket line sufficed for industrial action.

Uninspired by unmotivated and immobile colleagues who had been in their jobs since before he was born, Leo occupied several positions at Camden Council until he left in July 2008. As welfare rights adviser, he told council tenants what they were entitled to; as appeals officer, he made the decisions on entitlements and justified them in tribunals when they were disputed. Leo enjoyed the personal contact and became determined to help right the system in the interests of social justice. He talks with great passion – one of the few times in our conversation – about the pain and discomfort of those who have to survive on little money while they challenge decisions stopping them from claiming benefits: 'They invest a lot of emotion in it, they probably don't want to have to go up and sit in front of a lawyer and a doctor and explain what's wrong with them. It skewers the whole *Daily Mail* image – "These people are scroungers!" They're not at all.'

Progression meant managing people, not something Leo especially wanted, doubting his gregariousness, so he started studying for the legal practice course at night school in 2006.

It was not so much that his love of the law had been rekindled as a realisation that he wanted to change his career path, recognising that 'local government and career prospects don't go well together'. He applied to law firms in 2007 and started at Winckworth Sherwood in autumn 2008. His last year at the council was not easy, his colleagues' initial perception of him as a careerist having morphed into a silent jealousy at his escape from the numbing tendrils that clasped them. Now he works as a senior associate on the real estate desk of law firm Lewis Silkin.

Even in law, for Leo it is a case of so far but no further. While he was still at Winckworth Sherwood, he told me: 'I'm happy doing it at the moment, but I'm not sure I've got the stomach for being a partner, now that I've got a family. I can see a lot more now why people work for local authorities. My family time means far more to me than my work.'

When we met, his family consisted of his wife, whom he has asked me not to name, and baby Harry, born in November 2007. Since then he has had a second child. At the time, Leo was feeling his way around being a father and working through the issues that his own father had bequeathed to him.

After his parents divorced when he was six, Leo only saw his father for a few hours on Sundays, a dim influence on his childhood who flickered every so often until – one month before he died, suddenly, in 2007 – he cast a clear and unwelcome light. 'We went for dinner and he said he had an announcement. I had a fourteen-year-old half-brother, who I'd never met.' While it clarified his long absences, why visits to his house were forbidden, it left questions unanswered, questions ultimately rendered unanswerable by his death. His father said he had refrained from telling them because it would have upset Leo's mother, but Leo suspects his step-mother preferred to try and write her husband's first family out of their lives. He met his half-brother once and wrote him a letter to give him his contact details, but he heard nothing back, and does not seem too disturbed by this: 'He's related to me by blood, but I spent eighteen years not knowing him and I don't really like his mother and what she did to my family.'

Leo paints his father as a sixties radical who never quite got over it. As a child, Leo was embarrassed by his father's ponytail and his 'alternative' and 'esoteric' interests, like the anthroposophy books he found when clearing out his father's house. The 'spiritualist mumbo-jumbo' his father indulged in was in sharp contrast to his mother's pragmatism: 'All she was worried about was working and making sure we had enough and could pay the mortgage.' After his father left, his mater-nal grandmother moved to England from Malaysia to support them, living with (and later close by) her daughter, Leo and his brother for the many years – for Leo, an admirable and imitable family bond.

His father's legacy has been to inspire Leo to take the opposite path. 'My dad died when my wife was three or four months pregnant and it changed my attitude. I thought, I'm going to be everything he wasn't. That made me work a lot harder, be ambitious, be responsible, provide for the family. You could never rely on him.' There is an emotional incom-prehension in Leo's contemplation of what his father did: 'My father left when my brother was six months old. Having had a six-month-old baby, I think it would be the worst thing in the world to walk out on your wife then.'

He and his wife moved to 'glamorous Catford' in south London in 2006, three doors down from his in-laws, and they renovated the house – or, rather, his wife did. He assigns his impracticality to the tendency for his father's DIY efforts to end in breaking and swearing. He picks up the threads of his Greek by reading classical tales to Harry, 'in the hope that he is as interested in them as I am', although when we spoke by email he said that Harry 'was crawling around like a badger who has had too much sugar'.

One of my email questions, an ice-breaker, was about anything memorable that has happened to the previous owner of the book, and Leo said: 'Nothing particularly memorable has happened to me and I don't really have an overweening ambition to be successful or famous. I'm quite happy living a nondescript life with my family, cats and allotment, and so long as I've got enough to pay the bills and have the occasional treat, I'm happy.' What would he like to be remembered for? 'Being the best husband and father I could possibly have been.'

And it is now that Leo's solitude, so evident in his earlier life, finds its purpose. He no longer wants to be alone by himself, but alone with his family.

As I write, I like to think of Leo pushing his new baby around Nunhead's noble cemetery, one of his weekend pastimes – Odysseus at last returned home – solitary among the crumbled tombstones and crosses overgrown with weeds.

PUBLISHED BY BRISTOL CLASSICAL PRESS
GENERAL EDITOR: JOHN H. BETTS

These selections from Greek authors have been
carefully chosen to meet the requirements of
GCSE classes:

Homer: *Odyssey XXI* (The Contest of the Bow
     which only Odysseus can string)
Antiphon: Extracts from *Murder of Herodes*
Euripides: Scenes from *Ion*
Thucydides: Extracts from Books II & III (The
     Siege of Plataea).

The extracts are edited with individual introductions, comprehensive notes and vocabulary.

ISBN 1-85399-501-0

9 781853 995019

NORTH & HILLARD

LATIN PROSE
COMPOSITION

Duckworth

Fernández -Armesto MJA

Josh Spero
September 2007

LATIN PROSE COMPOSITION

UNIVERSITY COLLEGE SCHOOL
(2000–2)

My auto-isolated life at UCS did not continue in the manner to which I had become accustomed. My parents pointed out to me – very vocally, let's say – that my arrogant attitude had not won me any friends, and by the attrition of regular admonishments, I began to realise I did not have to be the pompous, haughty loner I had become. There was no problem at school, as such. I so wanted to be a grown-up and away from friendless teen-hood that I got on fine with the teachers. But I had alienated many people. Classics went some way to helping me redeem myself.

My Greek GCSE class had been small and there were only three of us in the AS-level set: me; Philip, an ugly-cute half-Greek skater-boy; and Ben, a louche, lanky bisexual American Goth who was not unfamiliar with categories A, B and C. In the sixth form, I could relax in a group that shared my interests, and I no longer felt all I had to offer was my patent rightness about everything. In a close set, I could also be myself more. Ben and Phil were two of the first people I told I was gay. (Another boy found out when we kissed in the fives courts.) I relaxed. I was *nicer*. They were not like the Jew Crew I had failed to crack, a wealthy, bitchy clique with their unattainable nights out. I recall my mother once yelling, in a desperate attempt to get me to go out, 'We'll *give* you the money if you want to go to China White with them!' I don't think they knew what China White was, nor am I sure I did, nor would they have approved if they *had* known, nor did I really have any idea how a sprawl of pasty but expensively dressed fifteen-year-olds would get in. It didn't take me long to work out that that was never going to be my milieu, and no loss for it.

Ben and Phil and their group of friends were liberal and heterogeneous. There was Diana, by her own description a 'big black bitch'. There were evenings at Heaven and G-A-Y when I told my parents I was at the Funkin' Pussy, some straight club I had never set foot in but on whose decor and music I could elaborate masterfully. The sticky floors of G-A-Y, however, and its 2 a.m. pop acts (Atomic Kitten! Westlife! *Scream!*) and the occasional handjob by the bar I was more than familiar with. Afterwards, we'd get back to Ben's in West Hampstead, which stank sweetly of marijuana, or 'draw' as we called it then, which his mother smoked for her MS – and Ben for his recreation – then ransack the fridge, play poker with naked-men cards and pan-sexually pile into bed together. To sleep, of course.

The days at school were almost as much fun, I can say, without fearing any loss of a cool I never had. First, the atmosphere was lightened now that I had knocked off my gravitas. But second, even sixteen periods of Latin and Greek a week were hardly sufficient for my unbound enthusiasm. I chewed up pages of Euripides and Homer and Ovid and Cicero. I took in points of grammar as fast as they were offered, as enticing as they were initially impenetrable, figuring out why a passive would be impersonal and why a gerundive attractive. Why did Caesar and Pompey come to fight in the Civil War? What were the mystical connotations of Vergil's Sybil who leads Aeneas into the Underworld? Mr Hyde, our wonderful, wry teacher, somewhat hippopotamian around the face – friendly jowls with a crunching jaw – gave me a scholarly article to read on ambiguity in the *Oedipus Rex* and I instantly became a structuralist. As I strutted around the refectory during one break, my copy of *Structuralism and Post-structuralism for Beginners* jutting out under my arm, my form teacher, Mr Plow, offered me one of his acidic dismissals that hid the hint of a compliment: 'Ah, Spero, always thirty years late to the party.' I took from that that it was impressive I had managed to find the party at all.

There was for the first time licit voracity and hours to indulge it. Our form room, which was also Mr Hyde's classroom, was one of the last unreconstructed rooms in the central school building. The parquet floors were worn down past their varnish, showing blond meat and blond splinters, while the paintwork had probably once been forest-green but was now over-boiled asparagus. (One of the Emperor Augustus' favourite sayings was 'as quick as boiled asparagus', as viewers of *I, Claudius* will know.) Large maps of the ancient world, hinting at the potential breadth of the subject, hung high around, and stuck on the walls were photocopied items from *The Times* on a faked history of Roman football or how a cheap copy of Horace could usefully serve in the absence of toilet paper. I adored this patchwork of easily digestible factoids, and such absorption in the extraneous would in later years bear an outsize reward.

The bookshelves, whose contents were as much Mr Hyde's as the school's, unveiled new authors to me as I curiously slid out this volume and that. A small corner office contained past exam papers and a fragment of a preserved papyrus from Vindolanda, the Roman fort by Hadrian's Wall, which, if I remember rightly, was part of a letter about some cakes. There was no thin blue carpeting or overhead digital projector as had invaded most of the other classrooms. It was the perfect classroom for a bunch of classical hold-outs who saw themselves as set apart from the modernity – thus, conformity – of everyone else. I think classicists always feel like this, even as we strive to demonstrate quite how relevant the subject still is.

The peak of geekdom arrived when I set up GAS: the Greek Appreciation Society. UCS had not had a classics society for a long time and so I reincarnated it to invite dons to give talks. Most would do it for their train fare and UCS's surprisingly good lunches – how many other schools serve canapés to their students? On a speaker day, I ate at the teachers' table with the guest, which probably didn't do much for my modesty but gave me a great chance to engage with them as I wanted, hungrier much more for the intellectual stimulation and the glimpse of life beyond UCS than for the cheese plate. Some of the best dons of the day came down to Hampstead. First was Oliver Taplin of Magdalen College, Oxford, talking about Homer. A couple of well-wishers have occasionally remarked that, as Magdalen was where I ended up studying, I needn't have bothered with any speakers after him.

Despite Oliver's appearance at GAS, I hadn't given applying to Oxford much thought by the start of my A-levels. I was, in fact, invited up by another speaker, Llewelyn Morgan of Brasenose College. Mr Hyde gave me a brief alliterative list of colleges to look round: Magdalen and Merton, Brasenose and Balliol, Corpus Christi and Christ Church. Some people claim it is the tutors, others the honeyed stonework, others still the deer park (do me a favour), but I chose Magdalen for no reason I can specify.

The interview process, a pleasant, stressful few days in Oxford in December, when the cloisters darken at three and your apprehensive comments materialise in the freezing air, was a combination of the fraternal and fratricidal as you got to know the others who were applying. Some current students stayed up after term to help out with interviews, making sure applicants knew where they were supposed to be and when, offering useful words to the confident and the crushed, the nervous and the over-expectant. I was staying in 71 High Street, a grim-green college building 'outside walls' above two shops that sold board games and knick-knacks and god knows what, and on my first night I woke up every half-hour as the Oxford Tube – oddly enough, a coach service – thundered past. Ned, who had become a good friend after I struck up a conversation with him while we were both looking in the same window of Waterstones in Hampstead, was already up at Oxford and bought me coffee in the Queen's Lane Coffee House. As was typical of Oxford, even this gaudy caff had a history of four centuries.

The interview itself was prefaced by a translation test, which I used when I was later tutoring and it came to interview time, if mainly to point out that the more recent ones were easier. Before the interview, which was held in Oliver Taplin's room, we had to wait upstairs in Andrew Hobson's living/teaching room. Andrew was the university's *Grammatikos*, its senior classical languages tutor, and Magdalen's resident linguistic specialist. His room, pale blue and with inviting sofas, was cold, liquid with quiet panic.

Downstairs, in Oliver's room, were arrayed Oliver, Mark Pobjoy, the college's ancient historian, and Amber Carpenter, a philosophy don, all across a table from me. Things started badly when Oliver wanted to discuss Homer, about whom I knew little, and I asked whether we could talk about tragedy instead. Off we went on the *Bacchae*, Euripides' play of dionysiac mania and filicide, and its contrast between the uptight city and the orgiastic countryside. Mark moved us on to Vergil – much safer ground, as I had studied *Aeneid* VI, one chapter in his poem of the foundation of Rome which tells the story of Aeneas' flight from Troy, his misadventures on the way to Italy and his war there for a local princess who will give birth to a dynasty that will eventually include Romulus and Remus. In Book VI, Aeneas goes into the Underworld (which I imagined as a blanket of green fields under a glossy black sky), where he sees all manner of fabulous beasts and legendary sinners and lost souls, and gets some rousing nationalistic prophecies from the shade of his dead father. And they say Jewish mothers never let go.

Finally, Amber took her turn: 'You wrote on your personal statement that you're a fan of Dorothy Parker.' Hmm. Where was this leading? 'Can you tell us her famous anecdote?' Which one? My teenage obsession with Parker had slightly receded by now, so I was damned if I could pick one anecdote out of a life composed of them. 'The one about horticulture.' Right. 'When asked to make a sentence using the word "horticulture", Dorothy Parker replied, "You can take a horticulture but you cannot make her think."' Laughter. Relief. And then Amber Carpenter again, serious: 'So, is this true?'

I got through an answer about notable classical courtesans – Aspasia was the remunerated consort of Athens' fifth-century leader Pericles and supposedly a shrewd politician herself – but as I spoke I realised I had had a close escape. Also on my personal statement I had written that I was a fan of the films of Jean Cocteau (I know, I know), and indeed I had been enchanted by *La Belle et la Bête*, which I had seen with Ned – but that was the only one I knew. Had Amber looked two lines lower, I would have been screwed.

In my final year at UCS, H. J. K. Usher, the former head of classics, died. A memorial service was organised and a prize set up in his name. As the first recipient, I was asked to read out his favourite ode of Horace in Latin at the service. Although all the talk of his 'bachelorhood' had thoroughly wound me up during the service – I did understand that being gay in that era was not easy, even with UCS's San Franciscan levels of tolerance – I was moved when I intoned the lines of poem seven from Book IV of the *Odes*, which contrasts the annual return of spring after winter with man's one and only death:

> *Diffugere niues, redeunt iam gramina campis*
> *arboribusque comae;*
> *mutat terra uices et decrescentia ripas*
> *flumina praetereunt;*
> *Gratia cum Nymphis geminisque sororibus audet*
> *ducere nuda choros.*
> *Immortalia ne speres, monet annus et almum*
> *quae rapit hora diem…*

The snow has vanished, already the grass returns
    to the fields,
and the leaves to the branches:
earth alters its state, and the slackening rivers
slide past their banks:
the Grace, with the Nymphs and both of her

> sisters, is daring,
> leading her dancers, naked.
> The year, and the hour that snatches the kindly
> day away, warn you:
> don't hope for undying things…

The poem ends with the image of the mighty hero Theseus unable to rescue his friend, perhaps boyfriend, Pirithous, from Hades. Perhaps this had spoken to Usher.

Incidentally, '*speres*' in line seven comes from the verb '*spero*' – 'I hope'. I think this explains a lot.

SEBASTIAN FERNANDEZ-ARMESTO
(BORN 1982)

There seemed a certain providence – or at least a complex chain of individually explicable yet altogether unfathomable steps – when I bought a second-hand copy of North & Hillard's *Latin Prose Composition* once owned by someone who had also been to UCS and to Magdalen. I was browsing round the basement of Quinto, on the corner of Charing Cross Road and Great Newport Street, whose upstairs was stygian, with ceiling-height bookcases looming over narrow gangways, and whose lower floor was fluorescent in the manner of a newly completed bomb shelter, with a similar series of capsular rooms. (Quinto has now been replaced by Patisserie Valerie as part of that general commercial movement in London from mental wealth to dietetic poverty.) North & Hillard's book, on the rules of turning English into Latin, is not as good as their Victorian competitors' attempts, but I bought it for the sake of completeness.

The name on the first page, written in an assertive, even nonchalant hand, was 'Fernández-Armesto MSA', which rang a bell – a historian, I thought, who had come up during my A-levels because he had written about early modern Spain – Ferdinand, Isabella and the like. Once I jammed his name into Google, our unlikely educational identity was uncovered. I cajoled a friend from university into giving me the email address of the professor's son, a friend of *his* from Eton, who then gave me his father's. Felipe Fernández-Armesto and I had spoken intermittently while I concentrated on other chapters, but eventually we agreed to meet during the semester he spends teaching students from the US university of Notre Dame in London. He is an omnivorous historian. On the Notre Dame website, it lists his special areas of research as 'Atlantic; Early America; Early Modern Europe; Environmental; Global; Imperial; Intellectual; Latin America; Mediterranean; Urban.' Quite what this leaves out is unclear.

His books – available in twenty-six languages – bear witness to this range. *1492: The Year Our World Began* follows voyagers – not just that sailor to the New World, but Muslims spreading through Africa, Jews fleeing Spain, Russians thundering westwards. If the claim is grand and never quite proved, the book had, for me, a much more interesting reading as a post-9/11 narrative, a history of religious extremism and a mirror to religious persecution – a plea for tolerance, too. There is no shyness in his subjects: *The Americas: The History of a Hemisphere*; *Civilizations*, which analyses how every kind of landscape has affected human settlements throughout history; *Millennium: A History of Our Last Thousand Years*; *So You Think You're Human?: A Brief History of Humankind*; and, perhaps inevitably, *The World: A History*. His next book, he told me as we sat in the pale yellow senior common room of Notre Dame's London campus just off Trafalgar Square, will cover something greater than any of his previous works, which can only suggest that the Almighty has consented to grant him an interview – or vice versa.

Professor Fernández-Armesto had already been more than cooperative by the time we met, returning my initial questions about his book with full answers about why he used it, when he got rid of it and what his book-collecting habits were. I had also been busy reading his books and reminding myself about the occasion he had been arrested and brutally mistreated by the police for jaywalking in Atlanta. 'The misadventure was, in retrospect, enriching for a middle-aged bourgeois professor of impeccable habits and fastidious tastes,' he wrote to me. 'My visceral liberalism is now backed by experience.'

He offered me tea and we sat across a luminously pol-ished low table. A cleaning lady pottered around by the coffee machine. I was, if I'm honest, at a loss as to what I should ask the professor about his book – his answers to my questionnaire had covered it fully and elegantly.

Q: How did you come to use/acquire this book?
A: It was one of those maddening school textbooks that pupils have to buy and then find that they use them so sporadically – owing to teachers' indolent habits or idiosyncratic tastes – that the cost seems a waste. I was educated – if you can call it that – at University College School, where I was part of what must have been just about the last generation of schoolboys to do more Latin than anything else...
Q: Please describe the role this book played in your studies/intellectual life.
A: I had many years of sometimes sound, sometimes inspiring teaching in Latin, and was already pretty good at prose composition by the time N&H came into my life. But although I'm not sure it contributed much to my Latin – we translated some passages, and I expect the evidence of how many will appear in annotations and interlineations I left in the book – I soon came to

find it intriguing as an historical document and literary
text...

I decided to show him the book – with some of the people
I've interviewed, handling the book has suggested memories
as effectively and involuntarily as a scent. Although even the
meanest classics book is pricey, it looked like a cheap paperback – no artwork on the thin scratched blue covers except
for the malevolent duck of the publishers, Duckworth; page
corners curling and creeping forwards.

The professor contemplated it for a second. 'No – this was
not my copy. No, not this one.'

Pardon?

'I did have a copy but it wasn't this one,' he said. 'It's probably my son's.'

Ah.

To: Seb Armesto
From: Josh Spero
Subject: Full circle

Dear Seb,
Quite a few years ago now, I emailed you and asked
for your father's email address, which you very
kindly gave me, for a book I'm working on. I had
written most of the other chapters when I decided
to try and meet your father, whose book I thought
I had, and yesterday we finally met – only for him
to say that the book was yours! If you are willing, I
would like to meet and talk to you.
Best wishes,
Josh

To: Josh Spero
From: Seb Armesto
Subject: Re: Full circle

Of course Josh. I'd be happy to help but I won't be
as good copy as my father. Let me know a few dates
that suit you and we'll convene.
Best,
Seb

O ne mystery was cleared up quickly when we met to
talk at the Hospital Club in Covent Garden. What I
had read as 'Fernández-Armesto MSA' in North & Hillard,
assuming the suffix was some sort of professional society,
was in fact 'Fernández-Armesto MJA', Seb's house at Eton.
After school, for professional purposes as an actor, Sebastian Fernández-Armesto became the more approachable Seb
Armesto, which name has seen him through the screen, the
stage and the page.

Eton, perhaps surprisingly, has produced rather a few good
actors in recent generations – Eddie Redmayne, Tom Hid-
dlestone, Damian Lewis, Harry Lloyd – and Seb is keen to
credit it. His drama teacher, Mr Dormandy, stoked his interest by taking his class to the theatre in 'exciting places', he
says enthusiastically. 'He took us to see a play by Complicité
– it was a revival of their first production called *A Minute Too
Late*. I remember watching it and I had never really thought
of [acting] as something you could learn or do, and I think
that was when I made up my mind that I was going to go to
drama school…I reckon before then I'd always just been going
on stage and just *pretending*, which is great, what it's all about,

but watching that I realised there was stuff you could improve on and learn.' It was also for lack of better options: 'I wasn't very good at anything else – I'm not very good at acting!' he says with jolly despair, or bouncing resignation. 'I didn't have any other options so that's when I think I made up my mind.'

He was not an unsuccessful actor at Eton. He played Faustus, Sir Anthony Absolute in *The Rivals*, Talbot in *Henry VI*, Willy Loman, Dromio of Syracuse. He also wrote and directed his own short plays for school festivals. But he did not get into RADA or LAMDA, instead ending up at a down-at-heel school in a South Kensington townhouse, Webber Douglas, which he makes sound Dickensian in squalor and charm: 'The school's theatre was called the Chanticleer Theatre and it was a bit of a fleapit. I remember stuck into the wall of the proscenium arch was half an onion that had just been painted over – crammed into the brickwork and painted over. I'm pretty sure it was structural. The whole building was like that – it was falling down, in disrepair, nothing worked. Mostly the students!' Again, the jolly despair.

Armesto can identify a certain genetic – or at least cultural – strain of acting in his family. He says his mother is good at accents and his father's lectures are 'an extravagant perform-ance'. 'When he was at Queen Mary, he played Le Beau and William the Yokel in *As You Like It*, in a student-teacher collaboration and his performance was…big and a large slice of ham, but the audience found it very effective.' He and his father share a remarkable voice – smartly louche, a little chewy, with the sort of *o*'s Katharine Hepburn would have recognised. Even as he talks of his parents being supportive of his choice to go to drama school, he says that he regrets not having gone to university – something to fall back on.

Although he was not supposed to work professionally during his three years at Webber Douglas, he went up to Edinburgh for the Fringe (which perhaps leaves 'professionally' untouched), sleeping in cupboards and doing three shows a day into illness. 'Unfortunately Edinburgh has partly gone into a blur and I've partly kicked it out of my mind because it's such an annoying place to be. It's so crowded and disgusting and you always end up getting ill and you're in these dank venues that are filled with urine and drunk Scotsmen. I used to do an improvised comedy show for three years with some Brits and then some Americans, and we did it usually around 11.30, twelve o'clock at night and it was – horrible.' Was he funny? 'Very rarely. Very, very rarely.'

Work has been regular but sparing since, and when he talks of being lucky to work he sounds like he believes it, a particular sincerity most actors never manage to conquer. In his case, I believe he does believe it. He is open about his disappointments with the industry and with himself: 'When I left drama school I had such grand ambitions and such integrity and I thought I was going to change the world and be devastating and brilliant – and the gulf between conception and reality ends up always being so vast. In fact, the job is so unlike what I thought it would be.' The trudge and struggle of auditions – sometimes creating a character from two pages of script with twenty-four hours' notice – throw him off, and he says he is nervous, inarticulate and unsure of himself at the first hurdle. 'It's a very difficult process and it's very unlike the next part which is entirely geared towards relaxing and getting the best possible work. It's about pressure and speed.'

When we meet, he has just flown back from LA after auditioning for the lead role in a new TV series. The experience sounds like a cross between the venality of *The Player* and the absurdity of *Curb Your Enthusiasm*. 'It's quite a frustrating process. They showed me into a tiny little room, five by five, and there were seven men in suits there and they'd been in there a while. The atmosphere was *sweaty*. It was in the dark and up at one end there was a very bright light shining on a chair which they showed me up to, and the whole thing felt like pornography in some ways. There was a large plasma screen over on the side wall and I was reading with the casting director, who's quite a large, masculine American man and wears sunglasses and who was playing the part of the love interest. At any stage in plays or films you're going to have to suspend disbelief because there's a camera or sixty crew, but I felt there was quite a lot of suspension of disbelief having to be achieved in this test.

'I could vaguely see my stupid head waving around on this screen in the background and I did it and I was very disappointed in myself because I didn't do a very good job, not because of the environment but because I wasn't on top of it – and I left.' He didn't get the part because he wasn't clean-cut enough for American TV, they told him, because he was too 'emotionally tortured'. Given that the series was about a young man being chased by supernatural demons while avenging his Illuminatus father who was trying to kill a US senator because said senator was in fact the Antichrist, 'I thought they wanted emotionally tortured.'

Even when he's telling an anecdote as bizarre as this, there is a precipitous resignation underlying Armesto's cheeriest tone. Perhaps it is the confronting fact of his recent rejection. Perhaps not.

It would be unfair to pass judgment on his acting skills because in most of his performances that I have watched he has not had the chance to exercise their full range. Indeed, he has already been typecast as, tragically, an Etonian. In *The Palace* (2008), a terrible ITV drama about an unexpected succession to the throne, he plays Prince George, the playboy brother of the new king – all he is required to do is look like he's loving it or is miserably hungover. He is a perfectly fluty, floppy Edmund Sparkler, son of the leopard Mrs Merdle, in the terrific BBC adaptation of *Little Dorrit*. He is in love with Amy Dorrit's dancer sister, Fanny, who repeatedly rejects him, only stoking his puppyish ardour all the more, then marries him to punish his mother. Every so often he ejaculates, 'She's a deuced fine girl!' or 'A damned fine woman with no begod nonsense about her!' and looks as if he may pass out from enthusiasm. Given that most of his roles force him to be chinless, it is ironic that in *The Tudors* (2007) he played Charles V with a Hapsburg chin so large Boris Karloff would have had jaw envy. Jonathan Rhys Meyer's Henry VIII – so handsome that the six marriages make perfect sense – gets to remark that there is nothing 'not to like about Charles…apart from the chin'.

It is not just the small screen that forced Armesto into a velvet straitjacket. Sofia Coppola cast him as Comte Louis de Provence, Louis XVI's brother, in her *Marie Antoinette* (2006), which has been denigrated for imagining the queen as an immature American teenager frolicking amid a rainbow of shoes and cakes at Versailles, and for using punk rock on the soundtrack. (Any film in which Rip Torn plays Louis XV is asking for trouble.) It works better when considered as video art than as a feature film. Its lavish tableaux of card games and parties and parterres, minimal script of snatched phrases and dissolute, unmoored characters are much more evocative of royal *anomie* than if Kirsten Dunst had had to offer well-researched opinions about the American Revolution or the scarcity of French flour. Armesto gets to party, pose languorously in the dawn sun and drag his tuneless wife off to bed, as she serenades a soirée, with the gallant words, 'Madame, shall we retire to make love all night?' which kills two songbirds with one stone.

The filming was as much of a party as the filmed. Because it was actually shot on location – indeed, Versailles is almost the only set, evoking the court's hermetic, hallucinatory carnival which only existed with reference to itself – French rules applied on set. 'They insist on a three-course meal at lunchtime and you have to serve wine and beer otherwise they won't work after lunch. It was the most amazing catering because normally you go and the catering is a bit of fried bread and an egg, and this was *delightful* celeriac remoulade and steak cooked to your choice.' The party scenes were no hardship either: 'They gave us real champagne. They'd struck a deal with Dom Perignon so there was Dom Perignon on tap, which was anachronistic but it didn't matter…There were all these cakes, so it was kind of like being at a very strange children's birthday party, with maybe Rip Torn as Smartie Artie.'

A subsequent film was *Anonymous* (2011), a Roland Emmerich picture that claimed that Shakespeare did not write Shakespeare but was a front-man for a plot involving incest and Elizabeth I. Armesto plays a vaguely foppish Ben Jonson, who subcontracts the specious role of playwright to Shakespeare, an illiterate rube interested in writing only as far as it can lead to rutting. A clever touch among the far-fetched plot points is having Vanessa Redgrave play the elderly

Elizabeth and her daughter, Joely Richardson, the young queen. At least the film helps solve one question of authorship – if an infinite number of monkeys wrote at typewriters for an infinite number of years, they wouldn't produce the works of Shakespeare, they'd write *Anonymous*.

As well as featuring in two plays at the National Theatre, Armesto has written his own, 'although I wouldn't call it writing. I know other young playwrights and they're writers – I'm not that. The plays I've done, I've normally sat in rooms with actors, played about with them and got them to do stuff and stolen from them. There's always a stage where you're sat down in front of a computer screen hating yourself, and hating everything around you, much like Latin prose composition actually.' He picks up North & Hillard, flicks its corners and turns it over and over. Given its age, it was probably second-hand when he acquired it for Latin A-level, and it went in a clear-out of his family flat's books. 'You sit in front of it and think, "I've got to translate this *wretched* piece of prose into Latin" – that's not dissimilar to what it's like writing the plays I've written. You're sitting in front of a collection of wretched notes that are chaos and boring and dull and you've got to make something out of it. You've got the kernel of what you need, but you need to put it into the language that's required.'

His plays have been put on at the respected avant-garde Arcola Theatre in Dalston, but he makes them sound not like a career path so much as lacunal occupations. This is a shame, because the version of *Moby-Dick* that Seb wrote, directed and adapted with his company, simple8, for the Arcola was economical, thrilling and profound. In streamlining Melville's million words into a two-hour eight-hander, you'd think there'd be no room for depth – either maritime or metaphysical – but into Captain Ahab's manic pursuit of the whale Seb wove fine philosophical threads. It was a wonderful achievement, but Seb, it seemed to me, received my praiseful email with something akin to pained modesty.

Just before we finished our interview, concluding with some gossip about our mutual friend, I decided to ask how Seb felt about the stellar success of his contemporaries at Eton – whether he thought their careers should have been his. I had been turning this over since early on in our interview, but I was in two minds. I thought that more was to be gained in insight than would be lost in the question's cruelty. Seb's deflation and ingenuous struggle at a generous answer showed that I had judged it wrong. He wasn't at all begrudging – his nature is much too sadly sweet for him to have been a pincushion of jealousy – but the question fixed him awkwardly, impossibly. I regret asking it.

Sebastian Armesto rests his legs in his drama school's
production of *The Man Who Came to Dinner.*

paperduck

Latin Prose Composition
North and Hillard

North and Hillard's LATIN PROSE COMPOSITION, which is a grade above Hillard and Botting's *Elementary Latin Exercises*, has for long been the standard middle school textbook. All common words and constructions are included. Special vocabularies are given for each exercise at the end of the book, together with rules for the order of words, lists of synonyms and prepositional phrases, and a military and complete general vocabulary.

Abbott & Mansfield
A PRIMER OF GREEK GRAMMAR

John Usher
AN OUTLINE OF GREEK ACCIDENCE

Hillard & Botting
ELEMENTARY GREEK EXERCISES
ELEMENTARY LATIN EXERCISES
ELEMENTARY GREEK TRANSLATION
ELEMENTARY LATIN TRANSLATION

North & Hillard
GREEK PROSE COMPOSITION
LATIN PROSE COMPOSITION
KEY TO GREEK PROSE COMPOSITION
KEY TO LATIN PROSE COMPOSITION

A. Sidgwick
SIDGWICK'S GREEK PROSE COMPOSITION

Sidgwick & Morice
GREEK VERSE COMPOSITION

H. W. Auden
GREEK PHRASE BOOK

C. Meissner
LATIN PHRASE BOOK

Duckworth
The Old Piano Factory
Gloucester Crescent, London NW1

ISBN 0 7156 1322 7
IN UK ONLY £5.95 NET

Homer

Poet of
the
Iliad

Mark W. Edwards

Emilie Vlemincx

2/03   Wadham College

Homer

Poet of
the
Iliad

MODS
(2004)

The rumour went that the suite of exams an Oxford classicist meets in their fifth term, Honour Moderations (or the seemingly friendlier 'Mods'), was in the Guinness Book of World Records for being the hardest set in the world. Others said it was second only to those one takes to join the Chinese civil service. Either way, this story was part of the undergraduate's arsenal of terror, used to oppress your classmate-competitors and to comfort, provoke or fortify yourself. It was an execution with eleven blows of the axe – twelve if you could hack it. My perversity took, of course, me to twelve.

I. HOMER, *Iliad* (translations from and essays on the poem, which covers five days in the Trojan War, climaxing with the death of Hector at Achilles' hands)
II. VIRGIL, *Aeneid* (the same on Virgil's version of Aeneas' escape from Troy and eventual settlement in Italy)
III. GREEK AUTHORS (translations from four set books)
IV. LATIN AUTHORS (ditto)
V. SPECIAL SUBJECT I: PLATO (another choice in philosophy was Introduction to Logic, which I could no more do than chew my arm off)

VI. SPECIAL SUBJECT II: HISTORICAL LINGUISTICS
AND COMPARATIVE PHILOLOGY (tracing words back
to Proto-Indo-European, the language from which
most European and many other tongues today descend
– think of Latin *pater*, Sanskrit *pitar*, German *vater*,
and English *father*)
VII. GENERAL PAPER (four essays on the books set in
papers III and IV)
VIII. UNPREPARED TRANSLATION FROM GREEK
IX. UNPREPARED TRANSLATION FROM LATIN
X. GREEK LANGUAGE (English prose into Greek)
XI. LATIN LANGUAGE (English prose into Latin)
XII. (Optional Paper) VERSE COMPOSITION OR
ADDITIONAL TRANSLATION

Thanks to the gods of timetabling, these exams were on six consecutive days, at 9.30 and 2.30, three hours each paper, with only Sunday interceding to prevent an incipient breakdown and/or a broken wrist. The short scream I uttered when I got my timetable was half for show, half for shock, which fairly accurately describes most of what I do.

The Oxford process of exams – much like everything else in Oxford – is wrapped in tradition but is none the weaker for it. Students must take exams in the get-up known as subfusc, which for men is a dark suit, dark socks, a white shirt, a white bow tie, your flapping academic gown and your mortar board, which cannot be worn until you have graduated but *can* be used as a pencil case. I will confess that, although I am not usually superstitious, I did wear what I felt were an auspicious pair of boxer shorts on the day of the first exam.

(I should probably have been grateful Oxford had not yet dictated the colour of those, too.) Women must be similarly sober, but instead of a white bow tie they have to drape a length of black ribbon around their collar in a manner no one is quite sure about. Some just run it inside their collar and let the two ends dangle at the front, others cross the strands over and fold one through, others still imagine it is a man's tie and half-Windsor it. I didn't shave during my week of Mods, my stubble a minor protest and also a way of ensuring I didn't accidentally cut my throat.

Although subfusc is the most obvious manifestation of Oxonian examination tradition, there are plenty of rumours regarding others. If you turn up in a full suit of armour on a horse, you automatically get a First; if you ask for a pork pie and a pint of cider, the invigilators have to get you one; and so medievally on. The truth is that subfusc *is* a suit of armour without the clanking or oiling. By putting on your subfusc, you move into the mental space marked 'exams' and replace the buffeting traumas of revision with the sturdy determination of one going into battle.

The Examination Schools themselves, which are normally used for lectures, elevate your mind to grander things, too. Seemingly just a porch on the eastern end of the High Street outside of which exam results are pinned up on blackboards, you enter an atrium whose floor has a witty mosaic of Aesop's creatures. All of the rooms – the smaller ones on the ground floor and the three magnificent Schools on the first floor, accessed over chequered marble paving and up broad marble staircases – are painted in jewel colours, the hues you imagine Catherine the Great demanding for her latest ballroom. They are hung with portraits of former university chancellors and other notables, including Wellington and Wilhelm II, who can be distracting in their austere grandeur. The North and South Schools have examiners' thrones which are exactly as large and imposing, almost papal, as their name suggests.

Of course, the reality is rarely as bad the imagination allows. My hand did not fall off, although I did have to go to the bathroom during one of the exams and in my haste slipped on the marble floor and nearly flung myself head-first down the stairs, a distinctly un-Homeric end. There were even bright spots. Thanks to an easily discernible rota of questions (and being taught by the exam-setter), the ones I had prepared for the linguistics and philology paper came up.

Just as I am writing this, I am looking at the actual papers I took, thanks to a matrilineal hoarding habit. It's astonishing that I could hold all of this in my head at once, especially given that I am now never further from a memory-substitute than whichever pocket my iPhone is in. I can even look over my jotted essay plans, reminding me of my trains of thoughts and making me consider to which terminals I'd send them now. If these trains of mine reached their destinations, at least after a fashion, it would be fair to say that Emilie Vleminckx's suffered quite the most catastrophic derailment.

EMILIE VLEMINCKX
(BORN 1982)

It takes quite some skill to get a Third. Perhaps more even than to get a First, which simply requires preternatural brilliance firing on all cylinders, no calibration necessary. For a Third, a degree with its own peculiar glamour, you need to be *just* disappointing enough. Not disappointing enough and you have a respectable 2.2; too disappointing and it's a pass, with its strong suggestion you perhaps ought not to have come to university. The gentleman's Third, as it has been known, today suggests a university career spent mounting the greasy poles of the Oxford Union or treading the clammy boards of the university's theatres instead of burying one's nose in a book.

You could argue, however, that a Third might in some way be a measure of unrecognised brilliance, of thoughts so unorthodox that myopic examiners feel compelled to reach for their red pens to protect their own dogmas.

You *could* argue this.

Emilie Vleminckx, I suspect, would not.

Emilie would most likely concede that her Third in classics Mods at Oxford in 2002 was probably not due to her unrecognised brilliance. No, it might well have been to do with her falling asleep in her Homer paper.

'That didn't help,' Emilie says as we talk in the Caffè Nero on the King's Road. 'We started with Vergil on the Thursday and the Homer was the Friday morning exam. I was exhausted and I thought, "I'm just going to think about this question," and I fell asleep for half an hour. It was the worst result of the whole lot.'

The Third was a badge of honour – she was 'excessively proud' of it – for its rarity and the skill it took to get it. It was heart-breaking, too, but in a pyrrhic way it proved a point to Emilie's classmates at Wadham College who would 'pretend' (her word) to be struggling yet still got a First, which is one of Oxford's mind games. There is an honest victory in being the one who was actually struggling. But it turned out that even the comforting of her friends about how Mods didn't count towards Finals and really didn't mean anything was hollow. The summer after Mods, Emilie says, she went to Paris and was mooching round Père Lachaise cemetery when she saw Oscar Wilde's tomb which dutifully records his First in Mods.

In many ways, her Third was 'a major relief' because it allowed Emilie to admit that she was on the wrong course, even if it did take sitting down to contemplate her next term's workload and bursting into tears to persuade her finally to talk to her tutor. He recommended that she switch to classical archaeology and ancient history, which covered material Emilie was interested in but did not require any language work. This change also meant that she was not sent down from Oxford permanently, as she had expected, and she went on to get a very good degree.

Homer is, in fact, what has brought us together. My paperback copy of *Homer: Poet of the Iliad*, by Mark W. Edwards, with its archaic warriors seemingly stone-printed in black on the turquoise cover, has on the first page the words 'Emilie Vleminckx / Wadham College'. The 'E' is really the letter *c* on top of a fatter letter *c*, and the *l* is a narrow loop. The *ck* is most striking, an elegant clover-like digraph where the *c* launches forwards and then turns straight upwards, curling backwards into a loop which thrusts through the middle of the upward stroke, before pulling back for another *c*, whose back rests on the stroke. Name aside, it is quite clearly the writing of a French person. Or indeed Belgian, it turned out, but I'll split the orthographical difference.

Edwards's book is one of the best modern introductions to the context, content and controversies of the *Iliad*. The *Iliad* – as anyone who has spent the eight weeks of their first term intensively reading it in Greek, thinking and writing about it, before putting it down and forgetting about it until their Mods term a year later, will know – is the story of five days in the last year of the war at Troy, which the Greeks are waging to get Helen of Sparta back. The plot of the *Iliad* itself is driven by the hero Achilles' withdrawal from the war after the Greek supreme commander Agamemnon steals his prize concubine. His sulk allows the Trojans to thrash the Greeks, even getting as far as starting to burn their ships, and it is not until his friend (boyfriend?) Patroklos is killed in battle, wearing Achilles' armour to fool the Trojans, that he returns, now enraged and insane for revenge.

By incorporating foreshadowings and echoes of the rest of the ten years into the poem, the *Iliad* adds a perspicacity and humanity to the bloody moil of the battle scenes that dominate. There are thousands of lines where swords pass through mouths and out of brains and where chariots stampede towards the imminently eviscerated, but Achilles also learns of and accepts his death, and wise men recall the examples of ancestors. There are panoramas of the Greek ships on the beach, and shots that swoop on to Helen and the elders of Troy sitting on the battlements. There are also speeches of exhortation or anger or supplication, and all human emotions are displayed. Most notable is the humanity of the poet towards the mortals who are falling victims to the gods' feuds and caprices.

But we must put the bard before the horse. The first thing one learns is that there is no such person as Homer, as I hinted earlier. Or rather, there may have been a person called Homer, but he did not sit down and write the *Iliad* (or the nostalgic *Odyssey*) as a complete product of his imagination. These two poems – 27,000 lines between them – were composed orally by bards who wandered around the Greek world, singing camp-fire tales for their supper and adding new stories and layers to the poems as they went, expatiating on one town's heroes as they arrived there or stressing the love or war themes as required. Although we may immediately suspect as impossible the feat of memory this would require, it is probably worth considering how many *libretti* or lyrics we have engraved in our brains. These lays would be passed from one bard to another and so on through the Greek world and down the centuries. At some point – perhaps the late eighth century BC – these poems reached a kind of fixity, and by the mid-sixth century they had been written down. An aid to composition was what are called formulaic epithets, fixed phrases – most famously 'rosy-fingered dawn' and 'swift-footed Achilles' – that easily complete the rhythm of a line, allowing the bard to focus on the next.

This was all to come when I picked up the book in the Oxfam on Broad Street and – sad to say – has mostly all gone since then. There are, however, many things that have stuck with me since I first read it, especially *Iliad* XXIV. In this final chapter, Priam sneaks into Achilles' tent in the Greek camp and begs him to hand over the body of his son, Hector. For the first and only time in the *Iliad*, after countless battlefield pleas for mercy have been met with a pointed response, the supplication is granted, for Achilles thinks of his own father and understands how Priam feels. It is this empathy that is so striking and is one of the most humane moments in Western literature.

What struck Emilie most were the nipples. 'Somehow the nipples come up. They come up the whole time. Homer has a massive nipple thing. The first time I read it, it went "nipple, nipple, another nipple". I'm sure other people have much more highbrow things to say.' Nipples do come up, although in the context of spear thrusts piercing chests between the nipples through to the heart, rather than anything exceptionally homoerotic. Once, the still-pulsing heart makes the stuck spear vibrate. More to the point, Homer almost never offers this sort of autopsy without an obituary and a eulogy. Part of the poet's humanity is that even minor characters are furnished with a back-story in the very moment of their death, often mentioning still-living parents and their homelands never to be revisited. Each victim is a person.

All of these themes and concepts (with the exception of an emphasis on nipples) are introduced in *Homer: Poet of the* Iliad. 'I got it in my first week [October 2000] when I'd been told what I needed to do for Mods, so I went to Blackwell's. I read it and re-read it, then I lost it – it vanished. I remember, a term before Mods, going, "Where's my *Homer*?" and going to buy another. Then, when I was moving out at the end of my second year I ended up with two copies – I found the first in a drawer.' Emilie took the first copy – the un-annotated, lost one – to Oxfam, the regular, ungracious receivers of her pint glasses filled with pennies, which is where I found it. You might think that rediscovering the first copy would have evoked an angry relief, but not at this point: 'It was just a bitter little reminder.'

Emilie's problem with Homer was something more funda-mental than exhaustion or a nipple-fixation: it had never engaged her in the first place. Her course – Moderations 1B, for those without Greek A-level – meant she only had to read four chapters in the original Greek and the rest in translation, rather than all of it in Greek, as for Moderations 1A and 1C (those with Greek A-level). Reading all of it in Greek cannot help but engage you, first on the panicked level of a flailing translator and then, once you gain some speed and fluency, because you get carried away by the story. Unfortunately, the elementary Greek Emilie was beginning to learn at Oxford prevented that, and a dull version in English failed to provide the excitement and narrative drive of the poem. Underlying it was the question of why she should be studying it: 'Reading something for work you should be reading for fun changes how you read it. We wonder if what we say should be better.'

The disastrous Homer paper was, if anything, the insult to add to all the academic injuries Emilie had already sustained. The underlying problem was that doing the European Bacca-laureate (not the International Baccalaureate) at the European School in Brussels, a school for the children of diplomats and bureaucrats, had not prepared her for classics at Oxford, where most people have an A-level in Latin and/or Greek and are primed to attack the shelves of text they have to read in the original. Emilie points out that in her junior exam she was allowed to use a dictionary, and that her four periods of Latin a week for two years were clearly inadequate: 'For some reason, people thought that we would be ready for [Mods] 1B, which was a big shock.' In contrast, most English students will have had eight periods a week for two years, and probably at least three years of fewer classes before that. Nevertheless, an inspirational teacher encouraged her ambition to go to Oxford.

It was an ambition Emilie had already been nurturing for years, but not one her parents approved of, and even when talking about her gratitude towards her parents, there is a frustrated edge – frustration at their lack of ambition for her. 'In their minds, I was going to be a translator in the EU or fulfilling some weird gender role as a personal assistant to someone important or a translator to someone important. Why couldn't I be that someone important?' Not that they had let her education slip, 'pulling quite a lot of strings to get me into the European School, because it's a school for people who work in the EU. They used friends or nepotism. I ignore the details as much as I can.' Emilie's father was a street artist, her mother an office clerk, and so their lives were Brussels-bound. Even though they would have preferred her to stay in Belgium, they supported her, and Emilie says – baldly, but faux-baldly, I feel – that her father worked himself into an early grave to pay for her education.

But they made a 'crucial mistake', Emilie says, employing the analytical tone of a detective explaining how they foiled a kidnapping. By having her visit a translator at the Berlaymont, the monstrously large Brussels office block that is the European Commission's headquarters, with floor space four times that of the Louvre's galleries, when she was eight, her parents gave her an insight into 'the booth [the translator] spent her life in and all the people wasting their lives translating drivel. From that moment on, I rebelled against it.' At the same age, a television programme introduced Emilie to Oxford.

Her parents' ambition for Emilie to be a translator was not an unachievable one. Indeed, Emilie says, she was bilingual, thanks to her Flemish father and French mother, by the age of eight. ('Vleminckx' is a dialectal rendering of 'Fleming / Flemish'.) At school she was 'the girl who spoke lots of languages', another one of which was Dutch, as her classes were taught in the language. Aged ten, she took up English, then German, as well as Italian, Latin and eventually Greek, and when we meet she is learning Scots Gaelic and has ambitions to start on Swahili. Spanish doesn't figure: 'People have always told me I ought to learn it but it's too obvious and that's why I don't want to. I can get round the world with what I have got, and gestures, and tough luck if I can't!'

But this choice of Latin and Greek at an English university is more significant that a simple desire to be a polyglot, or even having a natural facility (which Emilie clearly does). It reflects her youthful rebelliousness, both against her parents' expectations and against Belgium as a country. Emilie still seems powerfully to dislike Belgium for its meek nature, an artificial state that allows two languages to coexist with the pretence of equality. She must have been headstrong as a teenager. 'That's an understatement!' And apparently as a child, too: when her parents work out what her mother tongue was by her first word, it turned out that it was the universal 'papa', thus foiling them again.

Since Oxford, Emilie has been exercising her desire to remain in England, although initially without a grand plan. Her first job, while living with her boyfriend in Glasspool, Hampshire, was selling boric acid to the German market, 'which sounds more exciting than it was', so she did a course to become a teaching assistant in 2004–5. She was the only one under forty and the only one who wasn't a mother. When her boyfriend decided to move to Sherborne, Emilie realised that she would rather not be 'boring myself alive in the middle of Dorset' and came to London. After a year of being a French assistant teacher at Colet Court prep school in west London, Emilie did a full teacher training course – back at Wadham, her Oxford college, which certainly adds a different flavour to that of her first time there. When we met, Emilie was teaching French at another west London prep school, Ravenscourt Park, but she managed to slip in Latin lessons too, and ended the year with four devotees. The children suddenly *get* Latin, she says, when you explain that the name of the clothes store Urban Outfitters derives from the Latin *urbs, urbis*.

However, her life over here has not meant that Belgium has ceased to exert its pull, both maternal and practical, which continues to frustrate Emilie. Her parents wished she had stayed in Belgium, and now her mother pressures her with helpful suggestions about being able to babysit for Emilie's child. Emilie says she is torn by this, and the advantages of living in Belgium, such as easily affordable housing, are attractive. But getting a job in Belgium would mean choosing French or Dutch, and this has been a firm thread in her life – refusing to be pulled in one direction or the other by a decisive linguistic choice in an indecisive country. Instead, she has made a real linguistic choice by opting out entirely.

Seeing an article in the paper mentioning a vacancy for a headteacher on one of the most remote Shetland Islands, Emilie's interest was captured. The thought of teaching four children on an island with a total population of twenty-two, to which a ferry came only every six weeks, appealed – a compromise between her love of English and her desire for quiet, not easily accessible in London. A perhaps simpler compromise became clear when she and her husband moved to Kent, where she has taught French and a little Latin.

Emilie is certainly now anchored in Kent, with husband and child and library. Although she has four thousand books in Belgium, Emilie has amassed two thousand over here. Judging by some of her favourite authors and books – John Irving, *Lord of the Rings*, *Gone with the Wind*, the time-slip novels of Diana Gabaldon which move between the Second World War and the Jacobite Rebellion – we are not talking about two thousand slim, light volumes, either. She says there are books in every room, in piles around the bed and in the bathroom, one row sitting behind another on her bookshelves, simultaneously a guilty denial of her librovorism and a secret pleasure, never removing one book but discovering another, or making the front row foreplay for a desired book in the second row.

Emilie could no doubt be more precise than 'two thousand' if she wanted to be, at least as to how many she has gone through, because she keeps a notebook of what she has read. In the two years before we met, Emilie had read 135 books and recorded of each the title, author, publisher, date bought, amount paid and date finished. At school, reading eighteen books in a term would bring full marks in part of the English course. Emilie read 130. One of the most depressing things about her time at Oxford, she says, is that she did not read as avidly. This is a common complaint for arts students. After an entire day of wading through a treacly analysis of Athenian population figures or another one of Cicero's bombastic speeches, the last thing one wants is more black-on-white.

'A lot of people assume I don't read them very well, but I actually get really wrapped up in them. They're intense bursts of light. It's escapism and something completely different. I love it when I think, "That's true" or "I never thought about that" or "That's something that I went through." They can teach me something about my own life, too.'

If anything, Emilie has been teaching the books about her life, her contented existence in linguistic exile. Her *ex libris* plate, gummed in to identify her ownership, bears the legend *ubi bene, ibi patria* – wherever I'm happy, that's my home.

Emilie Vleminckx being admitted to Oxford

Classics

A Johns
Hopkins
Paperback

Homer: Poet of the "Iliad" is the perfect companion both for
readers deepening their appreciation of the poem and its form
and for those encountering Homer's work for the first time.
Mark Edwards combines the advantages of a general introduction and a detailed commentary to make the insights of recent
Homeric scholarship accessible to students and general readers
as well as to classicists.

Since interpretation of the epic requires an understanding of
the ancient oral tradition and its conventions, Edwards offers a
comprehensive analysis of the poetics of the *Iliad* and the
Odyssey. He also discusses essential elements of Homeric
society—its religion, history, and social values—to clarify the
style and substance of the poetry. In the second half of the book,
Edwards's scene-by-scene explication of ten major books of the
Iliad leads the reader to a greater perception of Homer's mas-
tery and manipulation of convention.

"A well written, substantial, reliable, and reasonable guide for
those who have never read Homer in Greek or in English and
even for those who have 'done' Homer in both Greek and English many times."—John E. Rexine, *Classical World*

"Thirty years of teaching Homer—the *Iliad* and the *Odyssey*—
and more of reading him are packed into these lucid pages. . . .
Edwards makes reading Homer exciting and meaningful. He's
alert to every aspect of his subject, including the problem of
translations. His book is an indispensable companion for anyone keen on drawing from this great source of wisdom and
delight."—Thomas D'Evelyn, *Christian Science Monitor*

"A very rich and valuable book."—*Greece & Rome*

MARK W. EDWARDS is professor of classics at Stanford University. He is the author of numerous articles on Homeric style.

The Johns Hopkins University Press

Baltimore and London

ISBN 0-8018-4016-3

90000

9 780801 840166

COVER DESIGN BY MARTHA FARLOW

Cambridge Greek and Latin Classics

VIRGIL

Aeneid

BOOK VIII

EDITED BY
K. W. GRANSDEN

CAMBRIDGE UNIVERSITY PRESS

M.B. M^{c}C. Brown

CAMBRIDGE GREEK AND LATIN CLASSICS

GENERAL EDITORS

E. J. KENNEY
Fellow of Peterhouse, Cambridge

AND

MRS P. E. EASTERLING
Fellow of Newnham College, Cambridge

UNIVERSITY CHALLENGE
(2003–4)

The only television programme I ever wanted to be on was *University Challenge*. The very theme tune releases endorphins in students, a post-scholastic chill. The least commercial of any quiz show (it has no financial prize), it rewards the seat of our self-esteem – our knowledge. Obscure, complex, trivial knowledge, but things known all the same. *UC* was a retirement home for superannuated factoids, the game-show equivalent of getting it off your chest. All those things picked up over the years – gleaned from the walls of Mr Hyde's classroom, or learning what a *Bildungsroman* was from the introduction to *Great Expectations*, one of my English GCSE set texts, say – finally had a purpose. We live in a purpose-driven culture where the aimless is the enemy of progress and productivity. In *University Challenge*, aimless knowledge becomes the aim.

Being at Magdalen, it was something to be taken seriously. We had won the show in 1997 and 1998, and a whole process, complex and time-consuming and thorough, had developed around selecting the team. Although Jeremy Paxman at the start of the first round announced that our team had come together at the college bar, the truth was that we had had an exhaustive term of practice matches, using complete sets of questions from previous series of *UC*, whittling down at least sixteen competitors into four and a reserve. This was no amateur operation. Thanks to a small grant from the college,

75

we even had our own set of buzzers. If you weren't quick, you were dead. Languid knowledge was no knowledge at all.

If that seems over-serious, well, it was over-serious, and no small part of that came from the nucleus of the team, Freya McClements, a Northern Irish modern history student in her final year, who pursued Paxman's grail with a frightening zeal. In 2002, Magdalen's team had failed to get on to the programme and so the 2003 competition was her final chance. Genetics had won through, too. Matt Holdcroft, an ebullient classicist and one of my college fathers (the pastoral system had fittingly but unknowingly given me a two-father family), was on the team. The supplier of our scientific knowledge was Dave Cox, mathematician and first-boat rower. We three boys had rapport, with similar senses of humour, which insulated us from Freya's demands that we should sit down and learn assigned lists of facts. When I tried to explain that I couldn't learn a list of architects, their dates and their major works even if Freya *had* determined that I would be the artistic-cultural prop of the team, she suggested I give up my place in favour of the reserve. I declined.

In Manchester, where the show was filmed at the Granada studios, about thirty feet from the cobblestones of *Coronation Street*, our hotel was packed with other teams since this June weekend was one for first-round matches, and when I stepped out of the lift up to our room I saw a member of another team wandering down the corridor, his head buried in a book of facts. Maybe Freya was on to something...As Granada evidently wanted to halve its hotel bill we had to share, so I stayed with Matt, who exhibited a trait he shared with one of my actual parents and tried to inhale the ceiling with his snoring.

Everything about our rooms was rubber – curtains, bed sheets, even the hot chocolate was synthetic, mis-sold to us under the alluring title of 'Cacao Fantasy'. Escaping the rubber room was thus a priority, and on the night before our match we wound up at a pancake restaurant where crêpes of all combinations were served on IKEA-ish delftware. We were as sensibly rowdy as you'd expect and when I told Matt years later, after a post-recessionary visit to Manchester, that the restaurant had been boarded up, we both sighed.

Before our first-round match the next day, Jeremy Paxman came and posed behind the desk with us for a team photo. People *still* say, 'Oh, it's a shame the score is zero.' In a dark crevice between the light-boxes which read HOLDCROFT and McCLEMENTS can barely be glimpsed my Spot the Dog, our mascot, cinched with a mini-Magdalen scarf courtesy of my grandmother who had, for once, directed her energies towards something charmingly creative rather than emotionally destructive. Sadly, less hard to glimpse am I, seated on the far right. At this time I was still sporting my highlighted hair, done into a post-trendy Hoxton fin. The highlights and the fin were the result of waking up next to someone inappropriate and feeling the need to change myself immediately, as radically as is possible for someone too cowardly to have a tattoo or a piercing.

Our win was halting – as, in fact, were our next two although we did still beat Nottingham 160 to 110, Sussex 165 to 130, and Royal Northern College of Music 190 to 130 in the quarter-finals. It was in the semi-final where we steamrollered St Andrews 265 to 85, finally putting in a performance of note. Since the quarter-finals, semi-finals and final were all being filmed over the same weekend in October, perhaps we had

built up a head of steam, or were releasing a rush of self-con-
fidence and optimism and maybe, just maybe…Freya and I
were still disagreeing, with her suggesting once again that I let
George Howe, the reserve – whom I liked a lot and who was
on the next year's team – have an opportunity to play, and me
suggesting she take her ideas elsewhere.

I still shudder at one question I got wrong, which I would
almost swear was put in especially for me: *Manhattan* is the
Woody Allen film in which he and Diane Keaton take refuge
in a museum during a rainstorm, not *Annie Hall*. I knew that.
Of course I knew that. I had frequently stayed up till 3 a.m.
on Saturdays as a teenager to record Woody Allen movies
from Sky on to video, and ended up with at least two dozen.
(Having no friends in the nineties at least had this, minor,
upside.) I can still quote Allen's prose pieces and stand-up sets
verbatim. And when Freya turned to me, my first answer was
Manhattan – but I second-guessed myself, which is the thing
you must not do in a quiz show. If an answer comes to you
instantly, it is probably right – the brain has a way of chucking
up the correct one, a reflex action.

Still, I'm proud of the starter questions I got right. *Bildungsroman*. *Objet trouvé*. 'My husband and I,' supplying the
end of a sentence from the Queen's speech at her fiftieth
wedding anniversary party. There were a few others, and I
would record some of them here if I could bear to watch the
video of the show.

Some while after the final had been broadcast in April 2004,
the trickle of fan mail began. (It never grew past a trickle.)
Magdalen started to receive letters from old ladies saying how
happy they were that 'our wonderful team spirit' had helped

us to win, and I like to think that we were unified in front of the cameras even if not wholly when the red light went off. One letter came directly to me from 'the Proverbial Secret Admirer'. If I may quote, for posterity's sake: 'Throughout the previous series, I was always particularly delighted when Magdalen won, for the very good reason that you are by far the yummiest specimen of gorgeousness ever to have appeared on the programme. Given the opportunity, I would have you for breakfast.' I expect I'd be a bit bony.

The victory in the final over Cambridge's Gonville and Caius College, 190 to 160, was especially sweet because it was the equivalent of a Varsity match – the Boat Race, but clashes with facts instead of oars – and we had led all the way. Bill Bryson presented us with the trophy, an open book cast in metal with each letter of 'University Challenge' rendered in a different alphabet or script or code, and he made the traditional remarks about how there was *nothing* to the rumour that students were getting progressively dumber. As we were the first team to win it three times, the producers let us keep the trophy, but internal college machinations meant that instead of being displayed somewhere prominent, or at least public, it ended up in a cabinet outside the Home Bursary, a dank corner of the college inaccessible to most and unwillingly visited by those who can. College *did* celebrate with an invitation to High Table at the Perrot Oration, an annual formal dinner where a speech in Latin commemorates the year's events.

Soon afterwards, we were asked to take part in a match in India against the champions of their version of *University Challenge* but Matt's Finals and my Mods militated against it. In 2009 we were dragged back into the limelight when the current champions were disqualified for having a team member no longer at the institution. Freya had also left Oxford by the time of the final in October, but had been assured by the production company that this would be no problem. Nevertheless, the newspapers dragged it up. Freya secured an apology from the *Daily Telegraph* for implying she had deceived Granada.

I don't often now think of *University Challenge*, and for a long time I could not even watch it. I felt it was a little like sex – once you're finished, you lose interest. It wasn't until I started researching Michael Brown that I even voluntarily brought it to mind. Today, our team photo is on my living-room wall and I can now watch it, even if I awfully, unwillingly, fall into the category of those who say it was so much harder in *my* day. It still flutters about when someone, grasping for a fact about me when making introductions at a party or, occasionally, a business meeting, mentions *University Challenge* – but I am never sure what to say. Do I come up with some recondite fact to prove the point? Should I start off with tales of Paxman? I normally just ask about the other person.

MICHAEL BROWN
(BORN 1942)

Herodotus wrote, more or less, 'Call no man happy until he is dead.' Death alone was insufficient, however: you needed to have a *good* death to qualify as one of life's winners, he thought. The word he uses for 'happy', *olbios*, is in fact also a word for 'rich' and so a credit check might do as well as an obituary, but his point, put into the mouth of Solon the Athenian sage when visiting uppity King Croesus of Lydia, is clear. And while he might be right that a good death is necessary for happiness, Michael Brown, I would venture, is happy. Perhaps not rich and certainly not dead when we meet, but happy – and it's only taken him forty years.

The immediate cause of his happiness is his release from classics-teaching duties at an Australian school, and his trip to England to revisit old schools and friends and to attend the Buxton Gilbert and Sullivan festival, from where he has returned when we met at his brother's house in Kew on a quickly darkening evening in September. (Some might feel that Australia is the perfect place to be when a Gilbert and Sullivan festival is occurring in Buxton, but that is beside the point.) Michael and his wife left for Australia when he retired as a classics teacher from Brighton College in 2003, and in doing so he seemed to fulfil a genetic destiny, or necessity, or at least capacity – his parents were both Australians who had left for Britain in the thirties, and his three children had by 2003 all emigrated to Australia, opening an irresistible horizon. His family had been planted in Australia when his great-great-great-grandfather, Simeon Lord, was transported after a conviction for stealing cloth in 1790. Lord went on to become one of Australia's wealthiest men.

The break for Britain that his father, Alan Brown, made – and which Michael has spent his life trying to repair – led to a life that Michael views with such admiration that, when I broached this book with him, his response was that I should be writing about his father. The modesty this reflects quickly comes to seem typical of Michael, who follows every point of pride with a self-effacing undercut, making him hard to grasp, a little frustrating even. (This must be what the rest of the world feels when confronted with the English.) Brown senior is worthy of study, no doubt. After his undergraduate degree and a spell as a barrister in Australia, he became the Fellow in Law at Worcester College and earned the nickname 'Meadow' for successfully preventing a road being run through Christ Church Meadow, one of Oxford's most pacific and appealing spots. He served on the city council and the university's Hebdomadal Council, its executive body, and was mayor during the Coronation year. Michael remembers the attendant benefit of being chauffeured to school.

His father had also served in the army. 'He was with the Scots Guards in North Africa and Italy. At some stage he was injured, possibly luckily for him because there was some ghastly battle which he missed, in which friends of his were killed, which had a heavy psychological effect on him.' That meant he could return home in time for some oddly specific family planning. 'He wanted to have his first child born on his birthday, so he took compassionate leave in 1941, from around August bank holiday, and lo and behold I was born nine months later on the precise day.'

Such rigour was not in the genes and Michael was an indifferent student at the Dragon, a prep school often seen as an incubator for Oxford, but a sergeant-major-style intervention by his father put the fear of god into him. Offered places at St Edward's in Oxford or Westminster, he chose Westminster on 'an inkling' that it was the more civilised place, especially since St Edward's did not at the time have doors on the toilets.

Civilised indeed it turned out to be, as Michael, who decided from his first year at Westminster that life was easier and the self more respectable with greater academic distinction, took to post-rationing London of the fifties. 'For me it was very exciting. In those days you didn't have all this health and safety risk, and we were allowed to go out into London on our own, do things children you were responsible for could never do now.' This included a form of fagging for the older boys, and Michael was sent across London by Corin Redgrave to collect books for the house drama society. Most boys went home at weekends, but Michael often stayed in London instead of returning to Oxford. 'You could walk round Hyde Park, listen to the speakers. A friend of mine was fascinated by looking at prostitutes in Soho. We were trying to make a census of where they were. That didn't last long.'

Westminster is one of England's classical powerhouses and it might seem natural, given that Michael was a classics teacher, and indeed taught classics at Westminster in the seventies, that he should have pursued that course at school, but from his description of his early experience it seems that classics was never the obvious, or at least most desirable, course

– an ambivalence that was to surface more than once. At the Dragon, where classics was so important you had to do it first thing in the morning while your brain was still fresh, he was not in the top set for Latin. At Westminster, the choice of prestigious lines of study was either the sciences or classics, subjects like English being for those incapable of the rigour of other paths, and rather than stressing his love of classics, Michael says he was so bad at science that his choice was clear. When I ask whether he pursued classics because of passion or pragmatism, he assents to the latter: 'It almost was. I think I've only come to love it since I've been teaching it, to be honest. It was *de facto* when I actually did it.'

Although he failed to win a scholarship to Oxford, Michael did get into New College to read classics a year before most of his contemporaries. When he went up in 1961 classics at Oxford had the same structure as now, but radically different content: five terms of Mods, where you had to read all of Vergil, all of Homer and countless other texts, and seven terms of Greats, where you studied philosophy and ancient history, and no literature for literature's sake. Indeed, the skills of literary appreciation that are now required at Mods were no part of that era's education, where textual criticism, a drier and more technical discipline revolving around manuscripts, variant readings and the transmission of the text, was the thing. Now, one has to analyse and *feel*.

Feeling was not a problem for Juvenal, the imperial satirist whom Michael chose as a special subject. His poems, in the grandiloquent hexameter verse of epic but with the foul mouth of invective and the passions of drama, reveal a feeling for (or rather against) many things: the gross obeisance and flattery that surrounded the emperor; the foreigners colonising

84

Rome; the capital's traffic and financial inequality; the morals of wealthy Romans, devoting their time to barren poetry recitals, greedy legacy-hunting and prodigious gossip-mongering. Juvenal's Second Satire rails against a 'plague' of homosexuality that has descended on Rome:

> Faces are not to be trusted. Why, every street is just full of stern-faced sodomites. How can you lash corruption when *you* are the most notorious furrow among our Socratic fairies?
>
> (trans. Rudd)

Best remembered for coining the phrase *panem et circenses* (bread and circuses), the encapsulation of the bribe of politicians for public acquiescence, Juvenal's persona is that of a scathing moralist, albeit one who probably protests too much. When we meet I have by chance been reading Juvenal and there is plenty a cosmopolitan could relate to, although I find the constant anger and sarcasm very wearing, so Michael's tolerance of Juvenal's haranguing – he still reads him in his leisure – seems to reflect a placid nature; the volatile are too easily driven wild by him. I cannot, in fact, imagine anyone less like Juvenal than the contented gentleman in front of me.

At university, classics once again seemed for Michael an interest rather than an obsession. After Mods, he gave it up and took English Finals. His reasoning is pragmatic: 'In the sixties, people were questioning things and things were being thrown out, and classics was under threat, so I thought I'd better have something to fall back on. It was the age of being free and easy, doing what you liked, and I suppose there's a rigidity and discipline about classics which people perhaps didn't like.' He benefited from tutors like Christopher Tolkien for Anglo-Saxon, John Buxton and John Bayley, but he says that after classical Mods, English Finals were 'a doddle'. (This type of masochistic pride-cum-snobbery is not uncommon in classicists.)

University held other pleasures, such as amateur acting in college plays. (There is no other kind of acting in college plays, in truth.) He played Fenton in *The Merry Wives of Windsor*, 'who does have quite a long part. They're lines that they think Shakespeare himself may not have written and you have to sum up who is meeting who where in these woods, so it's important to get it right. I wasn't a natural actor, so in order to get through it, I drank a pint of vintage cider beforehand and when the *Times Literary Supplement* reviewed the play, although it was a fairly complimentary review, they did say someone should have told Fenton not to sway so much.'

While at New, he picked the college's *University Challenge* team, who went on to win the second series of the show, in 1965. He is charmingly disarming about why he chose to select the team rather than be on it: 'I was the only member of the JCR committee who knew he wasn't good enough to be on it – I'm much too slow.' The prize that year on *University Challenge* was a series of prints of Hockney's *The Rake's Progress*. A set of these sold for £48,000 in 2005.

When Michael chose to be a classics teacher, it was as if two compulsions of differing valencies had met. The weaker one was his adherence to the subject – his enthusiasm for classics was underwhelming, but it seemed the right career choice. The stronger one only emerged after teaching for a term at Westminster Abbey Choir School, covering for a tutor who had had a breakdown.

After this stretch, he went to teach for a year and a term at Melbourne Grammar School in the country that has proved more magnetic to him than anything else in his life. This was not Michael's first experience of Australian scholasticism. In the fifties, his father had been invited to speak at the centenary dinner of Geelong Grammar School, his old school in Victoria, and in return he had asked that his four children be allowed to spend a term there. Despite being derided as a Pom, Michael's experience in the classroom was not all that different from his schooling in England, the didactic mode of the motherland having taken root in *terra nova*. There were Latin classes, and Greek came from correspondence exercises sent by the English headmaster. His main memento of his time there was his love of cross-country running, miles up and down great hills, determined to prove himself adequate. (Adequacy by Australian standards meant superiority when he returned to Britain.)

While a master at Melbourne Grammar School, a minor excursus removed him from the comfort of the Anglo-Saxon educational system and of his life thus far. There was a school trip to Papua New Guinea, an unsettled land fettered by colonialism and its landscape. By the time Michael visited in 1967, it had been under German, Dutch, British and Australian yokes, and it was not to gain independence from Australia until 1975. It had played a major role in the Second World War, the site of a prolonged struggle between the Japanese, Americans and Australians which cost over 200,000 lives, and its fabled cannibalism only came to an end in the fifties. Papua New Guinea has no easy geography either: the interior is spiny with rainforest-garlanded mountains, while its location near the clashing of several tectonic plates has rendered it volcano-ridden and earthquake-prone.

Something in Papua touched Michael. When he returned there in 1968 to teach English as a foreign language in a log-built school in Popondetta, his students were not like the urbane children of well-heeled Londoners he would have later when he went back to Westminster, but people who had had to walk miles to get to school, whose only hope of escaping a life of subsistence farming was their education. Nor were they necessarily teenagers – you could only attend that school after six years of primary education and if a school had not come to your village until you were in your twenties, you might well be in your thirties by the time you took Michael's class.

Didn't he feel as if he was there to civilise the natives, assuming an awkward colonialist mantle? His moderate response – 'In a way, you have mixed feelings about doing it' – seems typical of his equanimity, a trait that suggests either a life spent without extreme passions or a restraint appropriate to a stranger trying to provoke you with emotive questions, or likely a mixture of both. The word he uses – 'unreal' – seems right for the experience.

The Pacific had to be given up for the Thames in 1969 after Michael rejoined Westminster, but even then he could not stay away from Australia. He seems to have had an unexpressed infatuation with the country. Its latest manifestation came when he organised an exchange with Australia's oldest school, the King's School, Parramatta (the king being William IV). This was, he says, because his wife, Ruth, wanted to see the Australian side of the family, but I cannot imagine he was an unwilling traveller. He had met Ruth, a nurse at Westminster

Hospital, when visiting a sick elderly lady who lived above a previous girlfriend in Pimlico. The old lady – 'on her last legs – all that kept her together was whisky and cigarettes' – had succumbed to Michael's pressure to take medical advice and ended up in hospital, which proved fortunate for Michael in meeting Ruth, but less so for her, as she was transferred from the hospital to an old folks' home in Kilburn.

B y the late seventies, Michael had left Westminster – ideal for bachelors – for Eastbourne College, which was better for his growing family. This meant leaving behind more than a city. The hard-charging pupils of Westminster were replaced by the gentler students of the south coast, and the hard-edged pedagogy of military-drill public school was superseded by a softer, subtler kind of learning.

The austere grammar-led Latin teaching that Michael had both received and delivered was by now giving way to the gradual grammar and continuous storylines of the *Cambridge Latin Course*, perhaps today the most widely used series of textbooks. Instead of excerpts from ancient texts bowdlerised for pre-O-level students, pupils could follow the adventures of Caecilius, Quintus and a cast of aristocrats and slaves from Pompeii to Britain to Rome. A similar, less gaudy and melo-dramatic product of this era was *Ecce Romani*, 'Behold the Romans', which I used at school and, indeed, used until I gave up tutoring in 2012.

'For the less able,' Michael says, '*Cambridge* is certainly a more attractive course because you do read continuous stories, and they're very good. They give you the *flavour* of Roman society,' by teaching about town and country lives, weddings and funerals, dinner parties and the Senate. Since for most of Michael's life, classics had been under threat for its Victorian didactic strictures and lack of engagement with the world beyond the word, the *CLC* was a panacea. He says he thinks it saved Latin.

But instead of settling into life on the south coast, with a senior position at a good school, raising a young family and using the plentiful local hills for cross-country running, he became restless. 'In a fit of ambition, because I didn't really want to be a housemaster, I decided to apply for the headship of a school called St Anne's, Windermere, up in the Lake District, which to my surprise I got.' It was not a success. Burdensome administration and a lack of teaching time sent him back south after four terms, having taken his whole family up there. This is one of the few times in our interview that Michael uses a word of deep emotion, calling the whole experience 'traumatic', but this is soon countered by the 'lovely' school in Dorset he subsequently joined. St Mary's, Shaftesbury, is in an idyllic part of the world but suffers from rural isolation, and so it was back to the south coast, to Brighton College. All of these schools seemed *fine* – but none of them was in Australia, the place that truly sits in Michael's heart.

Just as Australia is part of his family's heredity, so seemingly is classics. One of Michael's brothers, Peter, was fellow and tutor in classics at Trinity College, Oxford, from 1968 until recently. The diaries of a former headmaster of Westminster, John Rae, were published in 2009 – Michael served under Rae when he taught at Westminster – and they are filled with examples of Rae calling the admissions tutors at various Oxbridge colleges and suggesting they admit this pupil or that one. Was there ever any Brown–Brown collusion? 'No, in fact with Peter my pupils had to be *better* than perhaps others so there should be no suspicion. I always thought *I* was doing *him* a favour, certainly not the other way round.'

In 2003, after his retirement from teaching, Michael made a decisive peregrination, a return to a land that had always, sometimes and never been his home. After his stints as a pupil and a teacher there, and with all three of his children now there, he and Ruth went to Australia for good.

Although he was in retirement he discovered a demand for his services and taught for a while, part-time, supplementing his lamentable English teacher's pension. Pymble Ladies' College, where he taught until his second retirement, is the only girls' school that offers Greek in the area, and Greek teachers are not easy to find, he says. (Not that there's a bubbling spring of Latin teachers, either.) The work ethic of his Asian pupils gave him his best-ever students, he says.

He had not expected to teach in Australia, so some of the victims of his move were his classics books, fifty of which had to be sold off. 'I am a natural hoarder,' he wrote to me, 'and it takes something extreme, like migration, to bring myself to part with books. Whenever I do part with books, I usually regret it later.'

We start to talk about the two books I have that used to belong to Michael, R. D. Williams's commentary on *Aeneid* V (1960), a faded paperback from Cambridge's green-and-gold-covered series of classical texts, and K. W. Gransden's commentary on *Aeneid* VIII (1976), now a dried-blood-red hardback without its original pale blue paper jacket. Respectively, these books discuss one average and one exceptional chapter in Vergil's poem of the foundation of Rome. The books themselves had not offered sufficient clues for tracking

Michael down – it had been a job for the super-capacious internet.

Because I had bought these two books in the Classics Bookshop on Turl Street to use for my Mods term on Vergil, I had assumed that Michael had done the same. In our email conversation, he gave a different reason: 'I acquired [both books] to assist in my teaching of Classical Civilisation A-level at Brighton College.'

Classical Civilisation A-level involves the study of Greek and Roman literature, philosophy, art and history in English, giving access to the classical world to those who do not have Latin or Greek. It is one of the ways in which the classical academic community has been breaking down the *de facto* barriers that surround its citadel, encouraging those outside the public-school system to learn about the ancient world – a well-intentioned Trojan horse, if you will. As you can now start a classics degree at Oxford with neither Greek nor Latin, Classical Civilisation has proved a success.

It is not problem-free, however, as some of my pupils have demonstrated. Because all they study is translations, they are sometimes seduced into believing that Vergil did in fact write 'I sing of arms and the man' instead of '*arma virumque cano*', which leads to odd acts of literary criticism. While the widening benefits of Classical Civilisation are clear, the residual feeling endures in me that you cannot properly access the thought of another culture if you cannot speak its language – after all, translations are mediated through the translator, no language can be fully mapped on to another, and thought patterns themselves are defiantly tied to linguistic expression. This can no doubt be construed as snobbery, but it isn't meant to be.

The chronology should have half-belied my assumption

anyway. Michael was at Oxford from 1961 to 1965, thus Gransden would not have been available then. Moreover, Michael
would have had no *need* for these commentaries. Before the
great reforms to Oxford classics in 1968, 'for Mods you merely
read through the whole lot, so I probably wouldn't have bought
a specific edition. You only did it for translation in those days.'
Commentaries certainly aid with syntactical elucidation, but
the advent of literary criticism and thematic essay writing,
the sort of thing commentaries are invaluable for, was one of
Oxford classics' concessions to modernity.

At university Michael had been quite happy with the syllabus requirement that students read all of Vergil. 'I am a total
Virgil fan,' he wrote to me. 'Bernard Levin is forever in my
bad books for describing him as a cold-hearted bore!' There
were particular aspects of Books V and VIII that appealed to
him, too. 'Being competitive and sporting by nature, I relish
the contests in Anchises' commemorative games,' he said,
referring to Book V's honorific funeral games for the father of
Aeneas. Once the Trojans have arrived in Italy, in Book VIII
Aeneas is taken on a tour of King Evander's city, which is on
Rome's future site. Vergil alludes to many of the features of
contemporary Rome: for example, describing the Capitoline
as 'now gold, then bristling with wild thorns'. It links Rome's
humble origins to its glory in Vergil's time, creating both the
expectation of growth and pleasure at its known fulfilment,
stirring pride in the intended readers and in Michael too: 'I
wallow in Virgil's patriotism!' Even his jubilant exclamation
marks give away his mild manner.

If Michael is no frothing Vergilian patriot – or epic slayer
of Italians – I do think he can stand comparison with Aeneas
in one respect: his near-obsessive quest for a foreign land, a

desire spanning decades. Perhaps it was latent, perhaps he did not or could not frame it as such, perhaps he could but is unwilling to admit to such a craving to a stranger, but I have rarely seen someone who has perceived a siren call and responded so strongly, so willingly, to it. As Italy was to Aeneas – a compulsion – so Australia has been to Michael. That he has finally settled there – well, wouldn't you be *olbios* too?

Michael Brown signing the wedding register in 1971

Book VIII is one of the most attractive and important
books of Virgil's *Aeneid*. It includes the visit of Aeneas to the
site of the future Rome, the story of Hercules and Cacus,
the episode between Venus and Vulcan and the description
of the great symbolic shield of Aeneas. Mr Gransden's introduction relates this book to the *Aeneid* as a whole and considers the text in various aspects: the topography, Virgil's
sense of history, his typology and symbolism, his literary style
and his influence on subsequent vernacular poetry. The commentary discusses points of special interest and difficulty in
interpretation, style and prosody and gives detailed explanation
of the many allusions in Book VIII to customs, legends,
traditions and historical events.

This is primarily a textbook for university students and
sixth-formers, but it also contains material which may be of
interest to students of English and comparative literature.

*The editor is Reader in English and Comparative Literary
Studies, University of Warwick*

C.U.P.
NET IN U.K.
£ 5·50

Also issued in hard covers

0 521 29047 3

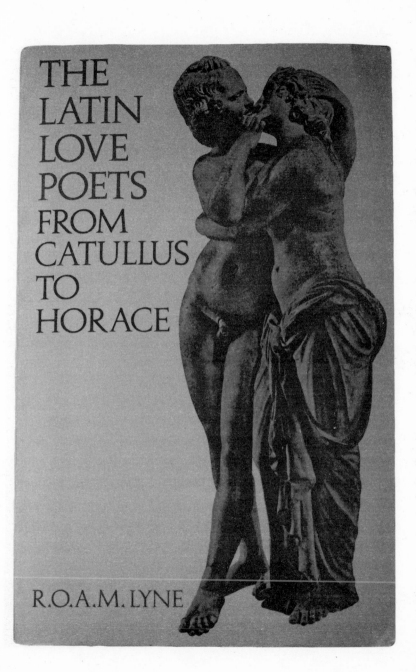

THE
LATIN
LOVE
POETS
FROM
CATULLUS
TO
HORACE

R.O.A.M. LYNE

Mark Richards
Coll. Katharine Oxon
MCMLXXXI

Josh Spero
Magdalen College, Oxford
January 2005

THE LATIN LOVE POETS

CHERWELL
(2004–6)

It wasn't a bad sign when the editors of Oxford's independent student newspaper, *Cherwell*, while interviewing me for a staff position as deputy features editor, congratulated me on *University Challenge*. Aled, an acerbic gay Welshman, and Elaina, a warm, smart Londoner, were holding the interviews for the next term's staff of a couple of dozen in the coffee shop in Blackwell's, and they said that although our victory was well known around *certain* parts of Oxford, *Cherwell* wouldn't publish it until the final was broadcast – the cosy media conspiracy, writ small.

I was hired alongside a girl called Rachel and even though she was manifestly uninterested in journalism beyond that term, I was still reflexively competitive. My responsibility was commissioning pieces for and laying out one page of the paper. As it was Trinity Term, I created a sidebar called 'Summer Saturdays', with things to do on a theoretical day off. None of these things have particularly stuck with me except for the one on skinny-dipping, written by a friend who would in the next term, when I was features editor, write a romance column for me under the unlikely pseudonym 'Adeline O'Horne'. My friend Miranda recently brought up a feature I let her write on masturbation, although it doesn't ring any bells with me. I applied for the editorship of the next term to stop my cousin, who was at St John's, becoming editor. We did not get on, but

I served under him as deputy before again failing to get the editorship the term afterwards.

I did not go up to Oxford intending to be a journalist – I wanted to be an academic for about the first five minutes of my first term – but my year on *Cherwell* persuaded me it was a potential, desirable career. One of the chief enticements was the kick of seeing my name five thousand times across the city, although it was more the inky reality of it rather than its frequency. Then there was the pleasure of giving people something to talk about for wholesome reasons, rather than the time I was caught with an inamoratus in a college kitchen against a glass door. There were the skills of producing coherent copy to length and to deadline – possibly the only skills in journalism, yet ones that many journalists lack. The artistic and technical challenges of designing a page. The buzz of gathering a news story – albeit I did this rarely. Directing, encouraging your team. The free stuff. The crepuscular camaraderie as the senior editors worked through to dawn on Thursday morning in our rackety office to meet the print deadline; the chocolate cakes I baked in my terrible college kitchen as a pick-me-up for the overnight staff; the fuzzy decision-making processes of those long shifts (was it theoretically justifiable for us to break into the Oxford Union for a story?). The pride in the product. These – cake-making included, dawn sessions excluded – have endured into my subsequent journalistic career.

One piece I had published in *Cherwell* was the obituary of Oliver Lyne, a classics professor at Oxford and a fellow of Balliol for thirty-five years, who died after a seizure while shovelling snow at his house in the Italian Marche in 2005. The editors of *Cherwell* at the time – my college daughter, Venetia, who thanks to a gap year was actually older than I was, and Daniel, who was at one of Oxford's odd theological colleges – somehow managed to print a mangled version of the obituary I gave them.

Lyne, who was lean and genial when I saw him lecture on Latin poetry, made a deep impression with his book *Further Voices in Vergil's Aeneid* (1987), which found subversive veins within the *Aeneid*'s marmoreal immensity. In the *Aeneid*, Trojan prince Aeneas flees the ruins of his city after the Greeks and their equine vector gain entrance and burn the place down. A storm tosses Aeneas on to the north coast of Africa, where he encounters fellow refugee Dido, who is building the city of Carthage; one divinely motivated love affair later and Dido is smitten, but Aeneas runs off. Admittedly, the gods are ordering him to go, but that hardly comforts Dido, who follows the obvious course and immolates herself on a pyre. Aeneas reaches Italy, descends to the Underworld for further instruction from his father's shade (he also sees Dido's shade, who still isn't too impressed and ignores him), and once back above ground launches a war to secure marriage to an Italian princess. The poem ends bleakly, with the unnecessary killing of the subdued Italian army's leader, when Aeneas' temper gets the better of him.

Traditional interpretations have seen the *Aeneid* as propaganda for the Emperor Augustus, self-claimed descendant of the Trojan hero Aeneas and Rome's fresh tyrant. We hear – for the poem was designed to be read out loud – a hero surviving the ruin of his homeland, renouncing his lover for divine duty, going into Hell itself for paternal piety, leading an army to success, to a dynasty, to an empire. If anyone needed justification through history and literature for a new imperial project, it was Augustus.

Lyne's book, however, makes Vergil seem more like a poet caught in a new autocracy, compulsorily patronised by the regime; in response, he injected into his work subtle criticisms and strains of doubt about the imperial project. The invader Aeneas' bloody struggle to secure the marriage and thus create the dynasty that would one day spawn Romulus, the founder of Rome, and Augustus, is in Lyne's reading less a triumphal march to imperial glory than a grievous campaign that injures or diminishes both the actors and the aim – where the balance between cost and reward is not as the smooth surface of the poem suggests, or as Augustus would have us see it. These further voices are dissenting ones.

It is another one of Lyne's books that connects me to Mark Richards. *The Latin Love Poets* was his first book after the publication of his doctoral thesis and it was pitched at the sixth-form and undergraduate level, but rather than leading to banal simplifications it had Lyne's literary insights elegantly distilled. Judging by its pencilled annotations and heavy lines marking paragraphs, Mark seems to have read only the final chapter on Ovid's *Amores* – sexy, witty evocations of love affairs in Augustus' morally straitened Rome.

Ovid, a sportive and subversive poet, addresses many of the poems to Corinna, who may, may not or may pseudonymously be a real woman. Their love affair is far from a chaste construction. The poet describes to Corinna the tantalising, lustful signs he will give her at a dinner party at which her husband will be present; he desperately apologises to her after he hits her; he tenderly regrets her abortion of his child, although, in true Ovidian style, he is unsure whether he is the father. This undermining of even the most serious of subjects is one of

Lyne's key themes in this chapter. He points out how Ovid will take established literary figures from love poetry – the lover as general or slave, the lover excluded outside his beloved's door – and use them for both sympathetic and parodic effect by stretching their literalness beyond logic and thus into humour. In Ovid, the lover etiolated through exclusion is so thin he can slip through a mere crack in the door.

Thanks to Mark's lack of a bookmark, the original receipt is still within the paperback, whose white cover is now cream verging on beige. He bought it from Blackwell's on Broad Street on 11 November 1981 and paid £5.25. It is now, with the quiet but energetic inflation of academic books, £40.

When I met Mark at the Jam Factory in Oxford, a cafe complex in a formerly disused building near the train station we spoke about his childhood in Liverpool, his years at Oxford, his passion for rowing, his career in computing and his love of ultra-marathons. At one point he started telling me about a post-university trip he made and it was the stuff of ancient poetry, as indeed it was meant to be. He sailed a reconstruction of the *Argo* from Greece to Georgia, imitating Jason's journey – albeit without fire-breathing oxen and men who spring from dragon's teeth – as described by Apollonius of Rhodes in his *Argonautica*. The story was thrilling, uncertain, dangerous, heroic – a modern epic.

MARK RICHARDS
(born 1959)

Beginning with you, Phoebus Apollo, I will retell the
glorious deeds of men born long ago, who through the
mouth of the Black Sea and past the Cyanean rocks,
at King Pelias's command, in search of the golden
fleece, sailed the well-benched Argo.
APOLLONIUS OF RHODES, *Argonautica*, I.1–4

'It was the first time a boat like this had hit the water in thousands of years. There was a sense of historical significance. It was a beautiful boat to look at, there was a real adventure about to begin. Nowadays people go to the North Pole, the South Pole, adventures are still there to be had – but we were breaking new ground. We were doing something no one had done before.'

Studying for his MBA at Manchester Business School, Mark Richards found himself bored, or at least disheartened, by the career choices his course opened up to him and so he set a new course. Not a new course exactly – an old course newly travelled in an old way. He dropped out of his MBA and recommitted himself to the heave and push of the years he had spent rowing at Oxford.

Hoping for inspiration, Mark went back to Keble College, Oxford, where he had read classics, and chatted to the chaplain, an old acquaintance. Providence provided, and the chaplain, aware of Mark's time in one of Oxford's expeditionary societies, suggested he contact Tim Severin, re-enactor of fabulous voyages, reading the palimpsest of the sea and retracing earlier sailors' strokes. His first project had been St Brendan's journey from Ireland to Newfoundland, a mythical passage of 4,500 miles across the Atlantic undertaken in the seventh or eighth century AD, which involved building a two-masted *currach*, wrapped in tanned ox-hides and held together by leather thongs. The next voyage was Sinbad's six thousand miles from Oman to Canton in a newly built Arab dhow, with cotton sails, sponsored by the sultan of Oman who was keen to attract some historical glory. By travelling these routes, Severin could compare the traditional accounts and see if they had any basis in reality – he was as much an explainer as an adventurer, a bunker rather than a debunker.

When Mark's CV arrived on Severin's desk he was planning his third recreation – or indeed creation, if the journeys truly were legendary – a three-month trip of fifteen hundred miles in a reconstruction of the *Argo*. 'He wrote back and said, "I've got a job for you. In six months' time we're launching this boat and we need a rowing master." So that was my job. He wanted someone to teach people to row. I had a lot of rowing experience on the River Thames but not a lot of experience with Bronze Age galleys.' Nevertheless, for an oar-loving classicist, this was a fine proposal.

Before he could take the three months off for the voyage, plus two months for training, Mark had to raise sufficient money to support himself for what is now called 'voluntourism', so he worked 'flat out at cramming schools, teaching Latin, Greek, ancient history and maths'. Being in Oxford, he could also assemble undergrads as a trial crew for the voyage, and they flew out to Greece to test the boat around Spetsos, where it was built, to see if it needed tweaks, to see how fast it could go. When the students returned, Mark stayed on to deliver the boat to northern Greece, to Volos, where it would be launched.

'It was built by a local traditional shipbuilder,' Mark says, 'who built Greek *kayikes* out of wood. It was built in the traditional Greek Bronze Age style, which was mortise and tenon joints, so the jointing of the planks butted on to each other.' There was supposedly no modern glue in it, but Mark is dubious. Aside from two small covered decks at each end, the ship with its benches for twenty rowers was open to wind, rain, and worse.

To enthuse the countries they would cross in their journey, volunteers from Greece, Turkey and Georgia were sought for the twenty. The Greeks and Turks, of course, would not be caught dead in each other's waters. Five or six Britons and Irishmen, including Mark and Tim Severin, went the whole way, but the others rotated.

A key question was whether they had made the galley seaworthy. The Greeks had left no blueprints for their boats and so it was sink or swim. 'When I first saw it, I thought it was fantastic, beautiful – just an amazing boat; the lines were lovely, and when it was launched, it slid gracefully into the water. It came to a halt on its hawsers and it just floated on its lines perfectly, absolutely balanced. It was wonderful.' So the boat floated – but the crew still had to fulfil.

'I suppose rowing is the strand throughout my adult life that binds everything together. I hadn't rowed before I came up to Keble, but being a fresher you're encouraged to think about taking up a sport – or at least you were in those days. I had never tried rowing before, although I had seen the Boat Race on the telly and thought that seemed like the thing to do at Oxford, so I thought I'd give it a go.' Mark proved proficient and even made Isis, Oxford's second heavyweight crew, but only for two weeks until a rowing legend, Boris Rankov, who had rowed five times in the Blue boat, returned for a sixth go.

Although he rowed at Leander, the smart Henley-on-Thames club, then at City of Oxford, Mark retired at forty, largely because he had worn out his back through years of hydrodynamic strain. (He returned to it, in the form of coaching, when his son took it up.) Rowing isn't (only) the rah-fest the Boat Race makes it seem, and Mark is proud of this: 'It's not just university areas which row. Anywhere where there's a stretch of water, flowing or still, which is probably more than five hundred metres long, you can find a rowing club.' He tries to rebut 'the Edwardian view of rowing' – public schools, Henley and such – by saying the sport has transcended its gentlemen-versus-tradesmen historical attitude

It is a demanding yet curiously forgiving sport, with the possibility of perfection in every fresh stroke, redeeming the slips and asynchronous movements. 'Essentially, it's a very simple stroke, but you have to get it perfectly right and you have to keep repeating it and that's the challenge, making each stroke consistently good and each outing consistently good and improving over time.' If you get three good strokes out of a thousand, that's victory. 'That's the challenge, in a period of strokes, particularly in a crew boat, where everyone's in synch, where the boat's flowing, where everything's going right, those are really rare moments and that's what you aspire to.'

The voyage of the *Argo* was a test of endurance of a different magnitude to the Boat Race – and, indeed, a challenge of a different quality. After twenty minutes and four miles down the Thames you're done, but there is almost always more of the Aegean to churn up. Ten, twelve, fourteen hours a day they would row, five oars on each side striking at once, any men spare enjoying five minutes' breathing space. Even with the heft of ten or more men the boat travelled at just two knots, which even a small modern boat with an outboard motor could exceed. This was with the wind against them; with a following gust, the boat sailed itself. When the wind was implacable they moored up and waited for it to turn, just as Jason would have done.

Aetiology was embedded in the journey, and as a classicist who had brought his text and translation of Apollonius with him, Mark could be the aetiologist, the interpreter of the environment, deciphering which natural features had been mythologised. 'One of things that we picked up on the journey was that maybe some of the Jason myth has some basis in reality,' Mark says. 'Apollonius of Rhodes wrote the *Argonautica* and so you have a third-century account of a mythical voyage. There are references to it in other, more ancient writers as well – Homer describes it as an event in recent history. They're all part of mythology, yes, but was there any historical background to it? You've got the gods involved, the Clashing Rocks, all sorts of monsters, and obviously these things aren't real,' but, voyaging and reading, the geography and the nautical conditions of book and reality often fitted. 'You could see how the myth had built up with the physical things they had encountered.'

As a historian, Mark had rational explanations for the

literary tradition: "Where do myth and reality merge? It may well have been the Argo was the first successful trading voyage that broke into uncharted territories and a myth grew up around it, that the reason no boat had gone into the Black Sea was the Clashing Rocks at the mouth of the Bosphorus.' Geography suggests a different reason. 'When you're going through the Bosphorus, what you have is the whole of the Black Sea emptying through a very narrow channel. You've got the big Russian rivers feeding the Black Sea, so you've got a massive weight of water that spills out into the Aegean. If you're on a boat like this, there's a drift coming out of the Hellespont through the Dardanelles. You feel the force of the Black Sea, you've got to row much harder.' He figures the story of the Clashing Rocks for the embroidery and embellishment of embarrassed sailors defeated by the swell.

That doesn't mean that the sailors were easily defeated, and he cites the lie of the Bosphorus, a twisting and shifting line. At its bends, the river flows more swiftly on the outside than in the middle, giving rise to eddies and countercurrents. If you can row into the right countercurrent, it will pull you along effortlessly; the wrong one requires a redoubled effort. Once you've ridden your current, you need to snatch the next one, and that means rowing straight across the river, rowing as hard as you can or you'll be pushed back, into an unexpected eddy or an unhelpful countercurrent.

They didn't have as many oars as the original *Argo*, which was a *pentekonter*, having fifty oars against the modern *Argo's* twenty. They had no idea if a twenty-oared boat could fight against the current; they weren't sure if their voyage was going to end then and there. 'We knew it was going to be tough. There was a risk that we would go across the headland, row across the stream and just get swept backwards.' The boat could go at four knots at a push, five at a sprint, and the water thundered out of the Bosphorus at five, meaning their maximum was just sufficient to match the torrent.

Failure would mean the Black Sea would be unsliced, their mission fruitless, Jason's myth unverified. They considered a tow a defeat, so they rowed, and just as Jason silenced the Clashing Rocks, so the modern Argonauts silenced them, too.

The sea doesn't appreciate effort or intentions, of course. 'There was one storm where we got blown out into the middle of the Black Sea. We left port and the forecast was a gale, but we carried on regardless, and we got caught out. By the time it was too late, we were too far out to sea, we couldn't row against the gale, which was increasing, so we abandoned ourselves to our fate. We had two life rafts on board and an emergency radio. The emergency radio didn't work.

'It was…frightening at times, because this was untested, we'd never been in a storm of that kind, it was gale force eight, nine, ten maybe, the waves – you could see the waves, they were above the boat. Only once or twice did they break into the boat, so we never got swamped, but you never knew if the next wave was going to break on to you. One night we slept wearing lifejackets, being ready to abandon ship at a moment's notice. We didn't sleep much.

'There's nothing…You can't row in those conditions, you can't sail because the wind's pushing you out, so we were blown out to the middle of the Black Sea. Too deep to drop anchor.

'If worst came to the worst, it was a boat made to float so at least we could stay with the hull. After two nights out at sea – one was extremely dangerous – once the gale had blown itself out we were sailing back – we were rowing back again. We were exposed to quite a lot then – but it made a great story, and tested the boat.' Without a keel, the boat bobbed along; a keel would have offered resistance and supplemented the sea's fury.

Enduring the Black Sea's temperament made Mark realise that the Greeks had been unwilling sailors. 'The Greeks, even in classical times, were afraid of the sea. They had a lot of euphemisms – the Black Sea was the Euxine, the Happy Sea. It's like when you're being attacked by a large Alsatian, you say, "Nice dog! Nice dog!" The Black Sea, the Dark Sea, that was its real name, because it was quite a threatening sea. The Euxine was a sea to be feared. *Any* sea was feared. The Aegean can turn with a gale, with a Meltemi in August it can sink ferries. The Greeks hated seafaring – it was seen as a dangerous thing for them. It was a necessary evil. A lot of them would go out and never be seen again.'

If Turkey offered a physical difficulty to ford, Georgia posed a political problem. In 1984, *perestroika* and *glasnost* were on the horizon but the Soviet Union was still cool on Westerners striking its borders with boats, even if those boats were nothing more than balsa wood and binding. The sea border between Turkey and Russia had been sealed to non-diplomatic shipping since the Second World War, yet even the Russians, it proved, were susceptible to the power of television. Tim Severin became friendly with Yuri Senkevich, presenter of the popular programme *Travel Club*. Senkevich himself had been part of a recreationist voyage, Thor Heyerdahl's boat *Kon-Tiki*, which proved that humans could have crossed the Pacific to populate Polynesia. Severin relied on Senkevich to sort out the visas. Senkevich relied on Severin for material.

The first thing the crew saw in Soviet waters was a gunboat. 'Are we seen as a hostile boat? Because we didn't know. We'd had no contact with them. No other boat had officially crossed that border, we thought we'd give it a go. We had our visas, but that's all we had. We didn't know if this gunboat was going to come and blow us out of the water.' The boat drew up alongside them. An official boarded and asked to see their passports – then welcomed them with delight. Even so, the crew knew that they had been vetted by the KGB, not least because one of them had been in the military, and that a paranoid state could as easily have pushed them all the way back down the Bosphorus.

As they later rowed into the port city of Poti, they encountered a quayside bristling with Georgians, a male choir singing in full voice. 'We were treated like national heroes. Because it was the voyage of Jason and the Argonauts, it's a similar kind of myth to Saint George in this country. For them, it was contact with the outside world, it was a great national thing – he slayed the dragon, stole the Golden Fleece, stole the princess Medea.' Georgian resentment of the Soviet yoke could also find expression in this celebration of a national hero. They were put up at the state's expense, fed, entertained, toasted and televised. When they finally arrived at their terminus, the Georgians had arranged for a woman to be dressed as Medea and for a Golden Fleece to hang from a bough – two pieces of evidence perhaps not to be adduced in the aetiological cause.

'We were bussed around. It was hotel to hotel, and it was so much that we were overwhelmed by everything we saw. They took us to their national sites, their local archaeology, their main historical and cultural sites, we were on TV, they had a show for us, we stayed at big hotels all the time.' The Georgians did not neglect their hospitality: at each banquet, an *arbiter bibendi* proposed toast after toast after toast. And after the haze of alcohol had cleared and the stupefying hangovers had slunk off, Mark flew home. To what, he wasn't sure. But home he flew.

A genre of love poetry can be seen to start with Catullus, continue with Propertius and Tibullus, and end with Horace and Ovid. Romantic love is defined, redefined, and then opposed by other ideas of love. Methods of putting these ideas and feelings into poetry are invented, tested, refined, rejected. In this book the story is followed and illustrated in copious quotations from the poets' works; all quotations are translated for the benefit of the Latinless reader — the student of English literature, of comparative literature, the 'general reader'. It is hoped that there will be 'general readers': this is beautiful poetry, at times delightfully witty, at times intensely moving; and it can still exercise its power even in translation.

The book combines literary history with literary criticism: it criticises as well as expounds the poems it quotes, and it sets the whole discussion against the social and historical background. Two chapters are devoted to an entertaining but relevant account of contemporary *mores* at Rome.

Finally it is hoped that the book uncovers something of the personality of the poets. Through their poetry these fascinating artists reveal, and mean to reveal, something of the sort of men they were.

Dr. Lyne was Teaching Fellow in Classics, Churchill College, Cambridge, 1969-71 and has since then been Fellow and Tutor in Classics, Balliol College, Oxford. His previous publications are *Catullus, a Handbook* and *Ciris, A Poem attributed to Vergil* (both C.U.P.).

OXFORD UNIVERSITY PRESS   ISBN 0 19 814454 7
£5.25 net in UK
Also available in hardback

GREEK VERSE

COMPOSITION

—

SIDGWICK AND MORICE

AN INTRODUCTION

TO

GREEK VERSE COMPOSITION

PROSE AND VERSE
COMPOSITION
(2002–4)

'Gilbert Murray thought that if you couldn't put something into Greek, probably it wasn't worth saying.' So Donald Russell told me as we sat in his north Oxford living room, with its view of the Radcliffe Observatory, surmounted by Atlas, in turn surmounted by his globe.

But when you do prose composition, turning passages of English into Greek or Latin, as some classicists still must at A-level and at university, it doesn't matter whether the sentiment is worth saying or not – you still have to do it. You learn not to look at the words but to burrow beneath into the thought. I will readily concede that the thought is frequently lacking, but even then you can see what the speaker is getting at, and this is what you have to render in such a way that a fifth-century Greek could understand it. Simple. Luckily, we were never given passages from Martin Amis, something even your Aeschylus-quoting Athenian-in-the-agora might have had trouble comprehending.

To improve our linguistic abilities, and thus the brilliance – or at least the workman-like accuracy – with which we could turn sample sentences into Latin and Greek, we had 9 a.m. sessions on Tuesdays and Thursdays in the Examination Schools for our first two terms. As the Schools were almost next to my room at 71 High Street, I could roll out of bed, fumble my way through the shower, snort some Special K and be in my seat in minutes, ready to regurgitate whichever arcane list of irregular adjectives we boys had had to learn for our test. I say 'we boys' because there was only one (mannish) girl in the top Latin set, and none in the top Greek. Sets had been assigned by self-rating your linguistic ability – which tells you more about girls' lack of boastfulness than about the state of their knowledge.

These classes were part of the MILC programme: Mods Intercollegiate Language Classes. The acronyms only got worse. In an odd avian pair, the Latin classes were known as PTERODACTYL (Programme To Encourage Revision Of Declensions And Conjugations Testing Your Latin) and the Greek as PTARMIGAN (Programme To Assist Revision [for] Mods In Greek Accidence Now). I suppose the most that can be said for these sloppy contrivances is that at least they're not in Latin or Greek – which would not have been all that surprising in Oxford, a university where you can still take an oath by saying '*do fidem*', Latin for 'I promise'. (Oath-taking was a surprisingly large part of university life.)

My Greek MILC tutor was Professor Christopher Collard, who was retired but had risen from the academic grave to torture a generation anew. 'Sixty per cent is a touch gener-ous,' he wrote on my first week's homework. The second week: 'Fifty, not good at all, Josh; talk to me about it after the class?' His epic handout covered every conceivable grammatical acci-dent and syntactical happening, and we certainly benefited from the knowledge he had accumulated over the past 180 years or so. After he finished teaching me I would occasionally see Professor Collard in the Bodleian. If he noticed me, he'd creakily smile and say, '*University Challenge!*' He was a grave counterpoint to my cheerful Latin tutor, James Morwood. I can still hear Morwood's high flighty voice declaiming his first exemplum, '*cantare me delectat*, boys!' ('I like to sing.')

At the end of every class, Professor Collard would present us with the compositional challenge of a modern English phrase or slogan to be rendered by next week into something an ancient Greek would understand. These included Humphrey Lyttelton's 'Double negatives are an absolute no-no,' although one he did not repeat with us from a previous year was the rude-boy affirmation 'sorted'. The story went that he had been surprised when versions came back with another meaning of 'sorted' – to be sufficiently supplied with drugs – yet had rendered that into Greek, too, unruffled.

Long-form prose composition – turning extended passages, with sentences that follow on from one another, into Latin or Greek, rather than discrete sample lines – may seem like a perverse parlour game for a subject whose relevance is constantly questioned. If Latin and Greek are dead languages, there must be even less point in learning how to *write* in them than there is in learning how to *read* in them. It is also a difficult discipline, which has made it all the less popular.

Some of my tutees after Oxford groaned when I broached it, because they knew that its cruelty was exactly the same as its benefit – it would force them to learn their grammar properly, to understand how the language works, how its sentences come together, to study authors' styles and then to apply all of this with precision to a foreign vocabulary rife with irregularities and subtle connotations. There is nothing quicker at exposing ignorance than sloppy prose composition; the infinity of fine distinctions in Greek grammar makes it a delight to read but a devil to compose. (Latin is less picky and thus less delightful.)

Take voices. The active voice is when the subject performs the action (I write this book), the passive when the subject is acted upon (the book *is written* by me). But there is also the middle voice, when one acts upon oneself or causes something to be done ('Henry VIII built palaces' doesn't mean he got his trowel out). Many Greek verbs are mysteriously middle.

Further hair-splitting. Consider the sentence 'He rented a room to cheat on his wife'. Does it mean he cheated *once* because he had nothing to do that night, or that he has a suite at a sleazy hotel rented out at the same time *every week*, a wilted rose always on the pillow, because his marital ennui is eternal? In Greek, it has to be clear, because the former case – a one-off action – demands something in the aorist tense, the latter – habitual – in the present. You need to know your aorist from your elbow or you won't be rightly understood.

Another thing one needs to concentrate on in Greek prose composition is how you connect your clauses, to show how the argument or the story flows. καὶ [kai] is 'and'. ἀλλά [alla] is 'but'. μεν [men] in one clause and δε [de] in the next means something along the lines of 'on the one hand…on the other hand', but can be lighter, merely contrasting two similar ideas or nouns. There is, in fact, a 660-page book devoted *just* to these means of connecting sentences, because their nuances are so subtle and the rules so important for clarity. (I've always thought Western philosophy developed in Greece in part because the language allowed such exactness of thought and expression.) Woe betide anyone who uses a μεν without a δε – it is like serving a meal with a knife but no fork. Being Greek, there is of course an exception. Aeschylus starts the *Oresteia*, his trilogy of tragedies about Agamemnon's return from Troy, his murder by Clytemnestra and the ensuing carnage, with a μεν, but there is no δε to be seen; it is as if he is establishing a problem that has no resolution. The audience would have been *desperate* for that δε.

Back at Magdalen, there were weekly prose comp sessions with Andrew Hobson (and a fair few green graduate students, as Hobson took a long absence of illness) in which I managed to make spectacular mistakes, the sort of things schoolboys would scorn. (Imagine using the Latin equivalent of 'bestest'.) One might fairly assume that digging down for the thought in our proses should not have presented too many difficulties in English, and that was largely true with some of Hobson's prescribed extracts – Boswell, Jowett, Thackeray, Macaulay and Churchill into Latin, and Emerson, Swift, More and Samuel Butler into Greek – but I can still recall the cold wash of incomprehension as J. S. Mill was laid in front of us, a text filled with 'incentives to industry' and 'imperfect protection of its fruits' and even 'anxiety'. When you could not work out how a Greek would think about these things – or in this case even properly understand the English – that was trouble.

One of my propellants was intellectual masochism. At Mods, for this perversity, I took verse composition, prose composition's nastier, more complex sister. The most difficult thing to do in the classical languages? Perfect.

What differentiates verse from prose is metre. Lines of Greek and Latin verse are built around fixed but somewhat flexible rhythms of 'short' and 'long' syllables, whereas prose has no required rhythm at all. In Latin and Greek, the rhythm depends in essence on the time it takes to pronounce their vowels (think *coat* versus *cot*); English poetry, by contrast, uses stress-based syllables. Epic poetry like Homer and Vergil has the dactylic hexameter (variations of *dum-di-di* six times, pretty much), which is flexible and allows for the rhythmic evocation of everything from horses' hooves thundering across a plain to a funeral cortège gravely processing from the field of battle. Greek tragedy employs the iambic trimeter (variations on *di-dum di-dum* three times) for its spoken parts, and a complex variety of lyric metres (any of an almost limitless combination of *di*s and *dum*s) for its choral interludes. In prose you have great freedom to juggle about the order of words and phrases, but in verse you are tightly bound to the rhythm – if the short and long syllables don't match the intended pattern, it's not poetry. It is not a case of shuffling them about until they fit. Some words will never go into certain types of verse because their very nature – an unacceptable combination of longs and shorts – prevents it; that's why you never see the number twelve in Latin epic poetry, only 'twice six'.

If you imagine trying to wallpaper a cave full of stalagmites, you're some of the way to understanding the difficulty. Your mind has to work along two paths at once, forming a complex thought into good Greek even as you try and fit it around the metrical scaffolding, rejigging the Greek as you find it doesn't fit but always thinking about the meaning, otherwise by the time you've got it to fit, 'Shall I compare thee to a summer's day?' will have turned into 'Now is the winter of our discontent.'

That is, unless you are Donald Russell, emeritus professor of classical literature at Oxford and a legendary figure at the university over the past seventy years. When he was teaching Greek verse composition in his flat to me and three of my year from Magdalen, gluttons for punishment all of us, he was nearing eighty-five and yet his mind was more agile than most people's will ever be. Rather than wrenching words and sense to fit, he moulded them elegantly around the metre, like a potter effortlessly shaping a fresh vase from pliant clay. He had seven decades of study and thought and practice on us, but I could never envisage having his deft way in the stickiest of disciplines, where a line can reach perfection only for you to discover that you mistook a short syllable for a long and that it must be wholly redone.

With Professor Russell, we passed a year's worth of happy afternoons, eating cherries he bought from the corner shop downstairs, first using Sidgwick and Morice's venerable *Introduction to Greek Verse Composition* (a thin, forest-green hardback copy of which he gave to me, or at least I somehow managed to retain), then fumbling about with Milton, Shakespeare, Robert Bridges and Goethe's *Faust*. The iambic lines took me hours, arranging and rearranging until my synapses ceased transmitting and the letters danced on the page, but it was what I took most pride in. That is, until I learned from Professor Russell about his time at Bletchley Park. Then I had a whole new source of pride, not in myself but in my mentor.

DONALD RUSSELL
(BORN 1920)

Verse came before service – but only just. In 1939, when Donald Russell went up to Balliol College, with hardly any practice in verse composition, his tutor asked him whether he did hexameters or elegiac couplets (a hexameter followed by a pentameter). Russell averred hexameters, with the suspicion that they would be easier, so his tutor set him twenty lines of Matthew Arnold. 'It took me *most of the week* to do it, to tell you the truth, with the aid of Winbolt's book, *Latin Hexameter Verse*,' he tells me. 'I sweated over it most of the week.'

Composition – both verse and prose – was key in classical studies until the war, Professor Russell says after I have brought in the coffee from the kitchen. At ninety-one, he uses a stroller to get around, making carrying a tray impossible, although he is not much harder of hearing than a decade ago when I sat at his dining table for verse lessons, and he is certainly no less acute – his mind oiled, if not his limbs. 'At one time these things were thought to be the most important part of classical education – that's long, long ago. Great prestige was acquired by being able to do these things properly and it was thought that this was a good sign that you were going to do well in the world.' He gives a brief cheerful laugh, suffixed by a rising wheezy *hmmm*, which does not express puzzlement but is more a rhetorical invitation to assent. 'But that's all gone really. That situation in the schools, late Victorian and Edwardian and early Georgian times, that certainly held. The people who did this very well, they're top civil servants or governors of India or something.'

The antiquity of this world of versifying viceroys is captured in the hand-me-down textbooks. The standard book, Sidgwick and Morice's *Introduction to Greek Verse Composition*, was written in 1883 and last revised in 1955, and there has been almost nothing for Latin verse comp this side of the war. Nevertheless, like those who would return us to the gold standard, verse-composers survive, mostly under Professor Russell's tutelage. (Boris Johnson commissioned Jesus College classicist Armand D'Angour to write an ode in Greek for the London Olympics.) Others don't like teaching verse composition, Professor Russell says, because it requires not just the skill of verse composition – hard enough – but also 'correcting the work with them with the minimum change. It's easier to start afresh than it is to modify what the pupil has done. That is a *difficult* skill.' You can't just give your version of the verse as the correct one – like a subtle editor, you have to respect the author's voice, even when the author is a bolshie second-year undergraduate, and work with what they give you.

There is an element of nature in being able to do verses, he says – an innate manipulative skill, the ability to conceive of the manifold repercussions of putting *this* word *there* within a complex system of rules, just like a chess player contemplating the board and its arrayed nobility. This must be combined with a capacious memory, able to draw on a line of Ovid or Euripides for support. Using words from the right era or dialect is important. He once damned a verse of mine by looking up some unusual word I had used and kindly querying, 'Clement of Alexandria, eh?' That was too late a word for Sophocles to have used – by about seven hundred years. Like all skills, however, it is improved by time and practice, neither of which Professor Russell currently lacks: 'It's been easier since I retired. I've probably written more verses in the past ten or fifteen years than I ever wrote before!'

Evidence of this is lying in front of me on the coffee table. He has composed an introduction in Latin elegiac couplets to a new collection of verses made by pupils at Merchant Taylors' School over the centuries. With his surpassing modesty – if that is not an oxymoron – Professor Russell earlier in his career refused to let his compositions be published; even if his ability was never in doubt, he said that he lacked the confidence. In his new poem he focuses on the composers rather than the composed, which tended to be standbys like Arnold and Shakespeare, with psalms and extracts from the Bible when in vogue. He captures the proud young poets (*gaudentes poetae*) who worked on verses because their teachers taught them that 'only classics could / give fortune, eloquence and moral good' (*eloquium mores virtutem cuncta parari / his tantum studiis credere moris erat*), the essence of imperial self-assurance. Foolish some call verse composition, but 'great men emerged from all that foolishness!' (*summos … hac e stultitia prosiluisse viros*).

If this view of verse composition as literary bran flakes no longer holds true, its endurance – like so much else in classics – is its own charm: students like to do it partly because 'it's got a tradition behind it and they like to be in it'. But there is something else, something not much found in education any more – creativity. 'When you've done it, you've made a little bit of handwork. I think that appeals, *hmmmm*.' Later, he comes back to this idea: 'It has a deeper side to it, an imaginative side to it, because you have to think about shapes and colours and events and people as well as manipulating the line.' He concludes with a satisfied *yes*. It's typical of Oxford that one of the few forms of creative writing that goes on is in classical verse.

Inside my copy of Sidgwick and Morice, at the end of the Authors' Preface, there is a Publishers' Note, which begins, 'The entire stock of this work was destroyed by enemy action in December 1940.' In December 1940, Donald Russell was in his second year at Balliol, probably anticipating Mods with its verse comp paper the following term, working with or without one of the unconflagrated copies of Sidgwick and Morice. If the book-bombing was an incursion of the war into classics, several of Oxford's brightest classicists, including Donald Russell, were about to find themselves repaying the favour at Bletchley Park.

In a lecture Professor Russell gave in 1996, eventually published in 2007, he spoke about his own undergraduate experience, and in particular what Oxford was like during the war.[1] Some of the most renowned German classicists had fled to England, Hitler's persecutions having an unintended benefit for Oxonian undergraduates. The days of 1940 and 1941 were taken up with study and with military preparation, with 'drilling in the Meadow, learning the parts of the Bren gun, and listening to improbable lectures: the poet Edmund Blunden on platoon tactics and a philosophy don, who shall be nameless, who managed to cast a cloud of metaphysical obscurity over the relatively simple topic of map-reading'. Despite the intellectual light, darkness was preponderant. 'For our real pleasures, we took our dimmed torches and scuttled through the dark streets of a blacked-out Oxford to Corpus or

Christ Church or Oriel. No lines of festal light, no welcoming lamps in college lodges, only wicket-gates to be pushed open, and a discreet glimmer within.'

Assimilating and mixing with those returning from the war, including those from Dunkirk who were camping on Port Meadow, led the students into an unwitting doublethink predicated on fearful self-preservation. Through 'youthful resilience – or callousness, or immaturity, or plain stupidity, or whatever it is', the undergraduates imagined an impermeable line between themselves and the soldiers, who had themselves been undergraduates a short time before. Although they were keen to contribute to the war effort, they could simultaneously 'compartmentalise', in Professor Russell's word.

Asked about when he got his summons, Professor Russell sounds almost a little impatient – not with the question but with the delay to his service (I hope): 'The call-up was not very quick – it was 1941 before I actually got into the army.' He also has a certain modesty – or reticence – about how he was picked for Bletchley. 'I expect through the university. It's all written up in the books on the Bletchley Park affair and how it was recruited and so on. Lindsay Moss was Master of Balliol at that time. He no doubt put a lot of names forward.' Several published accounts credit Oxbridge heads of house with selecting chess-playing, crossword-solving classicists. They joined an extensive list of notable classicists at BP.[2]

But Russell was not picked to work on the German codes at Bletchley – he was part of the much smaller band of Japanese code-breakers, needed after Pearl Harbor opened a new front. 'I was in the army, in the Signals actually. I had been in training really and then I was suddenly fetched out and I was sent to learn Japanese – it's well written-up – at Bedford and

I spent the rest of the war doing that.' He moves away from the subject of Bletchley but returns a little later to elaborate. 'I was on the third, I think, of these courses, and there were other courses. These course were held at Bedford, at a house in the middle of Bedford, and the person in charge, you'll find him mentioned in all these things, was Oswald Tuck, Captain Tuck, RN, the naval captain. Splendid man with a little white beard and a *very good teacher*. Really a gifted teacher.

'The whole thing was organised by that very brilliant cryptographer, John Tiltman, who was a regular army officer and had made great advances in the Japanese codes. And he recruited people, he thought that you could teach people enough in six months or so to be useful.' Two years was felt to be the minimum sufficient. 'The Americans didn't believe it, but he was proved right.'

His voice is kindly and didactic even as he scours his memory. 'There we all were, quite sharp at doing Latin proses and things, and we could all do it and we managed to do it. It was a curious business. I was there for some months. Most of my colleagues like Bill Sibley are dead now. The person I worked under, Chris Wiles, I think he's still alive, he's very deaf, and I didn't get a Christmas card this year so I don't know! His younger brother, Maurice Wiles, the Regius Professor of Divinity here, he was in it, too.'

Cambridge classicist Hugh Denham's account of his schooling in Japanese at Bedford was published in *Code Breakers: The Inside Story of Bletchley Park*. It gives some evocative details – Captain Tuck's first words to the students, for example: '"When I come into the room," he began, "you are to stand up. I shall then say *shokun ohayo*, which means 'all you princes are honourably early'. You will then reply *ohayo gozaimasu*, which means 'honourably early it honourably is'. I shall now leave the room and come in again, and we shall do this." Which we did.'[3]

The course's chief difficulty was teaching several Japanese systems of writing, all of which might be needed for translating decoded messages: *hiragama* and *katakana*, two fifty-character syllabic *kana* scripts (each symbol represents a consonant and a vowel); *kanji*, logographic Chinese symbols; and *romaji*, transliterations of Japanese into the Roman alphabet. Dictionaries were available, though in scarcity – Denham recorded his relief at receiving 'a treasure...the 2,294-page Japanese-to-English Kenkyusha dictionary' – and the students learned a thousand military and diplomatic terms.[4] Having an actual conversation in Japanese was another, impossible, matter, a skill taught mainly to those who would be interrogating Japanese prisoners. The need for all these alphabets was not because they would have to read the messages in them – decodes were rendered as *romaji* – but because the translators had to be able to look up the words in dictionaries. Even once you had decoded the message, it took a certain tilt of mind to understand foreign words the Japanese had used: 'CHI-YA-A-CHI-RU does not obviously spell Churchill to the untrained eye,' wrote Maurice Wiles wryly.[5]

Before translation came decryption. There were many types of codes used by the Japanese, some simpler, where the operator looked up a word in a code book and transmitted just that code-group (JN 4), some more complicated, where the code-group was 'reciphered' (JN 25, the main system of Japanese naval communications). The code Donald Russell worked on was that of the Japanese Military Attaché (JMA), a digraph code in which the basic *kana* syllables stood for themselves, and other two-letter groups stood for certain words or phrases commonly used in military communications. For example, AB stood for 'west' and AV for 'message continued'. The two-letter groups were then set out in a square grid in adjacent squares, sometimes horizontally and sometimes diagonally, and the letters were read off vertically to form the basis for the encrypted text. They were then enciphered using a prearranged 'literal additive', a series of letters that would be notionally 'added' to the letters taken out of the grid on the basis of a pattern laid down in advance on a separate table. Reading off the enciphered letter along the relevant horizontal line and the 'additive' letter down the appropriate vertical column would produce a super-enciphered letter which would be transmitted by the operator.[6]

The recipient, as someone once said of Ginger Rogers, had to do all of this, but backwards.

John Tiltman had broken the code but did not feel that his Japanese was strong enough to work on the decoded messages, so he set up the unit at Bletchley. 'That stage was being largely handed over to us,' wrote Maurice Wiles. 'We felt pretty ill-equipped...None of the thousand or so characters that we had so painstakingly learnt were there on the page before us. Something more was needed, for which we had no specialist training – an approach to problem-solving that our initial interviewers no doubt hoped had been ingrained in us by our interest in chess and crosswords.'[7]

Although Maurice Wiles said it was 'not the most difficult of codes' once they had understood how it worked, Professor Russell says it was not simple, either. 'I was basically a translator, but in the Military Attaché Cipher, the process of deciphering it could hardly be done without the cooperation of the people who knew something of the language. So I was involved in several stages of this apart from the final translation. I can remember spending hours and hours with *huge* sheets of paper, trying to reconstruct what they call the subtractor at the top of the page, going through all sorts of things.' They were called 'strippers', the people who found the subtractor and removed it from the received message.

Work on the JMA was fruitful, 'producing a good deal of intelligence...The codebreakers were able to read the messages of the Japanese military attachés without any problems...The messages provided a wealth of useful material on the movement and existence of Japanese military units.'[8] Messages that were a few weeks old could still be valuable, given the advance planning that a pan-Pacific campaign necessitated. The code often transmitted political and military affairs, whether fact or gossip, but individually significant messages were rare. They did discern the intention of the Japanese to have British POWs build the Burma railway, and there was one particularly notable message from 1944, of which Professor Russell had recently been reminded when an old friend of his late wife visited him. The lady recollected that 'in the weeks before D-Day, in the spring of 1944, the Japanese people in Berlin were shown the defences of the French coast by the Germans, they were given a tour of these defences and they wrote home about it.'

Professor Russell has a self-deprecating attitude to his time at Bletchley, despite the continual good work his unit did. It could be modesty, but on its edges frustration mingles with indifference. He says of the intercepted D-Day message that 'that was one of the few times when one thought one was doing something fairly close to the – ' and even though he breaks off it is clear he means something close to the action, something of importance. Were there other important messages? 'There must have been quite a lot. Some of it was nonsense. You learned at an early date that not everything that is a secret is important.' His laugh ends on a cliff-edge silence.

Other Japanese code-breakers had better cause to deprecate the time they spent at Bletchley. Hugh Denham was told in 1942, before the newly trained undergraduates arrived, that of the thousand Japanese naval messages intercepted every day, only forty got to Bletchley, and that the real work of decryption was done in Washington, Kilindini in Kenya and Melbourne. These other centres continued to be of greater importance throughout the war. One of Denham's colleagues in the Japanese Naval Section said, 'The recoveries that the section made and circulated were few, tentative and regarded with condescension' by the other units, and Denham recalled much greater satisfaction and achievement during his postings at Kilindini and Colombo.[9]

As the Brits at Bletchley worked away, the bulk of the deciphering was being done in America. The Americans had early computers and plenty of people at the navy decoding centre, OP-20-G, in Washington, which Professor Russell recalls without bitterness but without satisfaction: 'Whereas we had a small handful of people, they turned masses of people on to the job. The whole computer thing started in these circumstances. I was not involved in that at all – it was pencil and paper, our job.' He then occupies the traditional English redoubt: 'I'm afraid we thought their efforts were sometimes a little unscholarly.' I say that that's a very dignified way of putting it. 'We thought, just as you would – it was our classical training – we thought they were churning this stuff out and they made quite a lot of mistakes.' This suits as a microcosm of British perceptions of America during and since the war: brains and pluck on one side, might on the other; Britain's erudite Greece to America's brash Rome.

Elizabeth Ross, who worked on Japanese codes at the Park, recalled the competition with the Americans, straining to beat their computers with British intellect: 'If we got some way in there was always a feeling that we shouldn't tell them this time: "We can get there first. Don't let them know about this one." That was always the joke, of course. We always did tell them but we always felt that we did terribly well without the machinery and vast amounts of manpower they had.'[10] Maurice Wiles, in a generally acerbic account of his – and Bletchley's – role in Japanese code-breaking, concurs as to the mood: 'There is a sense in which they were for us the "enemy" against whom we were working, the spur to more vigorous endeavour.' When the Americans sent hints about codes, they were 'greeted with a feeling of failure and self-reproach', but 'times when we could show they had got something wrong were occasions of unconcealed glee'.[11] These happy occasions were made rarer because of a significant level of jealous territorialism and suspicion between competing military and intelligence hierarchies across the Atlantic.

Despite the successes of the various Japanese decryption units, Bletchley Park's role in cracking Japanese codes was of minor significance next to Washington's *and* next to the work others at Bletchley did on German codes. This infected the air, according to Maurice Wiles: 'We did not have the stimulus of knowing that the fruits of our labour were of immediate importance in the conduct of the war – something which, we dimly realized, characterized the work of some of those in other sections, even though internal security was sufficient to ensure that we had little idea how true those surmisings were.'[12]

Michael Loewe in *Code Breakers* agrees: 'All in all the value of this work seen in retrospect was highly questionable.'[13] And the author of *The Emperor's Codes* says that the successes of the Japanese code-breakers ultimately did not approach those of the German ones: 'The influence exerted by Ultra on the war in the Far East and Pacific only rarely matched its effect on the European war.'[14] When the end of the war in the East came, its sound was not that of scratching pencils in an English hut but of whirring machines in American laboratories. Two months after the bombs were dropped on Hiroshima and Nagasaki, some of the Bletchley Park code-breakers were ready to go back to university.

I ask Professor Russell how he feels about his personal contribution, but instantly I realise that this question is meaningless – anyone I have spoken to who lived through the war has been a generous communitarian. When they consider the war, they talk of duty and service, not achievement and individualism. So with Professor Russell: 'No, well, there was nothing personal about it really – we as a department probably did, we worked quite hard, but there was nothing personal about it. I think that was a rather good thing about it, compared with your usual ethos of academia, which goes in for personal achievement and individual effort. This was a team effort, very much.'

Bletchley was conducive to teamwork by hut, but the silent hours of decryption meant a default mode of keeping to oneself. Half a century after the war, Professor Russell's lady friend proved this: 'We discovered we'd both been at the

Park at the same time and we discovered that we must have at one time been working in the same room!' You never spoke to someone from another hut – let alone from outside Bletchley – about your work. There were also long years after the war when no one could talk about Bletchley – an intense and penetrating secrecy. 'It was rather uncanny in a way because there we were all back as young undergraduates in the late forties and half of us knew one another from this, but we couldn't talk about it. I suppose privately, me and my former colleagues, we might have made a joke or two about the old days.'

The silence of the Park is something that Professor Russell recalls, although it is hard to imagine, judging by a visit today, where stentorian, faux-jolly tour guides march blue-rinsed groups from hut to hut, delivering Enigmatic blasts of obscure facts. Several of the huts and blocks have been filled with informative displays, which are their own kind of noise: visual, verbal, historical. One hut tells how three brave sailors – including sixteen-year-old Tommy Brown – recovered code books from a sinking U-boat which helped those in Bletchley working on Turing's Bombe. Indeed, in Block B is a full-size whirring recreation of the Bombe and, a little further away, Turing's teddy bear, Porgy.

Finding the display in Block B about breaking the Japanese codes does itself require a little detective work, or at least persistence – also a cherished Bletchley quality. A small alcove tucked around several corners, it is not even visible until you stumble on it, and only then if you have forged past Tommy Brown's carriage-clock. Consisting of two vitrines of documents and a case with Japanese code books, card indices of deciphered messages and a scarf apparently belonging to a kamikaze pilot, it has been set out of the way so as not to distract from the more famous (and admittedly more significant) German code-cracking exhibits. Still, its materials are interesting: an intercepted Japanese telegraph message, represented as pencilled pairs of numbers; two code books lying open, with their columns of methodical combinations of English letters and Japanese symbols; translators' vocab notebooks (*shireichookan* = commander-in-chief); notebooks with Japanese characters above transliterations above translations; flashcards with single words on, the sort students still use today. With the Enigma machines and the massive Bombe and the explanatory video, you get a vivid sense of the process of code-catching and code-cracking; this Japanese display makes it seem only like so much labour-intensive paperwork. It's a deathly display away from the hum and crackle and electricity (literal and metaphorical) of its German cousin round the corner. Given the silence that Professor Russell recalled, perhaps this is fair.

This silence is, in another way, in another part of the Park, too easy to imagine. Neither Hut 5, where John Tiltman broke the Japanese Military Attaché code, nor Block F, where Donald Russell worked, has survived. The former had been demolished by 1954, the latter in 1987. If you want to hear the silence Donald Russell heard, stand in front of the crumbling steps and blank plot that are all that remain of Block F, in an unvisited corner of the Park.

All the time I have been reading about verse composition and the work at Bletchley Park, each has suggested to me the other, so I ask Professor Russell whether there is a symmetry between the skills needed for verse composition and those required for his activities at Bletchley – a dexterity with encoded texts.

He gives his dismissal in his kindly tone: 'I don't think you can make a case for verse in particular, but you can make a case for a connection with various kinds of classical scholarly activities. Frankly, I don't think the particular skills of verse were relevant. The skills of textual criticism were more to the point really – sorting out corruptions and that sort of thing. That was more to the point. And also the habit of thinking hard and deep thinking – the general habit of translating. I don't think you can say that verse-writing skills had anything to do with it.' Not even with the precise manipulation of syllables? 'Not particularly. You do manipulations in any case in any kind of translation, either way round, you manipulate when you're considering variant readings in a text. That sort of sharpness was probably more relevant, and as students in those days we did a lot of that, too.' Students in those days did a lot more than that, too.

Professor Donald Russell photographed for his sixty-fifth
anniversary as a fellow of St John's College

THE ODES OF PINDAR

The Odes of Pindar

translated with an introduction by

C. M. BOWRA

To Peter
with love and gratitude
from

maurice.

PENGUIN BOOKS

PINDAR
(2004–6)
and
THE TIMES
(2004)

I t was for one of my Finals papers that I had to find a translation of the lyric poet Pindar, author of obsequious and
abstruse *epinikia*, victory songs for patrons who had funded
the winners in one of the many games held across the Greek
world. While the Olympic Games have endured, there were
Isthmian, Nemean and Pythian games, too, all prestigious Pan-
hellenic festivals which included chariot-racing, running and
the *pankration*, a wrestling/boxing hybrid competition without
rules. Pindar was a poet of the laureate, and the unfortunate
consequence was sycophantic celebration.

'Water is the best thing of all, and gold shines like flaming
fire at night,' opens an ode to the Sicilian tyrant Hieron after
his team's victory in the horse race at Olympia. 'Look no more,'
he continues, 'for another bright star by day in the empty sky
more warming than the sun, nor shall we name any gathering greater than the Olympian.' There is a fawning, bombastic
climax. 'One man is great in this way, another in that, but at
the peak of all are Kings. Look no farther than this. I pray you
may walk exalted all these days of your life, and may I so long
keep company with victors, a beacon-light of song among the
Hellenes everywhere.' The mixture of pompous adulation and

sweaty-browed pleading still induces a slight nausea.

Nevertheless, he was necessary, and to avoid the gouging that the admittedly well-stocked Blackwell's perpetrates (as if paying two thirds of the *modern* price for a second-hand book is reasonable), I went to the second-hand Classics Bookshop on Turl Street, which left Oxford's classicists bereft when high rents later forced it to abandon the city. Upstairs in the narrow gallery I picked up the 1969 Penguin Classics translation of Pindar (from which I have quoted above), a small black paper-back with a Greek vase on the front cover, depicting two naked men seemingly engaged in some activity not wholly athletic. Its pages, slightly rough to the touch, were raw sienna with age and had the universal scent – sweet and dusty – of the forgotten contents of an abandoned library. The poems had been translated by Sir Maurice Bowra, the most notorious, if not most eminent, classicist of the last century – warden of Wadham College, vice chancellor of the University of Oxford, scholar, translator, poet, bitch.

When I got the book home, I saw that on the title page was an inscription:

To Peter
With love and gratitude
From Maurice

Logic suggested that this had to be *the* Maurice, since it was his translation. Maurice, a name that struck fear (or at least distaste) into friends and enemies alike, all of whom dreaded his tongue. The Peter was not obvious – to me, at any rate. Being a far more common name, I thought I ought to con-centrate on the obviously celebrated figure, but when I went to Oxford to talk to Al Moreno, my old ancient history tutor, and mentioned the inscription he suggested Peter Levi, and the preface confirmed this:

> I owe a great debt to Father Peter Levi, sj, who has read my text with generous care and made many wise suggestions. For the many faults that remain I must myself bear the responsibility.
>
> C.M.B. [CECIL MAURICE BOWRA]

Now who on earth was Peter Levi? As it turns out, one of the great barely remembered literary figures of the last century.

Poet-scholar-archaeologist-traveller-Jesuit-priest Peter – or at least a snatch of Peter – had been within my grasp before I had ever heard of him, and well before I acquired one of his books.

For anyone brought up with our traditional Latinised system of onomastics – Hector for Hektor, Achilles for Achilleus, Hecuba for the alien Hekabe – Martin Hammond's Penguin Classics prose translation of the *Iliad*, where transliteration is almost given free reign, restoring Greekness to timid familiar names, is a little shocking. This spare text lacks the elegance of Richmond Lattimore's poetic version, but it has an unadorned clarity. Plunging into it for my Greek A-level, I began to appreciate the omnipresent similes from the natural world and the tautness of the battle scenes, simultaneously rejoicing in gore and pitying the dispatched. (My favourite death in the *Iliad* is the one in Book XVI where the charioteer Kebriones is hit in the face by a stone, 'smashing the two brows together: the bone could not hold, and his eyes dropped to the ground in the dust right there in front of his feet'.)

One of the approving quotations on the back of my book read: "'A fine *Iliad* for our times" – Philip Howard in *The Times*.' This later came to mean something to me because during my second summer vacation from Oxford I got an internship at *The Times*, which was then in an old warehouse adjacent to Fortress Wapping. I worked first on 'The Register', where I wrote 'Life in Brief' obits for the minor leagues of the dead and then one for David Hare, who I pray lives a long life so that my inept potted biography, written without having seen any of his plays, never comes to light. Then it was on to the leaders desk. The leader writers themselves were inspiring marriages of intellect and verbal skill. Their office was a senior common room of the clever, the worldly and the engaging. Only Oxbridge firsts need apply, I was warned in jest, and in earnest. Hannah Betts had a doctorate in English from Oxford and wrote both leaders and *The Times*'s make-up column.

Leader writer Philip Howard, who also wrote the 'Modern Times' etiquette column, where godparents were complained of and the napkin versus serviette debate persisted, was a cheerful classicist who encouraged me, handing over his 'Wordwatch' column – *Call My Bluff* for the morning marmalade. The joy was not simply in rifling through the complete OED to find antiquarian, sesquipedalian words but – as I was gleefully encouraged by Philip – in making up the citations in the answer. Philip saw 'Wordwatch' as the perfect position for taking secret revenge on one's enemies. No one noticed my sniping but the subtlety of the slight was pleasing. (I would like to say that I cannot imagine being so petty today. I would *like* to…)

When I turned over my *Iliad*, Philip's name was what I saw, making me feel slightly closer to my goal because *I knew someone quoted on the back of a book.* Surely that seat on the leaders desk was not far away, as if association were a currency one needed to hoard until it could be splurged on a truly heroic name-drop. Perhaps it is.

Several years later, soon after I had started researching this book, I was translating tranches of *Iliad* XVI with a pupil for her AS-level, no doubt repeating what Mr Woodhead had taught me in his dusty, marsh-green classroom, complete with a fine example of the endangered species of blackboard and desks with antique graffiti. The lessons from my schooldays have stuck better than they ought, I often suspect, as I remember where I first learned many of my opinions. I was sure I could hear Mr Woodhead's voice as I spoke about Achilleus' mocking simile comparing his comrade Patroklos to a small nagging child. While I was waiting for my pupil to copy up our translation, I reread the back cover of the Penguin Classic. '"Martin Hammond's modern prose version is the best and most accurate there has ever been" – Peter Levi in the *Independent*.' As I would soon learn, Peter often hid in plain sight.

PETER LEVI
(1931–2000)

S tuffed somewhere between crumbling Penguin paperbacks
from the fifties and the eighteenth reprint of *Cujo*, on the
trestle tables of the book market that lives outside the British
Film Institute on the South Bank, is the only place I have ever
seen any of Peter Levi's books for sale. It was *The Flutes of
Autumn*, one of his memoirs, and although he became known
as a poet, I have never seen any of his collections in the wild.
His considerable and varied achievements as poet, scholar and
travel writer, burnished in life, have largely gone to rust in
death. It only eventually became clear to me why.

It was not even a long descent into desuetude. He died
in 2000 and his memory is retained among scholars, critics
and *littérateurs* of a certain age, but his poems have never
found their way into the wider affection and consciousness
or, indeed, on to academic syllabuses, although their tensions
between faith and reason, man and nature, animate them and
fascinate. He is Ted Hughes but with religion, a less surreal
Seferis, the Greek Nobel laureate, his favourite poet and a
friend. Despite the achievement of his lifelong ambition – to
become the Professor of Poetry at Oxford – in the 1980s, he
is not widely read or studied by scholars, or even requested on
Poetry Please. The Peter Levi who emerges from his own prose
and poems, and from interviews with his family and friends,
would never have expected or demanded such posterity, but

he deserves it nonetheless. This is the paradox of Peter, his modesty and his talent at unspoken odds with each other.

Inasmuch as most lives are conflicts between heredity and self-determination, mores and nature, expectations and actions and achievements, Peter's was a fertile battlefield, encapsulated in his name: Peter Chad Tigar Levi. Peter was an apostle of Christ, Levi a tribe of Israel. The Chad was a saint who evangelised to and converted the Mercians, the Tigar 'supposedly after a shipwrecked Spaniard from the Armada who knew no other word intelligible to the English but the name of the ship's dog'.[15] Perhaps salt water runs in the Tigars' veins. Peter records how he 'fell in love with the sea, and screamed with pleasure when I saw it from a train' as a child, and it would go on to be one of the key themes of his poetry.[16]

Peter's love of books, his desire to be a poet and his passion for nature are strands that wound themselves around his unsatisfactory schooling. Born on 16 May 1931 in Ruislip, Middlesex – then rural and not yet incorporated into London – Peter followed his older brother, Anthony, to Prior Park School in 1937, although at six he was too young to go, because he cried until he was sent with him.[17] He was bullied 'monotonously' and to escape he fled into the woods and read voraciously, poetry chiefly. Poetry was permitted as an occupation after homework had been finished, and his first effort was an imitation of Sir Walter Scott. Since then, he said, he never stopped writing.[18] Then, at Beaumont College, the Jesuit school Peter attended from 1946 to 1948, the training for his inchoate calling made 'me a poet and a kind of scholar. I was set free to read on and on in many unlikely section of libraries.' His love of nature was stoked by boredom, and frustration drove him to 'an intensity of vision'.[19] No one stopped him. The guilt the

Jesuit teachers felt towards poets after their harsh treatment of Gerard Manley Hopkins worked to Peter's advantage.

At Heythrop College, another Jesuit institution, where Peter studied philosophy from 1948 to 1951, he broke into the forbidden, 'intoxicating' theological library, scrambling over a roof to get in, an indicator of his agility and determination, fine traits for the mountain-climbing in Afghanistan and cave-exploring in Greece that he undertook.[20] He read everything he could, from the Bible to John Donne, but preferred to dally in the woods with their cows and foxes and flowers, all of which thrilled him when compared with the didactic torture of lessons in the baroque country house school. In his memoirs and in his poetry one can see that he does not just attend to the splendid varieties of birds, animals, plants, flowers, trees and streams with an encyclopaedic ardour for nature, but that he is also attuned to the spirit of places and is a master of evoking it. However, the earlier bullying and the later absence of authority that allowed Peter to develop his passions eventually made him unable to cope with the strictures of his calling.

Peter had more than one calling, in truth. His first collection of poetry, *The Gravel Ponds*, was published in 1960, when he was twenty-nine, and it and other early work earned him sufficient plaudits to be included in *British Poetry since 1945*, a 1970 volume in the Penguin Poets series. The introduction to his selection was positive, if backhanded: '[His work] can sometimes be compared with that of Elizabeth Jennings. Often, however, it seems an uneasy mixture of earlier literary influences: Wordsworth and W. B. Yeats cohabit in one and the same poem, and the tone varies wildly from stanza to stanza.'[21]

The title poem, included in the anthology, touches on themes (death or the imminence of death, suffering or the imminence of suffering), settings (the natural world) and moods (raging, resigned, empathetic) that he would develop throughout his poetic career, but its monosyllabic rhythm and sharp line breaks have an attention-grabbing violence, turning in the final stanza into longer, more elegant and rueful lines. More dramatic than much of Peter's poetry, it is an arresting opening salvo, if somewhat juvenile in its minor-key hysteria. It starts in tension, ends in calm:

> A tightening net
> traps all creatures
> even the wildest.

> Too late
> the young cry out,
> and the innocent,
> who were not wild enough.

> Bodies and tears
> are useless;
> so few years
> are helpless;
> free creatures are never wild enough.

> The noose closes
> making the tragic
> young the pathetic
> in slum clearance houses.

Never, O never in the long distraction
of the heart's inaction
never will a cry shake
that prison, or wildness wake.

The young were like those swans
which with folded wings
swim on the gravel ponds
on late June evenings:
like doomed stage characters,
pursued murderers
or slum lovers.

Peter quickly became a celebrated member of Oxford's literary set, and indeed his reputation spread more widely, giving him sufficient sway to entice Allen Ginsberg and Gregory Corso to Oxford. According to David Pryce-Jones, a friend of Peter's, this caused a shouting match at a reading between Ginsberg, who had read a poem in praise of dropping the nuclear bomb, supported by Corso and Peter, and 'all these little lefties in the audience, who were incredibly shocked because they were all pacifists and anti-nuclear CND people'.

The dedication of the opening poem of *Water, Rock and Sand* (1962), Peter's second collection, emphasises how much a part of the literary and artistic scene he had already become. It is to author and editor Francis Wyndham, friend and bail-bondsman of Henrietta Moraes, a bohemian petty criminal, model for Lucian Freud and Francis Bacon, and wife of Indian poet Dom Moraes, one of Peter's good friends. Henrietta and Dom are also regular dedicatees of Peter's poems. This social set chimes with Deirdre Levi's recollections of her husband's

'Soho life', as all of these were noted denizens of the Colony Room. Interior designer Nicky Haslam, one of London's most sociable people, recalls talking to Peter at a Beefsteak Club dinner about the Immaculate Conception; he could not believe that it was Mary who was conceived immaculately, as opposed to Jesus' virgin birth, and he made Peter write it out on a napkin and sign it.

For a religious poet, and a Jesuit at that, Peter's poetry has a raw and atavistic outlook on religion, as in the first stanza of 'Poem 20':

> What if the world were a horrible mad fit,
> human reason sand, and God a mere unknown,
> and no philosophies could temper it
> to shivering flesh and nerve, breakable bone,
> but the mind's vigour alone?

These angry lines harmonise with – or, rather, add to the cacophony of – Peter's attitude towards his calling, which he pursued at several Jesuit institutions: Beaumont College, Old Windsor (1946–8); philosophy at Heythrop College, near Chipping Norton (1948–51, 1960–4); and classics at Campion Hall, Oxford (1954–8), a permanent private hall – that is, a college based around a religious life. Peter had been kept away from Anglicans, his wife Deirdre says, by his religious mother, and the first time he met 'normal people' was at Oxford.

The problem was his attitude. Bullying at Prior Park, his first school, Peter wrote, 'was to leave me in spirit unteachable, almost intractable, difficult to handle, what the French call a *mauvais sujet*: not a bad thing for a poet, and curiously not at all unusual for a Jesuit'.[22] Not unusual, but not positive. Since 'the aim of the Jesuit training is to produce a perfect inner freedom, a conscious freedom in which God, life, death, oneself and the world and the Crucifixion of Christ, are all tranquilly and completely accepted,'[23] one can fairly conclude that the presence in his poetry of all these subjects, roiling rather than tranquil, meant that while literature benefited, Peter's vocation did not. Indeed, he recognises this himself: 'The training may be more successful or less successful according to the individuals concerned. In my case if it succeeded at all, it took seventeen years to do so.'[24] After seventeen years, in 1964, Peter was eventually ordained.

'Eventually' is exactly right. After the brothers postponed his ordination for a year due to his 'uproarious' behaviour (Peter's word), Peter had to face his friends, who felt he was doing the wrong thing. Given what later happened, they were probably right. David Pryce-Jones has said that 'a kind of medieval disputation occurred. In self-protection, he slipped lower and lower in his chair, until finally he was hiding under the table.' Now, with evident regret, he says they 'attacked' him. If the Jesuit training is a spiritual trial, Peter must have felt this disputation was one of the hardest tests to pass, finding his faith and his friends in conflict.

David was at Peter's ordination: 'It was one of the strangest things. It was in Eastbourne, and there were just two types of people who were asked: the respectable family, and Peter's unrespectable, disreputable literary friends. Peter lay face down on the floor with his arms forming a kind of crucifix, and people like Stephen Spender had never seen anything like it.' At the party afterwards, the presiding priest told a story about shooting champagne corks off a terrace at the Castel Gandolfo with the Pope to see whose could fly the furthest.

Peter had long felt that being ordained was the path of his life. He told David Pryce-Jones that in his childhood, while taking a walk, God had spoken to him. 'God said, "You're to be a Jesuit priest," and he said, "What's that?" and God said, "Go and find out." So he had some kind of vision, some kind of mystical experience.' Peter's younger sister, Gillian, now Sister Mary Anthony in the monastery of Our Lady at Hyning in Lancashire, says that Peter had always wanted to become a priest or a missionary. It wasn't the 'poverty, chastity, obedience and all that' that attracted Peter but 'the idealism. The following of Christ. The soldier for Christ. The rest of it is what you pay to get the other half.'

Not everyone approved. 'One of my father's friends, also Jewish, asked him once, as you do small boys, "What do you want to be, Peter, when you grow up?" and when he said he wanted to be a missionary, he put back in his pocket the pound note he was going to give him and from the other pocket produced a shilling. Peter was delighted, didn't know anything about it, but my father, who could see it happening, was furious.'

In an interview with the *Paris Review* in 1979, Peter indicated that his motives were not wholly religious. He said he became a priest because, being half-Jewish and half-Catholic, 'I'm very much on the edge of ordinary English society…But clergymen can move between classes and be accepted, always with a difference, by whatever class they are talking to.'[25] This is perhaps in tune with Sister Mary Anthony, who reports her eldest brother, Anthony, saying that Peter was never as devout as he should have been: 'Anthony told me after Peter died that Peter never said Mass for the day, because they're meant to say the office to themselves, and he said that Peter never, never said it.' (Sister Mary Anthony has her doubts about this.)

Later, Peter said that he went to Beaumont because his mother was afraid that 'I might take up with a dotty religious order she had never heard of.'[26] 'Myself, I just wanted to learn Greek, because Oscar Wilde had said the New Testament in Greek was the most beautiful book in the world, and I believed him. He was right too.'[27] But the Jesuit spirit seems to have been stronger than just the result of an over-protective mother.

What eventually possessed Peter was a spiritual empathy, not any particular religion. 'Humanism' in *Water, Rock and Sand* expresses his fellow feeling with Reformation-era Catholics and their like ('these / on the smashed ancestral glass'), but concludes:

> But I pray most to those
> whose act of suffering
> claims no tears or praise
> but is voluntary and strong
> in a long triumph of peace.

Humans and their spirit are a fit subject for poetry and piety; religion, by implication, is just rules. Indeed, his wife and his sister say that it was the rules of the Jesuits that he most disliked and which he strongly rebelled against. Peter, as a student at Campion Hall, would wind up the Jesuits, David Pryce-Jones says: 'I remember him saying at one point at the top of his voice, so that they could all hear, "It's wonderful to be studying theology, because I *never* thought that it was a serious subject and I find that it is." Another time he said, "Well, of course they all *hate* Jews." Peter was like that – he had no respect for anybody.' David also recalls Peter laughingly telling a story of a stay in a Roman Jesuitical house where he was given a 'chastity stick' so as not to touch himself when going to the toilet.

Deirdre Levi says something similar: 'I used to say – sometimes more or less in fun, but sometimes meaning it more seriously – "Why on earth did you bother to join because all you've ever done is try and fight against them? What's the point of belonging to them?"' His transgressions would be 'silly little things to an outsider', but within a closed community with antique laws approved by God they were clearly important. 'He would do things like having whisky in the tin that was meant to be used for the motor mower and then go to this hut in the woods with his friends or steal the bikes. It was like school really.' Deirdre readily agrees that this could have been a reaction to his mother's demonstrative Catholicism and the rules of all the other institutions that had dominated his life. Sister Mary Anthony says that 'he lived lightly to things like canon law'. It might pass for a free-spiritedness, but not in the light of everything else.

When Peter went to teach at Stonyhurst, the Catholic boarding school, 'He did everything to subvert the boys,' says Deirdre. 'He'd give them a cigarette, just what you're not allowed to do at school. He loved subverting and subconsciously he must have known that he was getting them on his side by always saying, "I'll meet you on the roof later," whatever he did say. He must have know that he was getting their loyalty. They all loved him.' This is borne out by a letter John Wynne-Williams sent Deirdre Levi after Peter's death:

He was our 'scoutmaster' (!) at Stonyhurst, during his stay there; the troop was somewhat unorthodox even before he assumed such duties. With him, we had summer 'camps' on the West Coast of Scotland, and also a relaxed tramp through the Massif Central, generally in the direction of Le Puis…Both expeditions had a limited link with BP's 'Scouting for Boys' traditions but they were highly entertaining!

Peter was greatly appreciated by boys such as myself who were increasingly frustrated by boarding school life and (pre-1960s) inflexibility. He became a 'pressure valve'; we were fond of him but respected him too.

…Peter's time at Stonyhurst was very rewarding for us, and he never allowed his personal frustrations to show.

David Pryce-Jones mentions another school trip when he got the boys, stuck at a French train station, to sing the ribald '*Il est cocu le chef de gare*' ('The stationmaster's a cuckold'). Peter was a *provocateur par excellence.*

Fram Dinshaw, finance bursar of St Catherine's College, where Peter was later a fellow, and a very close friend, went to classes Peter held at Oxford 'in an osmotic spirit of worship. One of the excitements about Peter was that you *felt* this transmission of scholarship going on.' This had been true the first time Fram met Peter, when Fram, as a pupil, had invited him to speak at Eton in 1969 or 1970. He remembers Peter spinning together poems and his thoughts on these poems into 'the most thrilling discourse'. Another attendee at one of Peter's seminars, Gerard Kilroy, describes how Peter 'was the first person to treat ancient literature as not just for translation but as literature', which was unusual and valuable.

Fram also studied Horace, the prime poet of Augustan propaganda, with Peter at Oxford: 'It was an experience like no other. One would wander in at eleven o'clock, the tutorial would be going on at three, we'd probably have had lunch in between, two or three people would have come in or out.' Peter did not separate teaching from his life, but rather integrated the two. Fram describes Peter's room in Campion Hall as 'an intensely exciting, romantic place', which stank of snuff, although it seemed 'rather in a scholarly-aesthetic way, quite an ascetic and bracing place. He never had a bed, it was always a mattress on the floor.'

The course of Peter's relationship with Deirdre could read like scenes from some pulp novel – a priest! a married woman! a love that can never be! – but their conduct harks back to Henry James, with a decency and subtlety and restraint that are almost unthinkable.

Deirdre and her second husband, Cyril Connolly, were staying in Oxford with the novelist Elizabeth Bowen in November 1963 and went to a party at All Souls College on All Souls' Night. They were talking to David and Clarissa Pryce-Jones about the recent drowning of Sir Henry d'Avigdor-Goldsmid's daughter Sarah, aged twenty-one, who is now commemorated with stained-glass windows by Chagall in All Saints', Tudeley. Just then, 'Peter came down some steps into this big room and it was love at first sight. He was the most beautiful, wonderful-looking man I'd ever seen.'

People were constantly falling in love with Peter, and a photo of him riding a horse in Afghanistan offers both a physical and emotional explanation. He is turbaned, binoculars hang around his neck, and he smiles a broad, amused smile. The image calls to mind T. E. Lawrence, or his cinematic imitator Peter O'Toole, with double accuracy, both for the desert setting and the cinematic handsomeness of the subject. Fram Dinshaw calls him 'startlingly good-looking…with a touch of exoticism', which came from his grandfather who sold carpets in Constantinople. Miranda Rothschild was deeply in love with Peter, according to Deirdre Levi, and used to ride on the back of his motorbike, and Sister Mary Anthony says that the Irish singer Mary O'Hara fell for him and wanted to marry him. They were not the only ones.

Ironically, Peter had come to the party for her husband. 'Cyril was his hero. He'd had *Horizon* [the magazine Cyril edited] when he was a schoolboy. He'd only gone to meet Cyril.' Peter later wrote that 'as she came down the stairs, I recognised the love of my life', but Deirdre never believed that. 'We had words later because in *The Hill of Kronos* he puts that he knew that I was the girl he would have married if he could and I don't think that's true. I always said that to him: "You didn't notice me at all, it was just Cyril. You just made that up for the book." But with me it was love at first sight.'[28] This love was about as complicated as either could have made it: Deirdre's husband and Peter's priesthood obstructed any possible advance.

They only exchanged chit-chat that evening, but Deirdre was already smitten. Over the next decade they saw each other at literary events or when Peter stopped at the Connollys' for lunch on the way to see his mother in Eastbourne, and at Peter's ordination in 1964, but what followed could only have been dreamed up by James. Deirdre stayed married to Cyril and 'of course nothing was said. We didn't say that we loved each other for ten years. It seems most extraordinary. He was a priest, he couldn't. We just met sometimes and every time one didn't expect anything.' Peter felt similarly: 'I was still determined to be an acceptable clergyman, and in that course I persisted for fifteen more years.'[29] Deirdre had him conduct her mother's funeral service in 1971, and after this came the first time they were alone together: 'I got Peter to do the funeral because she was a Roman Catholic. When we were all on the train going back to London, Cyril said, "Why don't you two have dinner?" I think that must have been the first time. Cyril was meeting his girlfriend and he wanted to get rid of me, although it was my mother's funeral.'

It was only in 1973, in the sitting room of Deirdre and Cyril's house, while Cyril was upstairs, that Peter and Deirdre said that they loved each other – a full decade after they had met and still one year before Cyril would die and four years before Peter would leave the priesthood. Today, Deirdre cannot even recall how it came up, but she remembers the relief they both felt, even though their constraints still applied. Cyril was suspicious when Peter and Deirdre were left alone, sometimes leaning over the banister to eavesdrop on their conversations, and later, with a typically erudite pun, he skewered his rival: 'I don't know what she sees in this Peter Rabbi.'

You can trace in Peter's poetry some key themes: the survival of reason, which shades into his religious self and the internal combustion religion can produce; the continuum of time; and nature, about which he writes like one whose pulse beats to the earth's rhythms. The strong rope of these threads forms Peter's most original theme, and clearly one of intense interest to him, as becomes very clear in his memoirs, including *The Flutes of Autumn* and *The Hill of Kronos* – how buildings and the wider natural landscape can retain and embody memories of emotions and events.

In 'Poem 27', he lets reason soar:

...Geese going over: high
in a trailing mist,
wingbeat, twist
of cloud, darkening sky.
So the flying reason
seeking its ancient places
moves scarcely seen among chases
of cloud, chimeras of this bitter season.

(To me, the sharp *g* and *t* of 'wingbeat' neatly suggest the crack of the bird's flapping.) In these lines he finds a pessimistic analogy in a natural phenomenon for the gradual vanquishing of reason; this accords with his vision of the universe, where reason and emotions and buildings and plants are all expressions of one guiding principle. This goes beyond metaphor and into a much more theoretical, even spiritual, notion.

The second pillar of Peter's grand theme sees the past, the present and the future as one long thread: we may break things down into eras and generations, but yesterday's light comes from today's sun. In 'Dream of a Hermitage', 'shivering day comes new from the same cold / that buried the old', and 'Future' suggests that ghosts, watchers of time beyond their own lives, may exist and that Peter would be a friendly one. 'Roman History' believes that time exists as a perpetual ribbon running through comets and stars down to seashores.

The final pillar – if you can forgive the rapid précis – is nature. In his address at Peter's memorial service in Oxford in May 2000, David Pryce-Jones said, 'Peter's poetry was religious in the sense that he celebrates the natural creation. Earth and stone, water and fire, are central to his imagery.' Reading almost any of Peter's poems will instantly show that this is true; they abound, throughout his poetic career, in the settings and metaphors of the earth, the sea, the sky. Heather Buck, in a review of *The Echoing Green*, three long laments for friends, quotes another reviewer who makes the important point that Peter may be a nature poet, but he is not one who creates a visible ecphrasis, a description of a place such that you could paint it. There may be an 'immediacy of his sensuous imaging', but there is no axis or horizon. This should not be taken to mean that his poems are random collocations of images. Some of his poems from the mid-sixties onwards, which were written, no doubt, under the influence of Seferis, are thought of as surrealist and do feature quite abrupt jumps, but they are really more like a Cubist painting where we are presented with many different facets of one scene.

Peter particularly seemed to observe and understand birds: swans, hawks, eagles, doves all recur repeatedly in his verse. 'Poem 27' has 'a pair / of flighting geese in a lonely exultation', and in 'Poem 15' he explores man's place in nature through the contrast between 'a mastered hawk [which] has no disloyalty' and the 'swans in a pair on the wing...defeating sense and understanding', recognising that the untamed spirit may be uncongenial, but wins 'passionate knowledge, peaceful desire'. He seemed attracted to their freedom, enjoying the idea that they were not constantly constrained by earthly bindings like gravity or stolid conceptions of morality and behaviour. Lightness was the thing.

There are more birds, again sprites of spiritual freedom, in a long narrative poem, 'The Shearwaters', which records a journey when Peter led a class from Stonyhurst to the Isle of Rhum (in fact, probably the expedition mentioned in John Wynne-Williams's letter quoted above). The poem builds from their tramp over open spaces beside the 'jangling dribbles' of a river, then up a mountain in 'that light falling which half defers / its suicide in the sun's own paleness'. And then they climb up the mountain and wait until the moon has risen, and eventually the shearwaters appear:

> Between dusk-coloured rocks like a ruin
> in the place where the mountain was most bare
> there was a sudden whirring in the air
> and the first shearwaters came in.
>
> Crying they swung as quickly down as if
> to split the wind to a structure of levels
> or a surdic intricacy of open cells,
> calling and rushing until the cliff
>
> murmured their thin cries and soft wingbeats,
> and threading through blown air like a surface
> they wove that massive dark with an alien grace
> which never dies or pauses or repeats.

The sounds and sight and simultaneity of this are evoked with the present participles drawing out the sentence so it can at once encompass his entire perception, running over two stanzas and ending with a tricolon which has a solid finality. Dawn comes and they eventually retreat down the hill in the fading dark.

Frequently nature appears in the abstract, as opposed to the chronicle above. 'Thirty Ways of Drowning in the Sea' (perhaps a dark pun on Wallace Stevens's 'Thirteen Ways of Looking at a Blackbird') started as a 'five-finger exercise' for

Peter but developed into a sequence of short poems. Number 2 begins with a simple thought, as if he felt he had to put down anything, but he immediately turns this into a vivid, almost suffocating picture, with a sudden first-person appearance halfway through:

> The sea is deep.
> Long columns of a green and salty light
> Trail downwards, finger for a floor,
> disappear in the sand-coloured water.
> I am below them in that deep current
> a trailing hand of light will never reach.
> Among whose grooves and wards the heavy sea
> shifts without turning, like a rusted key.

Rather than romanticise the sea, it is his direct engagement with its impassivity and terrors that makes these poems compelling: the sea is 'one pure chaos of brinish violence' (number 16); 'brutish and has no music' (number 20, refuting the ancient cliché). The sequence ends with Peter again immersed in the main, both physically and poetically: 'Wherever I move I am in the waves./The sea is in my ears and in my eyes.' (Vergil, of whom Peter wrote a biography, similarly saw in the sea a metaphor for poetry.)

Elsewhere Peter sees quite clear analogies between nature and poetry. In 'The Tractor in Spring', he describes how 'mother earth keeps us at it,/swathed in her withering rose and violet,/her thin liquids, her cold and lasting fire', how 'the tractor mumbling at its throatiest/speaks to earth in a kind of lover's voice', and concludes that 'I want words whose existence is this,/the rough soil and the root work in them.'

Poetry to Peter, at this stage, is an excavation of the human possibilities of the earth – or, rather, a way to understand his life and craft through the lens of nature.

In the letter from John Wynne-Williams, Peter's pupil at Stonyhurst, he describes how Peter engaged with nature, and classics, directly:

> When we visited the nature reserve of the isle of Rhum, we saw an eagle but Peter wanted to 'meet' the local seals, so, at the end of the day, he waded some way into the waves of the small bay and sat on a convenient single rock, before beginning to 'sing' an Ancient Greek chorus, in a gentle, high voice; very soon one and then two small whiskered heads surfaced, followed by more, until he was almost surrounded by a ring of very curious creatures; when he was quiet, they gently slipped away and Peter returned to us, happy and contented.

This is the sort of magic that revealed Peter's soul and why so many found him loveable in a profound, rather than a kitten-ish, sense.

The combination of all of these themes – reason's survival, time's continuum, nature's beneficent, cruel and impassive aspects – reaches their height in Peter's poems and prose that focus on the ability of buildings and landscapes to retain the history and emotions of men. In clipped lines from 'H.S.L.', he makes this explicit: 'A monument must stand / for the pain of remembrance, / it can contain / a complete passion.' This is a transcendent belief, one that does not measure existence in human lifespans but sees it as an eternal current, embracing everything and always accreting experience and history, so that a mere stone can speak of man, nature and god, if one reads it right. This is truly religious, as David Pryce-Jones said.

'Ruined Abbeys', a very long poem written as narration for a BBC film about the ruins of a Cistercian abbey in Yorkshire in 1968, is the perfect instantiation of this belief. The abbey ruins are not merely tokens of history but embodiments of all that happened in the thousands of millennia of their stones' formation, embodiments of the lives of the sculptors and builders, and embodiments of the abbey's environment. There is, in short, natural, geographical and human history all represented in the ruins.

The stone itself has captured its duration. 'Unquarried rock carries the print / of prehistoric origins', he says, as he considers the glacier 'which groaned in the rock / to lock this strength into this rock'. It 'can sing louder than a thrush…as clear as Christ in the gospel'. The abbey then expresses its authors. A pillar is 'still the work of somebody's hand:/ a self-portrait, a limestone hero, / a fantasy drawn in the light, / expressing self-knowledge as height'. 'The dead abbey still retains / the dead hand on the limestone reins.' Even though the fields and woods around the abbey die, as does all in nature, the ruins were witness to every 'unprinted sunrise' and 'fox in the gorse, wind in the tree, / raincloud, fellside, mystery'. The building, its material constituents, its makers, and its environment are in a constantly oscillating interplay and dialogue on history.

Nor are this abbey's ruins just the repository of this dialogue: they are alive, too. The poem begins 'Monastic limestone skeleton, / threadbare with simple love of life / speak out your dead language of stone', anthropomorphising the abbey yet going beyond this to imply that it can speak even after death for those who know how to listen. 'In the crude dark in the rank air / these clumsy harsh provincial stones / talk loud and clear like megaphones.' The abbey's 'speech' is one way of God conveying his message to man and of man praising God, for it is 'a hymn / shouted by heavy seraphim'. And even when ultimately it *is* ruined ('well desecrated, / safe for art history and capitalism'), as we all are, it can still tell its story. By the end of this poem, far longer because of its televisual purpose than most of his others, Peter has come to identify himself with the abbey, human life with its ruin, devastated but detectable in traces. He does, however, hold out the promise of resurrection, with the not-very-Jesuitical image of 'the Arabian bird in flames'. Life, death and future life are all here.

Reflecting a decade later, Peter was clear why he was a poet: 'Writing is like breathing, or it ought to be. One's got to write poems.'[30] Poetry, through its necessary precision, is a way of exploring one's emotional terrain, yet 'the words themselves, and the people themselves' are the true reason to write. They should convey these precise feelings to the reader, and though he stresses that no biographical knowledge is necessary to understand his work, he protests too much. He does confess that 'he can't stand the strain, can't hold it together' when he's writing, meaning he will finish a poem within two days because to drag it out any longer is to subject himself to agony.

One of Peter's idolaters, at least temporarily, was Bruce Chatwin, the novelist and travel writer.[31] Bruce – and later Bruce's wife, Elizabeth – was Peter's companion on the trip to Afghanistan in 1969 that formed the basis of his first travelogue, *The Light Garden of the Angel King* (1972).

(Reading *Light Garden* at a time when Britain has been

bloodily enmeshed in the valleys and mountains Peter explored, it is tempting to see today through his eyes – and indeed, Peter provides plenty of observations from history. He quotes the inadvertent prophet Lord Hartington, who was with General Roberts as he tried to expand British India north-westwards in 1880: 'As a result of two successful campaigns, of the employ-ment of an enormous force, and of the expenditure of large sums of money, all that has yet been accomplished has been the disintegration of the State which it was desired to see strong, friendly and independent.'[32])

Peter, being an archaeologist and historian, was at points almost over-keen to prove his theme, which was that Greek culture after Alexander the Great was a major influence in Afghanistan.[33] Given that Alexander the Great founded what is now Kandahar (which derives from his name), there is no doubt this is true, but Peter is interested in the ruins, or rather the remnants, of any fusion of Hellenism and Buddhism, a mixture of his spiritual and intellectual occupations. There are some convincing examples, such as the survival of Greek script for native languages and the use of frieze-like narrative scenes in relief on *stupas* (mounds containing Buddhist relics), but equally Peter can be of the school of thought that believes that if you squint hard enough, everything will look Greek.[34] For example, some marble 'was exactly like Pentelic stone...If you saw a piece of it on the Athenian Acropolis, you would certainly think it was a fragment of the Parthenon.'[35] Chatwin tired of this very quickly: 'It was one of the more unpleasant experiences of my life. Peter always believes there's a pot of gold at the end of the rainbow. He kept picking up bits of pottery and saying they were from a great Greek temple.'[36]

Chatwin admired Peter for his vocation as a writer and, if

this is not a contradiction, wanted Peter to show him how he could acquire the same vocation. According to James Ivory, Chatwin found Peter, with his poetry and travelling and priesthood, 'a figure of glamour', although Peter felt this was based on an unnecessarily romantic image.[37] (Still, it seems to be the same one that Deirdre Levi had succumbed to.) And if Chatwin trusted Peter for direction, well, that was not unexpected given that Peter was a pastor. But the admiration did not last long. As Nicholas Shakespeare says in his biography of Chatwin: 'By the time of publication, in 1972, Peter had fallen the way of Bruce's previous mentors.'[38]

As with all of Peter's travel writing, it is his poet's ability to capture a scene that gives the book its radiance. 'The Gorband valley is a sugarcane of sweetness winding through deserted hills…Even the snowglitter of the higher and the snakeglitter of the lower peaks seemed to be a function of light multiplied by wind.'[39] 'The small circles of oil-light in the booths of the bazaar were wan and unwelcoming and the hotels seemed a long way off. Unchained mastiffs stirred as we passed. The first copper star nailed itself into the sky. Then more copper stars and some silver stars.'[40] The rhythm, the metaphors, the coinages are poetry.

Peter is in love with the landscape, but he is not unrealistic about the people he meets or the situations he encounters. There is dizzying bureaucracy, and obtaining the correct stamps to access different regions is like watching the Marx Brothers.[41] They meet CIA agents 'plodding across the Anjuman pass in disguise',[42] and Peter buys off gun-pointing soldiers with snuff.[43] There is even a worrying (or kitsch) perceived affinity between Afghans and Nazis: 'Until recently the royal guards were dressed up as Nazi stormtroopers and the late Prime

Minister used to wear a black shirt and knee-breeches and carry a whip.'[44] No doubt the incongruity would have amused Peter, but it also bewildered him, for how could they care for this adopted fictional past when their real one was so much more interesting?

It would be climactically thrilling to portray Peter's decision to leave the priesthood in spring 1977 as a man's abandonment of his life's work and beliefs for the woman he loved, but the mixture of reasons and emotions behind it is complex and disputed. In *The Flutes of Autumn* he says, 'By 1974, as a priest I was falling apart.'[45] He elaborated in *The Hill of Kronos*:

> The year that followed [his return from Greece in early 1976] was a difficult one. I found that I was not able to do enough to justify my existence in any of my roles in life. I could not call myself a satisfactory priest or a satisfactory scholar, and I resented a kind of charlatan's success which was overtaking me, above all the way in which my life was becoming more public. I was very doubtful about my personal heart or soul, or whatever it should be called, and still more doubtful about the institutions to which I owed loyalty. I therefore decided to scrap my life and begin again. So I left the priesthood in what I hoped was a decently obscure manner and by due process of church law. With my religion, which had not altered, under one arm so to speak, and my books under the other, I started again. I was very much in love and had been for years, so we got married.[46]

'Whatever it should be called': not words of spiritual certainty.

Peter's ultimately lost struggle with Jesuitism – and his whole struggle with faith – is clearest in his most powerful poem, 'Christmas Sermon', from *Death is a Pulpit*, published in 1971, six years before he left the priesthood. It starts with a plain statement of faith based on John 3:16, 'God so loved us he sent his only son./In the name of the Spirit of God. Amen', but immediately moves into the room in which Peter, uncertain, conflicted, is writing. Here he is 'frightened by sanctity and light'. The poem subtly shifts between scenes of Peter anxiously anticipating Christmas Day, perceiving the desolate morning outside his house, and Christ's birth, which is not a joyful incarnation but is accompanied by 'the moon hid[ing] her equivocal face' and 'the axe banging in the trees'. Just as Christ's death is foreshadowed at his birth, so Peter cannot escape the death of his faith, the rejection of his studies ('theology is a mass of shadows'), the trap he is caught in ('I do not understand my religion;/I am always climbing back into prison,' the slight rhyme reinforcing the analogy).

His crisis of faith is partly sparked by his feeling that man can never live up to God's expectations, partly by his belief that God can only be understood as nature and reason, not as a religious construct. The conflict between his Jesuitism and his love for Deirdre is also evident here. Peter cuts away at himself with every line, brutally dissecting his doubt and paring back his faith. Like a storm that brushes a landscape with its first breezes, grows in force and fierceness, and then tears it apart as a hurricane, before subsiding into a breeze again, leaving a calm chaos behind, 'Christmas Sermon' ends – as it started – with faith, but this time an ambiguous affirmation whose careful tense suggests past certainties are no longer there: 'I have believed that the gospel is true.' By the end of 'Christmas

Sermon' there is nothing of Peter left but that ambivalent last line, and it is terrible to see.

Peter's sister, Sister Mary Anthony, thinks that he left because 'he was at a state where it didn't mean anything to him to stay. The priesthood had gone as dry as sticks,' which accords with what Peter says, although he expresses it almost existentially. It was 'an absolute catastrophe', his sister says, 'because he was leaving it all behind, because something he had given his whole life to obviously wasn't working'. He was 'in agony' about his decision, according to Fram Dinshaw. Many of his former Jesuit brothers found it hard to accept, and indeed actively scorned him. Deirdre recalls Peter being upset because a lay brother was not allowed to visit him after he left.

Sister Mary Anthony says that Peter's love for Deirdre, although it was a long-burning flame which outlasted his votive candles, had a powerfully pragmatic aspect, rather than just the romantic one he portrayed: 'He came out in order to help Deirdre, to marry Deirdre, to look after her. Peter felt that she shouldn't be left on her own to manage, she needed somebody. That's what he said.' Deirdre also rang a bell: 'When I met Deirdre, I thought, "Good heavens, he's gone for someone so like his mother it's not true." I never told her that. She had the same taste in fur coats, the same kind of very fair fly-away hair, blue eyes.'

The object of Peter's love is surprisingly realistic about it. Had he wanted to leave the priesthood solely for love, he could have done so when Cyril Connolly died in November 1974. Even after Cyril died, 'Peter wasn't going to leave. He didn't change anything. I think he wanted both [the priesthood and love].' Deirdre herself is not sure about the alchemy of Peter's choice: 'How much he thought about it we'll never know. In the winter of 1974, he went to Sicily instead of Greece, and something happened there internally, but I don't know what. I never probed, and when we were married I never probed about his religion because I felt that it wouldn't be right.' This fits in with the wall around their thoughts that Sister Mary Anthony saw in both of her brothers, which she partly ascribed to her being the youngest sister, but also to their innate privacy. David Pryce-Jones similarly says that he 'wouldn't have liked to probe' into Peter's private feelings: 'There was an inner protective core which he wouldn't let anyone penetrate. He was really quite a secretive person.'

For a classicist, Peter had got to Greece rather late. His first trip was in 1963, when he was thirty-two, and was typically prompted by his inability or unwillingness to follow the Jesuits' rules which caused them to postpone his ordination for a year and send him away (he blames his middle-aged delinquencies).[47] After he was ordained in 1964, he still wintered in Greece – for his health, always poor after childhood illnesses and the damp of his schooling, and because he had arrived at an 'insatiable' hunger for the country.[48] Later, in a beautiful but macabre turn of phrase, he says, 'Greece has twisted itself into my skeleton like a climbing flower.'[49]

The many flourishings of this flower he turned into *The Hill of Kronos*, published in 1981. Far more than recollections of unhappy incidents with ouzo and revelatory words about inspirational olive groves, *Hill* moves around a Greece traumatised by its occupation by the Nazis and its subsequent civil war, and Peter bears first-hand witness to the military tyranny of the right-wing Colonels (1967–74), playing a not insignificant role himself. The intertwining of past and present that he would perfect in his next prose work, *The Flutes of Autumn*, here allows Peter empathetically to depict Greece's eventful history. (*Hill* and *Flutes* were written in the early 1980s, evidently a fallow period professionally, before he became Professor of Poetry in 1984.)

When Peter first reached Greece, there were experiences available that modern ideas of archaeological preservation have put paid to. He slept in the temple of Apollo at Delphi and – like the Greeks – woke inspired by the god.[50] The temple, in ancient times, belonged to the snake-god Pytho, whom Apollo killed to gain possession of the oracle, and soon after Peter woke he heard that the locals had killed a two-metre-long snake that had slithered out of the temple. He also walked around the interior of the Parthenon, strictly forbidden today.[51]

Peter went out to Greece in 1965, and for a decade of winters after that, not just for his health but to research 'a translation of Pausanias with a long archaeological and topographic commentary', Pausanias being a Greek geographer (more like a guidebook writer and archaeologist) of the second century AD, whose eye for the past in present places inspired and complemented Peter's.[52] His reading material on his first trip to Greece had included a pocket Pausanias in three volumes and he soon 'discovered [his] thrilling relevance' when looking at temples and treasuries.[53] The project endlessly expanded as Peter tried to deal with every piece of information Pausanias provided, visiting every place Pausanias described in his ten volumes, contemplating hillsides and roads and ruins, trying to reconcile them with, or improve upon or correct, Pausanias' descriptions. His notes are extensive, explaining literary or mythological allusions and displaying an authoritative familiarity with the sites in question. Archaeology was, to Peter, a secular field of study, a break from theology, 'as clear and fresh as grass',[54] and a source for his work on Greek poetry.[55] Although it is necessarily imperfect, it teaches about history and humanity itself.[56] He was, in fact, archaeology correspondent of *The Times* for a year, back when newspapers could afford to have archaeology correspondents. Intriguingly, in his introduction he says: 'All [Pausanias'] scholarship and topography and encyclopaedic curiosity were a burden undertaken in the attempt to satisfy a deeper anxiety which had once been apprehended in religious terms.'[57] How relevant this would later seem to Peter! The two volumes of his work on Pausanias appeared in 1971, and were revised in 1979, and are still in print as a Penguin Modern Classic, proving his most enduring and popular work.

One of the things that made Greece so appealing to Peter was the great number of friends he made there. Indeed, he frequently refers in an almost child-like manner to the speed at which he made friends wherever he went, and the firmness of those friendships. Several were with major literary figures of the time, including Nobel laureate George Seferis, nationally worshipped not just as a poet but as a father of his country, and George Pavlopoulos, a poet from Pyrgos in the Peloponnese.

Peter does not seem to have been exaggerating when he said these friendships were firm. In a letter to Deirdre Levi after Peter's death, Pavlopoulos wrote: 'Since I learned about his passing away, there is nothing else in my mind than him and his nobility, his bravery, and his passion for life. Allow me to confess to you that he was my only true friend until the end, the only person in the world that I felt nearest to, despite the geographical distance which didn't let us enjoy each other's company as much as we yearned for.'

Peter does not stint in his praise for Seferis's poetry – 'There is a power and directness in his poems unique in Europe, I think. Yeats is hysterical and Eliot is obscure by comparison'[58] – or for his friendship – 'Later I came to love him as a friend, almost as a father, and to respect and admire him more than I can express.'[59] The material for this respect, which seems to have inspired Peter's own choices, was evident when Seferis, living up to his laurels, challenged the junta of the Colonels in 1969 with a statement broadcast simultaneously over several radio stations. He compared the valour of the Greeks in the Second World War with the 'compulsory paralysis' (Peter's translation) enforced upon them by the dictators, and used his unassailable position to agitate in a way that few others could without fear of the tortures the Colonels were applying to dissidents.

Peter himself, although customarily modest about it, was one of these dissidents, with a thick file held by the military who followed him in the street, bugged his flat and stopped him at checkpoints.[60] His decision to give a lecture on Seferis in Athens angered the Colonels, who tried to stop him. In a letter to Maurice Bowra from Athens, he mocks the situation, which is 'riotously funny: it is like watching policemen falling in a heap in a very old film, and then again and again. At present everyone is sending each other very stiff letters and the Ambassador is consulting his large dog…' He was arrested on occasion, and despite being 'a naturally unpolitical man' he fought back against the Colonels, who were suppressing the country and the people he loved, in any way he could, even if taunting the government was 'only the noise of the captive jangling her chains'.[61] He proved the mettle behind his words by helping to smuggle out of the country a student on the run from riots at the university law school in 1973.

It was an episode from a le Carré novel, complete with a false passport, a night sortie for a pair of glasses and a diversionary *Daily Telegraph*, but equally with the threat and reach of a repressive regime looming. In case Peter might be accused of overselling the danger of the situation, when the escapee boasted in Belgium about the Greeks who had helped him, one of them was arrested and tortured. Peter, then abroad, accepted full responsibility for the scheme so that he could help the real mastermind – a personal sacrifice since it meant he could not now return to Greece as long as the Colonels were in power.[62]

Following the massacre of hundreds of students occupying the polytechnic in November 1973, and a failed coup attempt by the Colonels in Cyprus in July 1974, the junta imploded. Peter was back in Greece that same summer.

Peter may have felt that his true calling in life, rather than Jesuitism, was poetry, but his prose travel writings do not shame him by comparison and they are certainly more accessible. Indeed, *The Flutes of Autumn* (1983), which mixes autobiography and the nature and history of the British Isles with the same alchemy as his poetry, is a special text.

Flutes has the ostensible structure of a memoir, starting with Peter's early life in Ruislip and memories of the northern Rigg family, the household servants, bicycle rides past Uxbridge's modernist swimming baths and the photos sent home by a school-friend's father who was one of the first British soldiers to reach Dachau. But so far from an annalistic autobiography is *Flutes* that anyone trying to pin down times is only given crumbs to follow.

There are still significant events from his life, such as the beatings he received at Prior Park, or the time when he was at Oxford that he was hit by a car, dragged for some distance and seriously injured. Peter says that during a walk with a friend outside the city, 'a little old lady in a little old car, being distracted by the lights, ran me over at a place where there was no pavement. I remember waking on my back on the tarmac and wondering why there were dead leaves in my bed.'[63] For two years he suffered from concussion. Sister Mary Anthony recalls the period as a ghastly one: '[The Jesuits] sent him down to Petworth to recover but he didn't recover. And then they let him go back and he was not well enough to do anything much and not ill enough to put his exams off for a year. He got a first in Mods, then he got a pass degree, and it just doesn't add up. And for the pass degree he had to add in English because he didn't have enough subjects.' During this time, to pile blow upon blow, their father died.

In 1976, Peter was a prison chaplain in Brixton, south London, tending to IRA members, some of whom were 'rough and passionate political extremists', others 'hardly more than schoolboys…who had just made an error of moral calculus, which they could now see for themselves'.[64] This empathy with the young, and belief in the possibility of redemption, are typical of Peter's sensitivity, focused through Catholicism but not derived exclusively from it – as was his realisation that a key problem in prison was that 'non-communication of every kind takes place'.[65] Deirdre Levi says that Peter loved and excelled at the pastoral side of his vocation, 'particularly with down-and-outs and very old men in the Jesuit order'.

One of the chief features of *Flutes* is the long and vivid descriptions of the landscapes that he was trapped in or was discovering voluntarily, and the blood that had soaked into the soil. Running through *Flutes* is an almost Homeric catalogue of brutality, as detectable in landscape: the Romans destroyed the British, the Danes the Anglo-Saxons, the Normans the English, the English the Irish, the English the native Americans. So disturbed was Peter by the animalistic violence of the Tudors that he says, 'It is one of the miracles of history that the poet of that age was Shakespeare and not Ted Hughes.'[66] Cultures flow into the British Isles through conquest and immigration, and while each may leave obvious traces in ruins, or subtler vestiges in place names, many are all but gone. He says, summing up his theme, 'The voice and genius of a place will speak silently and obscurely, after so many centuries.'[67] His own genius – the mental, rather than the locational, kind – was his ability to listen closely enough to hear that voice.

Rather than feeling any modicum of enjoyment in the perpetual savagery, like a bloodthirsty schoolboy, he is appalled, not to the parodic extent of bemoaning the humanity of it all, but deeply, humanely, at the thought of man causing such harm to man. He does not accept the glorious deterministic pageant of English history that neatly demarcates each era, as if in 1066 the English ceased to exist and the Norman age began, neatly smoothing over the suppression and the slaughter. The paradox for him is that today's 'civilisation' is a product of this bloodshed. 'How can it have taken so many beginnings stamped out, so many massacres and invasions, and the utter disappearance of languages and cultures, to produce the Britain we live in? This history is continuous, disastrous, endlessly repetitive. Neither God nor man can think it was worthwhile.'[68]

Peter's painterly skill in describing nature is nowhere truer than in *Flutes*. He is quite openly in love with the landscape, saying its details 'are written into the rags of my soul'.[69] On Midsummer Eve, he and Denis Bethell, a friend from Oxford, tried to walk to London:

> The sky scarcely grew dark until it was nearly light again. The last rose colours of sunset were still in the west when the beech woods swallowed us up as we climbed the Chilterns somewhere near Chinnor; by the time we got clear of the trees, and out onto the top of the hill, dawn was in the east. The night was cool and dewy; for three or four hours no traffic moved. The Chiltern beech woods were like Uccello's *Hunt in the Forest*, and the dawn chorus, just about West Wycombe, was the loudest noise one had ever heard.

A story of a walk like this will unfold into the life of an early saint, which will prompt a reflection on a local cathedral, which will turn into a story about the invaders who built it, which becomes a digression on their literature. There is something Herodotean about how Peter follows a thread through innumerable tales, and although it seems like it has been lost in a remark about how Oxford is built of 'antique ice cream', or the Vix Treasure, or George Orwell's last retreat to the Isle of Jura, or Vaughan Williams laying a wreath in Westminster Abbey in his carpet slippers, Peter is really showing how history and landscape bind all these together. The tone of *Flutes* may be melancholic – or, better, elegiac – but the intensity of his images and the curiosity of his stories are captivating.

I f Peter projected a jaunty satisfaction with his life after he left the Jesuits, Deirdre largely agrees, ascribing his happiness to his marriage and new family. Deirdre had two young children from her marriage to Cyril, Cressida and Matthew, as well as two older children from her first marriage. Nevertheless, even if Peter tried not to look back, occasionally he had no choice. His first job after he got married was teaching at Pembroke College, Oxford, and his room had a view over Campion Hall, the Jesuit institution where he had read classics.

It was much harder than he had expected to reintegrate into Oxford, even though he had never left, says Fram Dinshaw. 'It was quite shocking. Isaiah Berlin had always been quite happy to be close and jolly before,' but he refused Peter a post at Wolfson College, of which he was president, and gossiped about him as if he were a non-entity because he was now both a former Jew and a former Catholic – neither this nor that, so nothing. It was not a philosophical objection, says Fram, but 'theoretically philosophical. I thought it was pretty low stuff.' Deirdre suggests that people found it difficult to readjust their previous conceptions of Peter to fit the new version with which they were presented, as if something fundamental had changed. Indeed, she says it is remarkable that Peter had not been 'crushed by his terrible vocation – he kept his own identity very strongly'. His true friends did come through: Hugh Lloyd-Jones got him a lectureship at Christ Church, and Nicky Jacobs one at Jesus. 'But there was no doubt that, given what a figure he'd been before, it was a smack in the face,' says Fram – one that drove him more and more into his marriage.

His family offered Peter a great deal of pleasure. Cressida Connolly was three when Deirdre and Peter met, fourteen when her father died, and seventeen when Deirdre and Peter married. She did not live with Deirdre and Peter, unlike her brother Matthew, who is ten years younger. Cressida thus has the perspectives of both a mature, external observer and a long-term intimate. Visiting her and her husband Charles in Worcestershire, I found someone who knew him more as a friend than as a father-figure. (Coincidentally, Charles's father was at school with Peter and tried to protect the polio-frail, Jewish outsider from bullying.)

Peter was 'insanely generous', Cressida says, describing a man who would take her eldest daughter, Violet, to Toys 'R' Us and ask her what she wanted. When she gave the inevitable reply, 'This one and that one,' instead of a moderating parental urge, his instinct was to say yes to both. Her younger brother Matthew, who was four when Cyril died and seven when Deirdre and Peter married, agrees: 'It was my twenty-first birthday and he wrapped up his present to me, but instead of using sellotape, he used first-class stamps.' He was always indulgent.

Another side that emerges is of a jocular, quasi-Tourette's syndrome, where Peter would shout 'Unutterable scum!' at a newsreader or broadcaster – or, for some reason, on hearing Aberdeen mentioned would instantly yell, 'Bomb Aberdeen!' 'He had pockets of intolerance,' says Cressida, 'like turbulence on a flight.' It was part of his broader dogged loyalty, she says. Peter once boarded a train, waving his cane about and shouting the odds, to chastise a cousin of Cressida's who had been rude to her. He took cruelty to heart and stood loyal forever.

Despite his religious conflagrations and subversions of tyranny, it is clear that Peter had a sweet and humorous side, too, as in the pair of poems, a bouncing *bon voyage* and a welcome home, that he wrote for his younger sister, Gillian (Sister Mary Anthony) when she went abroad in 1953. 'Ballade for Gillian when she went to Germany (a ballade of last-minute conversation)' begins:

The train is in the station, & I hope
You packed your tooth-paste and your powder-puff!
You'd better put the ticket in your muff;
Here are the sandwiches. You're sure you'll cope
With all the customs people? If they're rough,
Here is a private letter from the Pope
(forged by a man who used to smuggle dope)
     – sleep on the journey: you'll have time enough.

The rebellion he displayed in his behaviour at Heythrop and to his pupils is evident here – rhyming 'Pope' and 'dope' might not be daring today, but for a Jesuit in the 1950s it was approaching the line. There is sweetness, too, in the affectionate final line of the stanza above, which is in fact the final line of all three stanzas and the *envoi*. In the interview with the *Paris Review*, Peter shows his dry humour, complaining about George Seferis correcting his English, 'which isn't bad, damn it'.[70] His humour could also combine a child-like and a macabre tone. After their mother died, Sister Mary Anthony recalls, 'We were walking up the street in St Andrews – Anthony, Peter and myself – and Peter said, "I'm an orphan now – nobody can tell me to cut my hair!"'

Peter's sense of humour also comes out in his drawings. Cressida says that Peter was a keen amateur artist. Matthew Connolly has collected dozens of Peter's drawings, from self-portraits to caricatures of their pets, and he showed me a particularly elaborate one, with 'everybody that he wrote about in one giant frieze, so Shakespeare, Milton, Lear, that's Peter, Tennyson and Pasternak, an Edward Lear parrot'. He also drew alphabets for children, with surreal poems and illustrations for each letter. One Christmas card has Peter, a dog and a cat dancing, with the message, 'Happy birthday Jesus from us'. Inside the copy he gave to Cressida of *A Private Commission: New Verse by Shakespeare*, his 1988 book about what he thought was a newly discovered poem, is a cartoon of a goofy Shakespeare with a bird on his head and the legend, 'Cuckoo! Cuckoo!' In another copy, a parrot says to Shakespeare, 'Wakey Shakey!'

Cartoons aside, the 'discovery' (no one today believes the poem is by Shakespeare) was a disaster for Peter. The publicity surrounding it and its debunking left him exposed and ridiculed, an amateur who had bumbled into the territory of serious academics. A. L. Rowse wrote pompously in the *Evening Standard* that if it had been Shakespeare, he would have known about it already,[71] while Peter Campbell, talking about the *Independent* in the *London Review of Books*, said that the newspaper's feebleness was exemplified by its taking a stand on 'the wretched case made by Peter Levi for the wretched poems which the paper went with him in attributing to Shakespeare'.[72] Another profile said, 'It made him look a fool, which he is not.' Charles Hudson, Cressida's husband, remembers Peter feeling 'cornered, like his publishers had pushed him into it'.

Peter could certainly push himself. In the nineties alone – like the early eighties, another productive period without high-grade academic occupation – Peter published biographies of Horace, Vergil, Milton, Tennyson, Lear and Pasternak (on whose grave in Russia he drank vodka with Russian poet Yevgeny Yevtushenko, according to Cressida Connolly). The reviews of his books were bad – the word 'vapid' appears more than once – but Fram Dinshaw says one should not accept that they were entirely correct: 'A lot of people sneered at them because they were full of mistakes. They were written quite fast and they were certainly written to keep money coming in. But he did take on big topics, and he didn't have that dry, patient, analytic thing of reducing them all to order: he was hopping about. He loved following up some strange byway of connection.' Peter was sanguine about his mistakes, says David Pryce-Jones: 'He used to say, "Oh, mistakes don't matter at all; I make them all the time – they're like plums in my puddings."'

The speed only increased his idiosyncratic, whirling, interweaving style, familiar from his poems, too: 'The kind of associations he makes are totally unexpected, not what a grown-up person would say,' his poetry publisher, Peter Jay, says, adding that his poems were just like his conversation. When Peter reads an interviewer a page from one of his note-books, he jumps from Aeschylus' *Agamemnon* to a French graffito to early photographs to a snatch of American speech to the image of a 'heavy tree sprawled like a dog in its own shade'. His poems come together from these fragments, and he 'usually would have a couple of lines on the boil. If they get really good, you write them down, or you get so excited you write a poem.'[73]

The Shakespeare 'discovery' typified the vicious circle that Peter's inability to get a permanent post in Oxford had created: stuck outside the academic mainstream, he produced his thin, poorly regarded books, rather than the scholarly works an Oxford berth would have allowed him to write, which in turn degraded his reputation, making him less likely to get such a post. The discovery was almost the natural conclusion of an academic life freed from the helpful restraints of a university.

Not that Peter was wholly excluded from Oxford's hier-archy. Once he had asked Maurice Bowra for some advice on what he should teach at Oxford, and when Bowra told him to consider what he was good at, he concluded it was Greek verse writers and Greek vase-painting. 'Pots and poetry,' Bowra said. 'Pots and poetry. No way to pay and promotion.'[74] Perhaps Bowra was right about classical poetry, but contem-porary poetry certainly brought Peter promotion when he was elected Professor of Poetry at Oxford, for a five-year term, in 1984.

This was a position of great prestige, if not one always filled by a poet of enduring merit. Indeed, Bowra had himself been Professor of Poetry just after the war, yet no one today knows many of his lines. It is more of a scholarly role than the Poet Laureateship, which requires verse on demand. The professor needs only to give three lectures a year and a biennial oration to thank Oxford's benefactors. There was a good run of Cecil Day-Lewis, W. H. Auden and Robert Graves from 1951, and Seamus Heaney, James Fenton and Paul Muldoon have held it in the past thirty years. But Peter's poetry has not proved lastingly radiant, so among this company he dims, unjustly, even further.

Deirdre Levi says the professorship was Peter's only ambi-tion, though she somewhat scorns it at the same time – when he needed to be earning money, this post was 'a peppercorn'. Similarly, Peter Jay says 'it hardly counts' as a post at Oxford, given its light duties. Still, election by Oxford's fellows and graduates is a significant mark of respect, and perhaps it went some way to salve any disappointment about the limbo in which his career – appreciated but not accelerated – found itself.

It is unfortunate for Peter that one of the custodians of his memory is more like Cerberus, three-headed hound of Hades, than is comfortable or necessary. It is easy to understand the desire of Brendan McLaughlin – in his own words (but no one else's), 'Peter's best friend for forty years' – to protect Peter's legacy, but at our first meeting at the Oxford and Cambridge Club on Pall Mall he attacked me with violent, inconsequential questions and demands. On a sunny terrace, I faced the hostile barrage of a human machine-gun. 'Quote your favourite poem by Archilochus.' 'Why do you mispronounce "research"?' 'What was the name of Seferis's wife?' 'Can you really have gone to Oxford?' 'Who taught you to think like that?'

A grey, rotund, unpleasant man, with teeth the colour and arrangement of roof tiles after a hurricane, McLaughlin seemed more defensive of Peter than either his wife or his publisher or his sister. This strange behaviour seemed to go against all the kindly instincts that dignified Peter. At one point he directed me to ask him questions as if he *were* Peter, a bizarre feat of poor impersonation. Prosopopoeia (literally 'face-making'), classical scholars call it.

All of McLaughlin's questions seemed designed to reassure himself that I was suitably inadequate to write about Peter, thus not stealing his memory from him. He delighted in dangling the possibility of reading his correspondence with Peter in front of me, only to snatch it back in favour of someone who could quote Archilochus. Nevertheless, if he was as close to Peter as he claimed – indeed, he claimed responsibility for arranging Deirdre and Peter's first meeting, although Deirdre did not mention this – I felt that I had to persist, so I sat there waiting for the next insulting, irrelevant question.

McLaughlin seemed to have an ambiguous relationship

with Peter. When I mentioned that Deirdre Levi had felt that Peter had been hard done by in his search for a position in Oxford, he said, 'Well, she would think that, wouldn't she?' Several times he implied that Deirdre's age had made her lax enough to talk to me. When I said that I felt that *The Flutes of Autumn* ('Tell me where that title comes from?' 'Trakl.' 'You mispronounced his name!') had a much greater sense of humanity than Patrick Leigh Fermor's most famous book ('Do you mean *A Gift of Times*?' 'No, *A Time of Gifts*.' 'I'm testing you!'), he laughed.

The only way to extract any information from McLaughlin was to trick him, to make a statement about Peter that he would feel compelled to refute. I started talking about the unclear contours of Maurice Bowra's relationship with Peter, which no one had mentioned, yet that had led to the affectionate dedication in my book, and suggested that there was some kind of sexual connection. 'Peter was not gay,' he snapped. 'No, Peter was madly in love with many people in many different ways.'

Regarding Peter's connection with the most prominent figure in Oxonian classics, it is quite clear from his writings that he respected 'that great man', seeking out his advice and quoting his *bons mots*.[75] Deirdre Levi says one of his favourite Bowra-isms was that someone 'thinks he's his own worst enemy, but not while I'm alive'. Peter says explicitly that Bowra didn't have 'an enormous influence on me', other than that he was generally enlivening, although Peter did become a friend and 'an admirer for life'.[76] Their eras as dons at Oxford overlapped, thus the 'gratitude' of his inscription is explicable as from one colleague to another, befitting Peter's 'wise suggestions', as recorded in the preface. But this still leaves the 'love'. Bowra was an old friend and occasional house-guest of Deirdre Levi's during her marriage to Cyril Connolly, and he invited Peter to dinners and parties, but no one I interviewed could recall any particularly close relationship between the two. A letter from Peter to Bowra, friendly but nothing more, survives. Interestingly, Peter was asked to write Bowra's biography, but refused.

It is possible that Bowra tried to cultivate the handsome, successful poet as one of his young acolytes, thus writing to him with fey affection, but it would have soon become clear that his forked tongue would not have been replicated in or appreciated by Peter.

Despite the blindness, spreading out from the centre of his vision, that diabetes brought on him, Peter continued to write poetry, and his last book, *Viriditas*, was published in 2001. His concerns are still nature, birds, the sea, poetry, but he writes with a calm, almost transcendental tone:

> Now I must climb high up the wooden and white
> stairway above the brick comfort of this house,
> above learning, above poetry, above sight,
> to gather thoughts like birds and let them loose,
> shadow hunt shadow till the hunt goes right
> and then these stoop on those.
>
> Though it is only shadow-poetry:
> I recall your real poems, your real tones,
> the shelly trumpet grumbling distantly,
> the sea-grind of the light, sea-groan of bones,
> honoured among the dazzle still to be,
> honoured among sea-stones.[77]

Viriditas is one of his most accessible – yet not simpli-fied – books. The poems allude to Vergil and Basho and the thirteenth-century 'Sumer is icumen in', but all glow with beautiful descriptions of nature and his eternal understanding of its phases, its rises and falls.

Peter had a pacific approach to his own approaching death, but he endured the deaths of friends far less sanguinely. In one of his finest poems, an elegy for Colin Macleod, an Oxford classicist colleague and friend who committed suicide by setting his head on a train track in December 1981, he grieves with anger and horror. Peter understands Colin's rejection of religion and life: 'What other pride is proper in God's eye / than the refusal to be comforted?' And terribly, vividly, he gives us the moment Macleod's death is reported: 'Then when you died the fellows in their gowns / ran cawing like a colony of rooks / disturbed in airy quadrangles of stone.' It ends in unutterable bleakness:

> God has crumbled the stars in his own sky,
> nothing is breathing but antiquity,
> our world is broken, it lies where it fell,
> under the crust earth is an iron bell
> heaving its awful weight around the sky:
> it is swinging and clanging silently.
> I say your likeness is to an old stone:
> upright, raineaten, mooneaten, alone.[78]

It may seem odd, prurient even, to talk about Peter's sex-uality, but its contemplation leads to a more elusive truth about him. People have suggested that he was gay, and Deirdre Levi perhaps alluded to this interest by commenting on how someone else interviewing her had been looking for 'scurrilous things', which she would not find. Indeed, Peter once told friends that falling in love with Deirdre was a relief, as he had assumed he was 'queer' before then – probably from the plain lack of women in his environment until that point, David Pryce-Jones surmises. 'Peter was one of those sympathetic people,' says Fram Dinshaw, 'who, like most imaginative people, was very responsive to either sex.'

However, Peter Jay says: 'I don't think Peter's sexuality bothered him in the slightest, I doubt if he gave it a second thought, I think he was too busy. I know that sounds silly but I think it's actually true. His real activity was in his head.' This lack of thought about sexuality turns out to be congruent with Peter's wider personality.

When talking to Deirdre about what attracted her to him, she says that 'one thing I noticed about him all the time was that he was quite childish in a way, from being institutionalised. Except when he was in Greece, he'd always been in a institution. He joined up pretty well from school really.' We develop this idea of his child-like nature in our conversation, since it seems an unusual way to describe someone as accomplished as Peter and whose poetry is as insightful as Peter's. Was it physical? Social? Emotional? No, she says, he was considerate, sweet, organised. 'Innocent' seems to come close, but not with wonderment. 'Callow', perhaps, given schoolboy provocations like holding up communist newspapers in public in France.

It is not until I am speaking to Peter Jay a few weeks later that it finally becomes clear what Deirdre was trying to articulate. Deirdre had made a lot of the fact that Peter had never held a permanent post at Oxford, describing his rather desperate search for a job, and when we were talking about what the Bowra–Levi connection might have been, Peter Jay picked up on her theme: 'Peter did not have the type of social skills that would have allowed him to reach Bowra's eminence. He couldn't work the system, that was Peter's problem. He. Could. Never. Work. The. System. At all. If he had been able to, he would have had a job at a college.' Did it not occur to him, or did he simply not like meeting the right people, saying the right thing? Despite Peter Jay's soft manner, his voice acquires force here. 'I think he simply didn't know how to do it. I don't think Peter would even have thought he had to do it. I think he was as he was and hoped that the Oxford world would take him on his merits. Well, they should have done, but he was wrong and they didn't.'

Peter was un-cynical, I suggest. 'Totally un-cynical.' This lack of scheming is exactly what Deirdre was describing: Peter was guileless. David Pryce-Jones said at his memorial service that 'there was in him all manner of squibs and what the French call *boutades*, but no trace of malice or unkindness'. Once you consider Peter's life through a lens without guile, many things fall into place: his inability to secure an Oxford post; his unlimited capacity for love; his disregard for sexuality; his poetry, too. Fram Dinshaw emphasises the innocent way unexpected opportunities clustered around him: 'Peter told this wonderful story about how Johnny Craxton [the artist] had been walking around in Greece and pulled this fifth-century head out of a hedge. Well, with Peter came the possibility that, on a walk in some wild place, a fifth-century head might be waiting for one in a hedge. That's what he meant to me.'

Although Peter eventually became entirely blind, he secretly wrote a diary to be given to Matthew as a birthday present. Sometimes his ink is used up and he continues writing, other times his new lines run over old lines, but his words are as poetic and surprising as ever. The most poignant note is in his introduction: 'Here is a year's journal, I hope so because my only ambition is to live another year. It seems to me a preposterous hope but it does include the millennium.' He died on 1 February 2000.

Peter Levi in light and shadow

Penguin  Classics

THE ODES OF PINDAR

TRANSLATED BY C. M. BOWRA

Arguably the greatest Greek lyric poet, Pindar
(518–438 B.C.) was a controversial figure in fifth-
century Greece – a conservative Boiotian aristo-
crat who studied in Athens and a writer on physical
prowess whose interest in the Games was largely
philosophical. Pindar's Epinician Odes – choral
songs extolling victories in the Games at Olympia,
Delphi, Nemea and Korinth – cover the whole
spectrum of the Greek moral order, from earthly
competition to fate and mythology. But in C. M.
Bowra's clear translation his one central image
stands out – the successful athlete transformed
and transfigured by the power of the gods.

The cover shows two athletes, in a detail from a
Greek vase, about 430 B.C., in the British Museum
(photo John Freeman)

United Kingdom 35p 7/–
Australia $1.20
New Zealand $1.00
South Africa R0.85
Canada $1.50

D. Rundll,
Coll. Magd.,
Oxon.

6 Feb. 1948.

Josh Spero
Magdalen College
Oxford
November 2005

THUCYDIDES
(2004–6)
and
DALSTON
(2011)

As I write I can hear police sirens, spreading fear and safety, speed in front of and behind my house, shrieking in unsynchronised stereo. It is 8 August 2011 and I have been stuck in my flat between riots all afternoon and evening, one ten minutes to the east, and another on the Kingsland Road five minutes to the west. Fires have been set, barricades thrown up, shop windows smashed in, the police attacked, small businesses in Dalston defended by their Turkish proprietors menacing rioters with makeshift clubs and iron poles. I have riots on the brain, civil disturbance prickling under my skin.

Earlier today, I had been writing the introduction to this brief chapter about my least favourite ancient historian, Thucydides. I had bought David Rundle's old copy of the Oxford Classical Texts Thucydides, volume two, as edited by Enoch Powell (a noted classicist before a notorious politician). This introduction would have been about how poor a historian Thucydides is – it still is, to an extent – but the riots have made me remember why I grudgingly came to admire him: if anyone understands civil strife, it is Thucydides.

Ancient history was what I was determined to do most of at university, because I loved the drama, the foreign-ness of the worlds, the great figures and their great acts. Sometimes I think obsessive childhood watching of *Dynasty* and *Melrose Place* gave me a head for complex political manoeuvres. (Who was Alexis Carrington if not Livia with shoulder pads?)

At Oxford classicists used to be able *only* to study ancient history or philosophy for Finals. All of literature – Homer, Vergil, Sophocles, Horace and the rest – was apparently serious enough only for getting up your reading rate at Mods and a little light criticism. In my time, however, you were allowed to take up to five papers (out of eight) from the ancient history menu, and I picked the densest dishes: in Greece, from 776 BC to the Persian Wars, with Herodotus' *Histories* to hand, and the fifth century from the Persian Wars to the Peloponnesian War, (mis)guided by Thucydides; in Rome, the fall of the Republic in the second and first centuries BC, and the rise of the empire, from Julius Caesar to Claudius. My fifth paper was a thesis on a Roman rabble-rouser and proto-socialist called Clodius, one of Cicero's antagonists.

The period papers involved the gross consumption and digestion of large chunks of well-known historians (in the original), as well as contemporary inscriptions chiselled into stone by anonymous hands. Inscriptions are surprisingly valuable: they offer hard facts (no joke intended) about legislation or finances which ancient historians do not report, and they are found both in metropolises and in colonies or imperial territories, making up for our lack of local historians. Inscriptions would undo Thucydides in the end.

His narrative starts as Herodotus' finishes, with the Persians hightailing it back from Greece after the surprise defeat of their invasion. It then covers both the *Pentekontaetia* ('Fifty Years'), the golden decades of Athens's military, imperial, artistic and intellectual primacy in the Greek world from 479 to 431 BC, and the war of aggression they started against Sparta in 431. This war ultimately consumed Athens's money, manpower, dignity, stability, government, empire and freedom.

Thucydides says that Athens was forced into war by Sparta, its regional rival. Both had strings of affiliated colonies and territorial empires, but Sparta was jealous of Athens, fearing its encroachment into its sphere of influence. Athens's empire, at its height, stretched outwards from the city into the region of Attica, across the islands of the Aegean and on to the coast of Turkey, seeded with Greek colonies – a wealthy and expansive union. Provocative and brash, Sparta goaded Athens until Pericles, the consensual if not quite official leader of the city, had enough and was left with no choice but to fight Sparta's sorties, Thucydides says. A thirty-year war ensued, bringing debt, disaster and two anti-democratic revolutions to Athens, before its final defeat. Thucydides, however, gives us only one side of the story, as is his wont. The truth came in fragments.

Unearthed in the Agora, the main space for social and political life in the city, the Athenian tribute lists revealed to historians a whole new way of looking at the Athenian empire. Once the lists – large carved blocks of stone, some in hundreds of fragments – had been reassembled, they showed the true story, the one Thucydides hides. The lists record how much gold the cities and islands subject to Athens had to send in tribute (or rather, it tells us the one sixtieth of this amount given to the treasury of Athene). We can also work out, from their disappearance from the lists, which tribute-payers had rebelled and, from their reappearance, if and when they were retaken. This is an actual accounting of the burden of the empire, and Thucydides does not even mention that these lists exist, let alone most of the vicissitudes contained within their figures.

So, instead of Thucydides' quasi-fascistic, monumental mode, which purports to give absolute truth while only purveying his personal bias towards Athens, we now have a rich picture of the grand workings of a fractious empire. This truth disturbs some people because the received image of Athens is of a peaceful and intellectual society, spreading philosophy and theatre. But it's the truth, nonetheless.

While the sirens wailed by, I thought not about Thucydides' poverty as a historian but his excellence as a psychologist, the first perceptive analyst of human nature in the Western tradition.

This is borne out in two of the great set pieces of his work, the plague in Athens (II.47–55) and the civil war (*stasis*, not a word that has connotations of immobility as people commonly assume today) in Corcyra, modern Corfu (III.69–85). The former takes place in 430 BC, one year into the war, when Athens has brought all the citizens from local villages behind its walls. Conditions are bad, with insufficient space to live in and water to drink, and then a plague descends. Thucydides describes the course of the plague – bleeding, vomiting, fever, violent diarrhoea, loss of limbs or blindness or amnesia, if they were lucky, death if not – with a doctor's eye and a patient's pain, for he says he survived it. Many did not. However, the plague causes not just physical deterioration but social and moral breakdown: 'The catastrophe was so overwhelming that men, not knowing what would happen next to them, became indifferent to every rule of religion or law.'[79] People forsake pious burials of their relatives, spend their money lavishly in case they might die soon, act shamelessly. 'As for the gods, it seemed to be the same thing whether one worshipped them or not, when one saw the good and the bad dying indiscriminately. As for offences against human law, no one expected to live long enough to be brought to trial and punished.'

The *stasis* is worse, worse by far. In Corcyra, the democrats, supported by the Athenians, and the oligarchs, supported by Sparta, begin a violent civil war while Athenian ships lie at anchor nearby, doing nothing. The oligarchs start to kill their enemies *en masse* and to persuade suppliants in a temple to kill one another or themselves. Oligarchs kill democrats, democrats kill oligarchs. Their victims were accused of conspiring to overthrow the democracy, but in fact men were often killed on grounds of personal hatred, or else by their debtors because of the money they owed. There was death in every shape or form. And, as usually happens in such situations, people went to every extreme and beyond it.

Fathers kill sons, men murder in temples. There are 'unheard-of atrocities'. 'Fanatical enthusiasm was the mark of a real man.' The one who strikes first survives. The key section is this:

> Then, with the ordinary conventions of human life thrown into confusion, human nature, always ready to offend even when laws exist, showed itself proudly in its true colours, as something incapable of controlling passion, insubordinate to the idea of justice, the enemy to anything superior to itself...Men take it upon themselves to begin the process of repealing those general laws of humanity which are

there to give a hope of salvation to all who are in distress, instead of leaving those laws in existence, remembering that there may come a time when they, too, will be in danger and will need their protection. (III.84)

What is going on near my flat is not on this scale of barbarous atrocity (from the cultured Greeks, don't you know?), but Thucydides was right then and he's right now: in a situation, whether auto-manufactured or imposed, given the chance of some consequence-free trouble, most people will act according to their worst instincts – and rejoice in it, too. The rioters, most of whom have no prospects, no ambition, no responsibility, no hope even before they gloried in their violence, see no point in conforming to the laws of the land, or even of morality. Isn't violence the atavistic response, the base trait, when you have no future? Clever old Thucydides.

DAVID RUNDLE
(BORN 1929)

Dear Mr. Spero,

I have received your letter via the Development Office at Magdalen. A year or two ago I offered my collection of classics books to the classical department at the college. For reasons of sentiment, but mainly out of laziness, I had kept all the books I used for Moderations and Greats, although I don't think I ever looked at them again. They were accepted by a young female lecturer whose name I have forgotten (I forget many things these days). I suspect she may have offloaded some of them, so perhaps that is how you come to have two of them. I have no recollection of the Headlam translation, but I remember the Jones and Powell edition of Thucydides. I suspect that not many of the people who only remember Enoch Powell for his 'rivers of blood' speech realise that he was once a professor of Greek in Australia (if I remember correctly).

As regards the rest of your letter I can't help you very much. The whole of my working life was spent in the employment of the ████████████████████ ███████████████████████ The constraints of the Official Secrets Act, by which I am still bound even in my retirement, forbid me from discussing my work and activities there, except to say that, unsurprisingly, my classical studies bore no direct relevance to my work ---although I hope they helped to train my mind!

I'm sorry I can't be of more help.

Yours sincerely,

David Rundle

THORNTON & S
Booksellers,
11 The Broa
Oxford.

Josh Spero
Magdalen College
Oxford
March 2004

T. J. Dunbabin
C. C. C.
Oxford,
March 13, 1931.

HERODOTUS
(2004–6)
and
EUROPE
(2005)

It was on the Tube ride to Heathrow that I realised I'd made a terrible mistake. Not on the plane to Paris or on any of the boats or trains we took between there and Istanbul, or even in any of the ancient cities we visited over our month-long summer vacation – no, before we had even left Zone One I knew that going on holiday with my friend Sarah was a mistake. Put it down to similarity: she and I both have to be right all the time, and we kept an uneasy peace in between trivial arguments fraught with one-upmanship. That was the pattern of our relationship at Magdalen, where she also studied classics, and it was no different in different time zones. I can plot our holiday by the stupid quarrels we had: over the relevance of the British monarchy while walking along the northern edge of the Lido in Venice; over the place of *Monty Python* in the history of catchphrase comedy at a restaurant on Aeschylus Street in Athens.

The holiday was meant to be the Grand Tour refracted through the budget of classics students. Politics students can all be individuals on the faux-hippy trails of Thailand, and geographers can discover much-discovered South American tribes – we classicists were heading to the motherlands in search of the Spirit of the Ancients. I needed it: my love of classics had been waning for some time and I was hoping that breathing the air of Pericles had (only now smoggy with Athenian pollution) might put the pep back into the Peloponnesian War in time for my final year, when I would incarcerate myself in Magdalen's library for revision. (In the event, I did actually build a little prison cell for myself, surrounding my library desk with towering walls of books.)

We had all the experiences you would expect: a march up the Acropolis; sunburn on the beaches of Samos; at several sites, that special awe you know you are meant to feel but cannot really, so you settle for ersatz awe, a facial expression of awe even as your brain wonders how long it can keep your eyes this wide and where the nearest Coke stand is. There is little doubt that if I had known more about Greek vases I could have felt some real awe, but having idiotically spurned the classical art papers at university on the basis that I was going to do *serious things*, I was left to coo over so many black-figured *kotyle* cups without any honest appreciation. Young male classicists tended not to treat the artistic side with any regard, a truly pointless chauvinism, a prizing of words over objects.

Imitation emotion aside, there were plenty of genuine pleasures. Nero's Golden House on the Esquiline Hill was in summer 2005 open for one of its brief spells in between the Italian government repairing some damage and causing some more. Within forty years of Nero's suicide, this grandest folly, with its rotating dining room and golden facade, had been buried, to be topped in all senses by greater imperial benefactions. Walking down into its chambers, it was almost as if we (we the other tourists – not we Sarah and I – Sarah stayed outside after we'd had another argument) were the first to discover the Domus Aurea. Descent into the dank puts you much more into that mystical frame of mind than the sunlit reception of the Forum. Similarly, I loved the little-visited ruins of one of Rome's oldest temples under the Capitoline Hill, and there I felt mystical, too, but perhaps that was just the spooky music they played.

In Venice we were treated to fireworks, only two days after being in Paris for the Bastille Day *feux d'artifice*. We had watched the Eiffel Tower fizz brightly with its sodium-strontium-copper combustions from the Champs de Mars. The Venetian fireworks were for the Feast of the Redeemer, commemorating the end of the bubonic plague of the sixteenth century, which took away Titian. A bridge is built across boats, the only day of the year the southern island of Giudecca can be reached on foot, and whoever holds the antique, empty office of Doge crosses the bridge from the mainland to the Church of the Redeemer on Giudecca. The sky burns.

One of my most pleasant memories from Venice is kissing an American who was staying in our gulag-like youth hostel. We walked up and down Giudecca in the evening and talked about Homer and Rugus Wainwright. The next day we kissed on a vaporetto as it churned past Venice's poorly hidden industrial sites and council estates. I could remember his name for a long time, but I don't now.

Nick.

But romance was a brief distraction. Sarah and I spent hours at a time on trains, whether in the airless six-bunk sleeper carriage from Paris to Venice, or the cliff-skirting train from Patras to Athens, or the train taking us away from hated Naples as we cursed the city and swore never to return, which stopped halfway to Bari and returned. There were hours to fill and my suitcase was labouring under the delusion it was a library. I finished two books I had three times started: *Portrait of a Lady*, whose interminable scenes and tiny shocks of rudeness had not initially compelled me; and Philip Roth's *Sabbath's Theater*, whose wrenching climax had me choking for breath. (It was really quite a performative holiday, all in all.)

There was also academic reading to be done. One of my Finals subjects was Greek history 776–479 BC, from the date of the first Olympian Games, which the Greeks considered the beginning of real, non-legendary, time, to the end of the Persian Wars, when Darius and then Xerxes failed to conquer tiny Greece with the might of their empire – twice. The guide to this was and is Herodotus, perhaps the best of all classical historians, for he does not avow accuracy, only curiosity, and on our trip I had several chapters to read in his peculiar Ionic Greek. (Imagine if Gibbon had written in a West Country dialect.) Herodotus takes us on a tour of the known world, writing about everything from Egyptian burial customs and the gold-digging giant ants of Persia (a tale long scorned but apparently true – they're Pakistani marmots) to why the Persian Emperor Darius decided to invade Greece and how the battles themselves played out. Everywhere you turn is a story within a story within a story.

His genius lies in his broad interests – geography, ethnography, mythology, theology – and his application of critical judgment as to the reliability of sources and the reconciliation (or otherwise) of contradictory tales. He took a multifaceted, postmodern attitude towards his history of the Persian Wars, comparing one account of an event with another, suggesting the truth might even be unrecoverable, a novel idea at the time.

There were no good modern commentaries on Herodotus at that time and the only decent one I had was that of How & Wells (1912, corrected 1928). With its thick, wine-red hard covers and a spine that was detached from one side and flapped feebly every time the book was moved, it was too heavy and too delicate to be taken with me, so only a text and a translation travelled. But I had already inscribed my name on the first page of How & Wells, next to 'T. J. Dunbabin / C.C.C. / Oxford, / March 13, 1931'.

Although Herodotus is, among other things, a guide to the geography and customs of Greece, one place he does not cover in great detail is Crete, whence come Greece's earliest myths, about Minos and his brood, and its earliest decipherable script, Linear B. The Cretans demurred from helping the mainlanders fight the Persians, thanks to an unpromising oracle, and so they get short shrift from Herodotus, who is interested in Greece pulling together. Nevertheless, it was Crete – its people, its oppression, its defence – that defined the life of T. J. Dunbabin, my companion in Herodotus.

TOM DUNBABIN
(1911–55)

1. *Introduction*

Counter-espionage is a combination of the activities of various Governmental Agencies and is usually concentrated into one controlling service, e.g. police, immigration, customs, treasury, government security service, radio security, military security.

'That's just my idiot cousin,' the Cretan villager told the German soldier who had entered his house and was pointing at the bedraggled, olive-skinned, unshaven figure gobbling down his food. The soldier took him at his word and moved on to the next house. Luckily for Tom Dunbabin, Cretans are proverbially famous liars, and have been ever since the days of Odysseus. Had the soldier known that the idiot cousin was in fact not just an Anglo-Australian Oxford don but a major in the Special Operations Executive, the most senior Allied officer in the resistance efforts against Crete's Nazi occupiers, the capture would have been swift, the torture long, the village-wide reprisals brutal.

If Dunbabin had opened his mouth, he might not have instantly been given away. A classicist who had spent years in Greece archaeologising, his Greek would have been better than passable. And his appearance – 'angular high cheekbones, deep brown hair, a fine dark flush of the skin and an off-hand, remote splendour of physique', says Dilys Powell – burnished by his years under the Greek sun, thinner and rougher from the privations of his life in caves and on mountainsides, would not have been too out of place.[80] A photo from a picnic at Eleusis on mainland Greece from February 1937 testifies to Powell's perception: as two friends lark about in front of him, Dunbabin sits on a boulder on a hillside, smiling a bright white smile and looking raffish and handsome in a crisp, open-necked, bright white shirt. It was not the same Tom Dunbabin who left Crete eight years later.

Thomas James Dunbabin was born in Hobart, Tasmania, on 12 April 1911, the only son of Thomas, a journalist and author, and Beatrice Dunbabin. The earliest Dunbabin to come to Australia was, by family legend, 'a fine upstanding yeoman who had emigrated to seek a better life'. The truth, unknown before Tom's children's generation, was that he had been a Welsh or Border farm labourer who had been transported for stealing a horse, his death sentence having been commuted. Tom's father was successful in journalism. His break was being one of the first people to interview Amundsen on his return from the South Pole, and at one point he worked for the *Sydney Morning Herald*. (Journalism was soon to be dominated in Australia by the Dunbabins' distant kinsman Keith, father of Rupert, Murdoch.) According to Tom Dunbabin's daughter, Katherine, her grandfather was anything but the archetypal journalist – 'an odd man, extremely antisocial' – and there was a shyness that recurred in her father.

An announcement in the *Herald* on 7 March 1928 testifies

to Tom Dunbabin's evident academic capabilities. Headlined 'Brilliant Scholar', it tells how Tom, who attended the Sydney Church of England Grammar School, had just won the Cooper Scholarship for classics in his university entrance exams and would be attending at a younger age than was normal; he had also come joint first for the attendant prizes. It goes on to detail his academic record thus far: aged twelve years and seven months, he had got six grade As in his Intermediate exams; he had 'shared the Burke prize for highest general proficiency in his school in 1926'; and, aged fifteen and a half, he had taken first-class honours in English, Latin and Greek in his Leaving Certificate. His academic achievements continue for several lines. While this ability was plainly impressive, one suspects it may have been his father's influence with the *Herald* that secured him several inches on page sixteen.

B.4. GERMAN ARMY: GENERAL ORGANISATION

A. *The Wehrmacht*

   5. *Hitler – Accelerated Expansion*

In January, 1933, Hitler became Chancellor, and expansion of the [military] services was accelerated and secrecy was gradually abandoned.

After Albania, Greece. While Hitler was plotting his eastward expansion, Mussolini was looking south – having conquered Albania in April 1939, Greece was next. He invaded on 28 October 1940, pushing in from his Albanian base, but was soon repulsed by the Greeks, who made up for the harsh conditions – rocky terrain, poor weather – and inadequate military hardware with a heroism that echoed that of their ancestors who had turned back the Persians two and a half millennia before.[81]

Among the bravest of the Greeks was the Fifth (Cretan) Division, composed of 'the pride of its manhood'.[82] One Cretan regiment routed an entire Italian division in January 1941, and the Italians were penned back into Albania.[83]

This bravery, though essential in repelling the Italians, was of no use when the Germans invaded. Stuck in Albania, where they continued to contain the Italians, and unable to retreat thanks to stubborn central policy, the Greek army with its Cretan division was cut off after Hitler's simultaneous invasion of Greece and Yugoslavia on 6 April 1941. Had the Allied expeditionary force, sent out to Greece in March with Churchill's will and Eden's authorisation, beaten back the Germans, the Cretans might have been able to escape from Albania, but the opposite happened. The German advance was relentless and the British W Force itself, under General Wilson, was driven back. Between 22 and 24 April it was evacuated from the Piraeus, Athens's harbour, to Crete, whose best men were still in Albania. Mainland Greece taken, Crete was Hitler's next target.

The loss of Crete has been too well told to be rehearsed in miniature here, but one refrain suffices to illustrate how the Cretans felt their bravery on the mainland had been not just in vain but actively injurious to their domestic hopes. Despite the Allied forces present on the island, Hitler's aerial invasion triumphed. 'If only the Division were here!' cried the Cretans.[84] The initial resistance of the Allies and the rag-tag Cretan brigades that had been formed on the spot lasted from the invasion on 20 May to 1 June, when the Allies surrendered. Thanks to British naval efficiency, most of our troops were evacuated, but a vital Allied outpost, linking Europe to Africa, the Middle East and beyond, had fallen.

Despite the scholarship, Tom did not complete university in Australia. When his father was offered the chance to become the British correspondent for the *Herald* in 1928 or 1929, Tom went to England with his parents and was admitted to Corpus Christi College, Oxford, in Michaelmas term of 1929. It certainly helped that the elder Dunbabin had been a Rhodes scholar at Corpus and, according to Katherine Dunbabin, another kinsman had read classics there, too. Her brother John says this was 'Cousin Leslie' Dunbabin, who went on to teach classics at Hobart University, becoming, briefly, vice chancellor. He was an eccentric man: 'When I was about six, he wrote me letters in Latin that my mother had to translate.' John would go to Corpus in turn.

The record held at Corpus of Tom's university years, despite its bare bones, glows like the *Herald*'s article: '2nd Classical Mods 1931; 1st Lit. Hum. 1933. Haigh Scholar 1933; OU Derby Scholar 1933; BA 1933; MA 1936.'[85] The A. E. Haigh Scholarship carries a substantial financial prize, while the Derby Scholarship is awarded to a classicist to enable six months of research abroad – entrants have to submit three letters of recommendation and a 5,000-word essay. Given the strong interest in archaeology Tom had manifested, the Derby would have been an apt boost and would allow him invaluable time at site. Strangely, for a man reputed to be terribly shy, he was also president of the Sundial Society, Corpus's debating society.

All of these exams and awards are fitting for one of high scholarly achievement, but the next prize Tom took was perhaps the supreme academic honour in Oxford, confirming him not just as a brilliant mind but as one of the greatest of his generation: a fellowship at All Souls College. Normally only two people, who must have obtained Firsts in Finals, are admitted to a fellowship each year. Previous fellows have included Isaiah Berlin, T. E. Lawrence, A. L. Rowse and Joseph Stiglitz. To gain a fellowship, you have to take six exams: two on your subject, but with left-field questions; two on broad philosophical questions; a translation paper; and, until 2010, an essay for which you were given a one-word title, such as 'chaos', 'possessions', or 'miracles'. If you are adjudged to be of sufficient merit, you are then invited for dinner – after all, college is as much about conversation as contemplation.[86] John Dunbabin, however, says, 'In a 1937 experiment (not repeated), my father and one other person were admitted not by written examination but by "thesis".' The change in method does not denigrate the achievement, for the supremacy of your intellect still had to be plain, and Tom remained a fellow until his death.

A.I. OBJECTS AND METHODS OF IRREGULAR WARFARE

5. You will be a cog in a very large machine whose smooth functioning depends on each separate cog carrying out its part efficiently.

It is the objective of this course to clarify the part you will play and ensure the efficiency of your performance.

B efore and after the fall came resistance. John Pendlebury was a Wykehamist archaeologist with a glass eye who had been curator of Knossos, the site of 'King Minos' Palace', under Sir Arthur Evans from 1929 to 1934, and he returned to Crete in May 1940 as British vice consul, a poor cover for his real activity, organising guerrillas,[87] on behalf of one of SOE's precursors.[88] Such was the respect won by Pendlebury for his work that his friend Dilys Powell, wife of the director of the British School at Athens, devoted the largest section of her memoirs of this period in Crete to Pendlebury, paying tribute to the 'obstinate romantic' in love with Crete, whose work with the local bandit leaders laid the foundations for Tom Dunbabin's.[89] While the Germans besieged Heraklion, Pendlebury's consular base, on 22 May 1941 he ventured outside to continue organising the *andartes* (bandits) and was shot in the chest. He was treated by a doctor and recuperated outside the city overnight, only for more Germans the next day to recognise this convenor of fearless *francs-tireurs*. This time they shot him in the head.

When Tom arrived in Crete on 15 April 1942, this was the danger that faced him. He had been sent out by SOE to replace Monty Woodhouse, a captain in the British Military Mission to Greece and another old Wykehamist, yet the shoes he really had to fill were Pendlebury's. They had known each other in their academic capacities in Crete, and although Tom respected Pendlebury and his work in both archaeology and espionage, Pendlebury was suspicious and perhaps a little jealous of Tom, believing that Tom, rather than he, would become the next director of the British School at Athens.[90]

Tom had been trained by SOE in 1940, learning – if we can judge by an SOE syllabus published by the Public Records Office, which provides this chapter's headers – methods of self-protection and counter-espionage and spreading propaganda, how to burgle a house and subvert troops and kill a man without a weapon.[91] John Dunbabin recalls that his father, on one occasion, had to ride a motorbike from a location on one side of Salisbury Plain to one five miles away on the other: 'The motorbike turned up but he didn't! Oxford had been a bicycle town.' Katherine Dunbabin says that one of her father's colleagues in training was the grandiloquent Enoch Powell: 'My mother went down to see him at weekends. I only remember that because Enoch Powell was apparently on the same training course and he didn't like him. The one thing I remember she told me about him was that he said, "I have put this uniform on and I will not take it off until Hitler is conquered."'

When Tom did arrive, a year into the occupation, what he found dismayed him. The Cretans had come through a winter during which starvation had killed 100,000, and they were suspicious of the British, feeling abandoned in the teeth of the Germans. Pendlebury had earlier established that 'Anglophily is rampant!' in Crete, no doubt augmented by his own personality and relationships, but this goodwill had been wasted.[92] The British were hardly having a better time. 'It was perhaps not fully realised in Cairo [SOE headquarters in the Middle East] under what difficulties they were working,' wrote Tom.[93] Monty Woodhouse had not been able to fulfil his major task of evacuating the British soldiers who had been left behind after the initial exodus. This Tom had to do, and when he had completed the mission in 1942, smuggling the soldiers to the south coast and thence into boats bound for Cairo, he was awarded the DSO. It was also given, among other things, for his tree-top surveillance of an airfield from which German planes could have operated over Libya and Egypt.[94]

Just because Greece invented democracy – or, at least, a dimly recognisable ancestor of democracy – does not mean that it endured in that nation. Democracy was originally a by-product of factionalism in Athens, not a noble philosophical aim in itself. Some politicians realised that they could cripple their opponents by extending the franchise, and suddenly every male citizen got the vote. It had no good reason to endure, and it didn't. Greece enjoyed Macedonian tyranny, Roman tyranny, Ottoman tyranny and imposed foreign kings right into the early twentieth century, and a series of republican and monarchist coups and counter-coups culminated in 1936 with the right-wing dictatorship of Ioannis Metaxas. This was just before Tom Dunbabin arrived as the assistant director of the British School of Archaeology at Athens.

The school was a customary staging-post for British archaeologists out in Greece for fieldwork and was a natural place for Dunbabin to gravitate to (although he specialised in Sicilian and south Italian archaeology), both as an undergraduate and then later in a staff position. This is where Dilys Powell knew Dunbabin, and her first recollection of him (quoted above) was from when she met him as a bewildered undergraduate in an Athenian police station. Much of Tom's time at the BSA between 1936 and 1939 was spent not in Athens but at its outpost in Crete, which was based at Sir Arthur Evans's elaborate Villa Ariadne, near Knossos, which Evans had built to facilitate his excavations of Minos' Palace nearby.

The Villa Ariadne was an attraction for notables and dignitaries on the island. During Tom's time, the King of Greece visited, accompanied by the dictator Metaxas. Metaxas had drunk too much at lunch and crawled off into the first bed he could find, which happened to be Tom's. He was woken by the housekeeper screaming. During the same visit, according to John Dunbabin, a dove was presented to the king. 'He obviously couldn't take it round in his arms and so gave it to my father, who was also at the reception and who put it under his ceremonial top hat. The dove was kept at the Villa Ariadne for some days, but then escaped and presumably went back to its village, which no doubt concluded that its goodwill offering had been rejected.'

Tom's archaeological papers, photographs, drawings and correspondence are now part of the Beazley Archive in Oxford, and they give a flavour of his pre-war years in Greece. There are, naturally, countless photos and details of vases and pottery sherds, and translucent beige envelopes with heavy glass slides. Tom had kept the obituary of Humfry Payne, head of the British School at Athens and Dilys Powell's husband, who had died earlier in the summer of 1936, from a Greek newspaper. Payne warranted a whole page and a large photo. After Payne died, Tom continued his work on the Corinthian site of Perachora, excavating the pottery of the eighth and seventh centuries BC, and the resultant publication established a new chronological–artistic framework for the period which has, in outline, endured for seventy years.

There are dozens of shots in the archive from digs, serious photos of ruins and rubble, Englishwomen with dainty head-scarves at Knossos, looking at something beyond the edge of the picture; but there are also photos evoking the camaraderie of a group of young archaeologists let loose on someone else's patrimony – the picnic at Eleusis mentioned above, for example. If Greece's fascist present was intruding, those immersed in the past show no signs of it here.

A.4. MAKE UP AND DISGUISE

1. *Definition of Disguise*

(a) It does not mean covering your face with grease paint and hair.

(b) It must have as its basis the art of being and living mentally as well as physically in this new role. EXTERNAL IMITATION BY ITSELF IS NOT SUFFICIENT.

As the most senior officer in Crete – first major, then lieutenant colonel in 1943 – Tom filed a report on this period, the only known copy of which survives in the archives at King's College London of Count Dobrski, a senior figure of mysterious origins, at SOE HQ in Cairo. On the first page, Tom observes that the British officers 'each had a great personal following among these people, sharing their hardships and also their festivities, joining in their sing-songs and christening their children…These Officers acquired a personal influence which went far beyond matters of duty.'[95] No small part of this affinity came from the classical education of many of the officers. It was no coincidence that so many archaeologists, already possessed of a passion for Greece, found their way out there. Further in their favour, they were most likely already able to speak modern Greek, or could at least pick it up quickly.

There is also a manuscript written by Tom in a large exercise book which is in the possession of his son, John. It covers his first year in Crete in prose that, conscious of a certain stiffness, strives for vividness and anecdote, and includes an ethnography, with long sections on the clothes, houses and geography of Crete, and on the Cretans' crippling fondness for vendettas – making up for Herodotus' lack of coverage. There is little military to-do, but as it ends in 1942, a year of inactivity in Crete while the North African front raged, no doubt matters military would have intruded later. On the back page Tom has plotted out his ten chapters, ending with 'The Blessings of Peace', indicating that he was intending to retrace all of his steps on Crete. His distinctive full stops, miniature plus signs, punctuate the elegant writing.

In the manuscript, Tom discusses his living conditions,

recalling at one point 'a series of supremely uncomfortable caves', at others the cheese huts and cherry trees that provided shelter, shade and sustenance. 'Not every cave was suitable for a habitation. Some, like the Idaian cave, the fabled birthplace of Zeus, were too well-known and attracted tourist traffic; others were on an open hillside, visible from afar; others again had a north aspect and the roof leaked in winter.'[96] There was one cave that was 'a hole in the ground just large enough to wriggle through, which enlarged lower down to accommodate three or four'.[97] The likes of 'Matthew's Hermitage', where Corporal Matthew White, a wireless operator, lived for months, were too familiar to Tom: 'It was always dripping with water, rain or no rain, and everything there was permanently soaking.'[98] Lice were constant companions.

Sometimes there were not even caves, and Tom reports sleeping on open hillsides – fine during the summer – or in thick scrub by rivers, or in 'a sort of eagle's nest, lined with springy thyme bushes' on top of a tree. He preferred sleeping on stones, says John Dunbabin, 'because they stayed where you put them', whereas sand 'humped and hardened under your weight in the course of the night'. 'We marched straight up a mountain-side, it seemed, and lay and shivered, rather than slept, on a threshing-floor at its top,' wrote Tom. 'There was a north wind, and we were glad enough to see the dawn and resume our journey.'[99]

Conditions were not always terrible and it could be peaceful as they waited with their radio equipment. At one point, Tom recalls that 'for hours we just sunned ourselves, sitting there out of the world and above it, our only contact with reality coming from Alec's wonder-box, snatching messages from the air.'[100] There was a part of Crete that Tom and the other English soldiers had a particular affection for, naming it Lotus Land after the *Odyssey*'s oblivious playground – it was 'that lovely little valley of trees and running water and friendly people', sounding more like an eclogue than a wartime account.

By establishing friendly relations with local farmers, solitude and the worst of hunger could be alleviated. Tom remembers how 'they would always bring us a lamb or a kid, bring up a flask of wine from the village'.[101] They often relied on the kindness of the Cretans, who despite having little in a time of terrible inflation still gave. In one part of Crete the villages were 'second to none in the support they gave us, we had them always as a place of refuge'. Tom writes that, despite a general terror of the Germans, 'everywhere we found someone to take us into his house and give us a meal, the Cretan tradition of hospitality triumphing over fear'.[102] The manuscript is filled with affectionate recollections of Cretans who helped – priests and schoolmasters, farmers and shepherds.

There could be levity, too. George Psychoundakis, one of SOE's many native message-carrying runners, participated in an orange fight in one of Tom's hideouts. Captain Dick Barnes disapproved, only for Tom to aim several at his head, before continuing with sticks and stones and charging the others with a stick-cum-bayonet: 'I had never seen him in such high spirits before,' wrote Psychoundakis. 'Then it was the turn for water – whole bucketfuls were thrown about, until we were all drenched to the skin. There was shouting and horseplay until nightfall.'[103]

Appropriate disguises were needed. After months in a cave, a ragged farmer-look – unshaven, tanned – would not be difficult to acquire, but the costume had to be appropriate. Although he arrived looking like 'a dock-labourer rather than a hillman', a local tailor kitted Tom out, presumably with what the British called 'crap-catchers', capaciously bottomed trousers, a white shirt and a black *sariki* headscarf.[104] Boots were a problem: 'Tom and Paddy [Leigh Fermor] between them had only one sound pair,' Dilys Powell wrote, 'which they took it in turns to wear. "I crippled myself over those boots, marching in a pair too small for me when Paddy borrowed the good pair."'[105] Perhaps for this reason, 'none of us acquired the gait of a Cretan hillman, for all our practice'.[106] Nevertheless, according to Tom, 'English colleagues with months of dirt and sunburn could pass for Greeks when they kept their mouths shut.'[107] A moustache was 'indispensable'.[108]

Although the Cretans favoured and helped the British, their 'garrulity' (Tom's word) could be dangerous. Tom's main base was on Mount Ida, overlooking the Amari valley, and 'everyone above the age of five knew more or less what was going on, but no-one was found to give it away under pressure'.[109] Shepherds knew more than anyone, but rarely told. In another manuscript in the possession of John Dunbabin, apparently a speech or lecture from the way it addresses an audience, Tom says of Greece in general, 'There was no country in Europe where the Germans found a poorer crop of quislings,' and no doubt he would intensify this for Crete. There were also 'bad Greeks' (note: not 'bad Cretans'), traitors despised by their communities who worked with the Germans, although the Cretans, thanks to their garrulity, were able to pick them out and avoid them. At one time, Captain Xan Fielding escaped some German soldiers who had been given his location by ninety seconds, though the greater tragedy that day was the loss of his diary to a hungry pig.[110]

Residence in Crete, though enforced, does not seem to have been wholly distasteful to Tom. As Dilys Powell writes, he could get exasperated with Cretans' gossiping, but he respected, admired and was grateful to them. 'The attitude is different from John Pendlebury's. John in his joking paternalistic manner was proud of the Cretans. Tom felt deep affection as well.'[111]

Tom did more than just acquire photographs of vases between 1936 and 1939, his stint as assistant director of the British School at Athens. During his first months there, he met Doreen de Labillière, a student at the school and the daughter of the Bishop of Knaresborough. He proposed to her on the roof of the Villa Ariadne, then the British School's headquarters in Crete and later the headquarters of the occupying German generals. They went up in search of a cat that had recently had kittens and came down betrothed. ('They were both always remarkably fond of cats,' says John Dunbabin. 'My father wrote that he had put "travel" as a recreation in his *Who's Who* entry, since he could not very well put "cats".')

For a footloose pair, Greece offered all sorts of Romantic (and romantic) possibilities. 'It was still rather the heroic age of exploration,' says Katherine Dunbabin, when you could travel around Greece by clapped-out bus and happen upon this undiscovered grave site or that forgotten temple. John Dunbabin recalls how his mother told him about a moonlit trip up Mount Hymettos, near Athens: 'She was pleased that my father was wearing a very fine white linen suit for the occasion. She was less pleased that he maniacally hurtled down the mountain at twice her speed and someone else shoved her down!' According to John, they read *Paradise Lost* to one another. They worked together, travelled together, lived together, and a love of Greece found its way into their bones even as they fell in love with each other. In less than a year they were married.

Katherine Dunbabin asserts that one of the reasons her parents had a successful marriage was because they were 'complementary: he probably brought her out a bit. He had a rather more relaxed attitude than the one with which she had been brought up.' The differences between an Australian upbringing as the son of a journalist and an Anglican upbringing as the daughter of a bishop are perhaps not as extreme as might initially appear, however. Anglophilia was in their bones, and they were both from the well-off and highly educated professional classes. After Tom died, Doreen never remarried, and to her last day, says Katherine, 'she adored him.'

G.I. MINOR TACTICS

Para-Military training is the basis of the type of warfare known as diversive or guerrilla warfare. Operations of this nature are usually carried out by bands of patriots in countries over-run by the enemy, and behind the lines.

While these operations are of necessity limited in extent, owing to the difference in size of the opposing forces, a small well trained and well led band of partisans can do damage to the enemy which is out of all proportion to the size of the band.

One of Tom's key missions in Crete was to foment local resistance. He would certainly meet an enthusiastic reception, the freedom-loving Cretans not only having the will but the weapons. But was it always the wise thing to do? As Tom quickly realised, every raid brought a reprisal.

There were three legendary *kapetanoi* (bandit leaders) in Heraklion, the central division of Crete, who could command insurgent forces, with whom Pendlebury had been dealing: Antonis Grigorakis, also known as Satanas, diabolical connotations intended, who had shot off his dice-rolling finger in anger at an unsuccessful pitch; Manoli Bandouvas, precipitate but powerful, with two thousand men at his command; and Georgios Petrakageorgis, lean-faced, beak-nosed, 'a courageous merchant of considerable loyalty and common sense'.[112] Tom had particular respect for Bandouvas, admiring his 'courage, his natural gift for leadership and the affection of half Crete', but despairing of his 'uncontrollable impetuous nature'.[113] Tom was personally popular with the Cretans he encountered, too, who warmly called him 'Yanni' or 'O Tom' or 'Mr Tom'.

By no means were these men pliable to the Allied will – they had their own constituencies – nor did they even always look to their own long-term interests. Tom wrote that, after the armistice of the Italian troops occupying the east of the island in September 1943, Bandouvas started attacking Germans and mobilising his men in anticipation of imminent liberation, despite Tom's order not to do so. This immediately led to one of the most savage German reprisals of the war in Crete, the burning of several villages in the area of Viannos and the massacre of the villagers, while 'the guerrillas were obliged to look on impotently'.[114] Once, after the *andartes* had murdered some treacherous Cretans, and a subsequent (but not consequent) raid under Captain Lord Jellicoe had hit Heraklion aerodrome, a key base, the Germans killed fifty hostages: 'All guerrilla activity stopped; Crete this time was cowed.'[115] At another point, the Germans set fire to a village and left the bed-bound to burn.[116] Villagers did not share the reflexive violence of the *kapetanoi*, for they knew that at the very least the Germans would seize their sheep and goats in return, inflicting a much less endurable hardship on them than vice versa.[117] Especially towards the end of the occupation, when the Germans had retreated to a narrow strip on the north of the island, the guerrillas had to be restrained in case they pushed their luck and provoked their weakened but not defenceless enemy.[118]

This attempt to avoid reprisals probably extended to the best-known incident of the war in Crete: the kidnap and rendition by Patrick Leigh Fermor and William Stanley Moss of the German General Kreipe in April 1944, as told by Moss in *Ill Met by Moonlight*. They left a note in the car from which Kreipe was kidnapped: 'To THE GERMAN AUTHORITIES IN CRETE …We would like to point out most emphatically that this operation has been carried out without the help of CRETANS or CRETAN partisans.' That did not stop the Germans razing Anoyia, where the general had been stashed on his route south.

Tom was far from gung-ho for such adventuring. 'Whether Tom Dunbabin approved of the plan I very much doubt; level-headed, he may have feared the consequences for the Cretans,' wrote Dilys Powell.[119] Tom's report reflects his ambivalence: 'Much of the purpose of the operation was lost' since the unknown General Kreipe had replaced the cruel General Müller.[120] Tom was supposed to play a role in the operation, contacting SOE HQ in Cairo on his wireless, but he was deathly ill with malaria and fell out of contact.[121] Sinclair Hood, an archaeological colleague, says that he believed Tom did not approve of the plan because of the possible reprisals, and anyway it was not the monstrous general whom they captured.

The *kapetanoi* could turn on their allies, too. After an ammunition drop, Bandouvas tried to prevent Tom from storing the
contents in his cave and claimed they were all meant for him,
although Tom was the arbiter of the distribution. Failing with
words, Bandouvas cried to his men: 'Stand to your arms!' Tom
then sat on top of the stores and said, 'Go ahead then, gentlemen, and shoot an unarmed man.'[122] Whether a bluff or bald
courage, it is easy to see why the *kapetanoi* respected and were
willing to work with him.

The deep irony underlying all of Tom's efforts to build up,
placate and restrain these guerrillas, so important for the eventual uprising, was that there was no eventual uprising – and for
very good reasons.

In the years following Tom's return from Greece, his ascent
up Oxford's academic hierarchy was swift. He was appointed
university reader in classical archaeology in 1945, a position he
held until his death, and in 1948 he was deputy to the Lincoln
Professor of Archaeology and Art, Sir John Beazley, the most
eminent scholar of Greek vases of the twentieth century.

One of his responsibilities was to give lectures. Donald
Russell recalls that 'although Tom was very learned, he was a
bad and hesitant lecturer' on his pet subject of Greek Geometric
period vases. Sinclair Hood mentions his 'very slight tendency
to stammer'. According to John Dunbabin, his father recalled
starting a lecture at the appointed time, going on for a while
and then glancing at the clock, which appeared to have moved
backwards. (It had, in fact, moved backwards, after a power cut
had sent it into reverse.)

He also took up administrative tasks out of the same sense
of duty that threaded through his war service. He was Senior

Proctor in 1949, the chief disciplinarian in the university. In this era, the proctors were supported by the 'Bulldogs', the university's private police service, which had powers of arrest over undergraduates within Oxford. He was responsible for university examinations, too. A correspondent from the University of Maine wrote to him after his year in office was up: 'You have let down your Proctorial duties, I suppose, and no doubt with some thankfulness!'

C.3. PROPAGANDA PRESENTATION: FUNDAMENTAL PRINCIPLES

Introduction

Good advertising is based on set principles; good
writing on deep feeling. Good propaganda needs both;
and the good propagandist will use the latter to mask
the former.

Even if Tom was never able to cry havoc and let slip the guerrillas of war, he did support the Cretans and subvert the Germans with words. The former was important lest they think the British had abandoned them, the latter to unsettle the occupiers in a land where they were widely hated. Much of this was also done by Stephen Verney, an Oxonian classicist sent to Crete in 1944 as part of the Political Warfare Executive, a dedicated propaganda unit.

The initial use of propaganda was anything but sophisticated. Xan Fielding 'had to conduct his own propaganda campaign by word of mouth, giving pep talks from village to village'.[123] But, like the resistance with its discrete groupings, the propaganda movement sprang up in numerous locations, a thousand wild flowers across Crete, using whatever technology came to hand and supported by the officers of SOE. One of the main means of production was the Roneo, a rotary duplicator where ink was passed through a stencil. Tom attests to two papers – *Nikê* ('Victory'), published by 'the young people of Intelligence Group' in early 1944, and *Deltion* ('Tablet'), which communicated directly with the Germans.[124] The *Kreta Post*, published by journalist Xenophon Hadjigrigorakis in a cave, tried to convince German soldiers that if Hitler fell a better Germany would come about. Hadjigrigorakis also published a Greek-language paper.[125]

The Cretan 'runner' George Psychoundakis recalls that these efforts could be officially endorsed, or at least supported: 'We often went to Kyparissé as well, for that was where the Greek Government representative, Air Commodore Kelaïdis, had his hideout. A duplicating machine had been set up, and they published a newspaper called *Elliniki Phoni – The Greek Voice*. A very good boy and fellow-worker of ours, Stavros Biris from Zouridi, worked the machines and turned out the little newspaper.'[126]

Tom, Patrick Leigh Fermor and Xan Fielding, as well as encouraging propaganda, produced their own. Early in 1943, they wrote pamphlets to demoralise the German soldiers, and 'a particularly ingenious touch was to have these German-language leaflets stamped with swastika-bearing eagles, and messages in Greek asking anyone who found them to hand them immediately to a German soldier,' writes Antony Beevor in his book on the war in Crete.[127]

Graffiti offered a more permanent, more public, more anonymous form. Imitating disaffected Germans, people daubed 'Scheiss Hitler!' and 'We want to go home!' on barrack walls.[128] As part of Verney's efforts, the letter *K* (for *Kapitulation*) started appearing all over Crete, etched with acid into German windscreens and painted on every available surface.[129]

It is hardly provable whether any of this brought the end of the occupation faster than it would have otherwise come about, but as a way of disturbing the uneasy equilibrium, words were weapons.

The preface to Tom's 1948 book, *The Western Greeks: The History of Sicily and South Italy from the Foundation of the Greek Colonies to 480 BC*, contains a modest euphemism that would been understood by all of his readers. In the final paragraph, he explains that 'an early version of this book was in 1937 submitted to All Souls College for examination for Fellowship by thesis. Circumstances have since prevented me from spending the long periods in Italy necessary for revising it.'[130]

The full extent of the classical world is often unappreciated. Greek cities, both on the mainland and the Ionian coast, sent out colonies in the eighth and seventh centuries BC as trading outposts and land-grabs, planting cities that endure today, such as Marseilles. Tom's book was a study of the origins of the Sicilian and south Italian colonies, their relationship with indigenous Sikel culture and how they interacted with other cities around the Mediterranean through trade and through war. What made it important was its wide survey of the area, unifying the diverse cities for the first time, tracing the connections. His daughter Katherine, an eminent archaeologist in her own right, says, 'I would have thought it was groundbreaking for its time. I've certainly met Italians who absolutely swear by it. It's the synthesis [of all the cities] that was of value.' When I ask her about *The Western Greeks*, Katherine goes over to her bookshelf and picks it out immediately.

A modern classical archaeologist might kindly say, however, that the book is very much of its time. Tom states in the preface: 'It cannot be expected that the archaeological evidence will always combine harmoniously with the literary history; but here is the attempt.'[131] Today's approaches shy at such reconciliation, preferring to draw lessons from archaeology and suspecting the biases and assumptions of literature.

More importantly, when a cultural collision such as colonisation is considered today, we stress the commingling of the two rather than the compression of one by the other; we live in a world where cultures are celebrated for their miscibility. Statements such as 'I am inclined to stress the purity of Greek culture in the colonial cities, and find little to suggest that the Greeks mixed much with Sikel or Italian peoples, or learnt much from them,'[132] would be debarred by the modern observation of cultural exchange.

As Tom himself acknowledges, he is retrojecting his own views as an imperial and anglicised Australian on to this period: 'I have drawn much on the parallel to the relations between colonies and mother country provided in Australia and New Zealand. Here political independence is combined with almost complete cultural dependence, on which the colonials pride themselves...This unity is the pride of most colonials; so probably in antiquity.'[133] There is certainly an imperial snobbery in here, involuntary, inbred, based on his blithe and misguided perception of his homeland – that the indigenous or Aboriginal peoples welcomed the arrival of the British settlers bringing 'civilisation'. Just so, he thinks, the native peoples of Sicily and south Italy not only had their own cultures wiped out by the Greeks but welcomed it, too.

There is nothing strange in this mindset. Katherine

Dunbabin readily concedes 'that it probably does reflect the attitude of a certain class of Australians in the 1920s, and certainly of Tasmanians'. John Dunbabin says that his father had 'no qualms' in giving up Australian for British nationality, as 'he had grown up as a citizen of the Empire'. Love of the nation that had exiled his ancestors was amnesiac and overpowering, and the natives were nothing.

1.5. WEAPON TRAINING

Firing Practices

You will always fire two fast shots at every target. The reason for this is as follows:

1. You must *kill* your man. One shot *may* kill him but it is better to make *absolutely* certain by putting two shots into him.

The SOE syllabus, quoted above, focuses for its last five lectures on training, combat and weapons. Under 'Close Combat' come instructions for blows, holds, knife-fighting, disarming, spinal dislocation and the like, including the 'mad' half-minute, a violent free-for-all.[134] The weapons training is detailed, describing how to shoot when moving and with different kinds of gun. And while it may so far seem as if Tom's role was limited to organiser, arbiter and propagandist, he was a soldier, too – and soldiers, faced with violence, must sometimes respond with violence.

He could countenance others killing, but barely. When a communist leader was shot by a nationalist, fighting began, and Tom had to drive round the town placating both sides. The killer was sentenced to death and Tom 'became convinced that he should support Papadakis in confirmation of the sentence', in order to prevent a civil war.[135] John Dunbabin's godfather, Sandy Rendel, 'more than once told me that this was the hardest decision my father ever had to take, and insisted that it was only so that an explosion was avoided'.

The first time Tom killed – or the first time we know about – was in 1943. When presented with two local traitors who were trying to entrap him, Tom 'not only took the decision that they had to die, but felt obliged to do the deed himself', writes Beevor.[136] The possibility of his location being revealed to the Germans was too much to risk, could wreck the important work SOE was doing. Wine laced with suicide pills failed to kill the men, so Tom took them outside the cave. Gunshots.

In August the next year, the Germans were preparing to withdraw, as the war was on the way to being lost. Tom was going to meet Group Captain Kelaïdis in Kyparissos, where he was producing his propaganda. On their way there, two Germans suddenly fired on them. Tom returned fire, killing one instantly and wounding the other. One of Tom's Greek companions had been hit by the initial fire; the Germans attached him to their car and drove until he died.[137]

These were two strikingly different incidents, one a reflex action during a fire-fight, the other a rational calculation. They do not just convey how, in a war, one had to make horrendous choices and perform deeds for which one might not be able to forgive oneself, but they also embody the complex role Tom had to play, splitting himself between strategy and action, mind and body. Both ended in blood.

It was only after his return from the war in 1945 that Tom could spend a prolonged period with his children. John had been born in 1938 and Katherine in 1941, and most of Tom's years since then had been in Crete. Indeed, Doreen had left Tom in Crete in order to have John back in England, so he would not be liable for Greek national service.

Their memories of their father are not of the severe face he presented when lecturing, nor the harsh face he had to put on in Crete – nor the silent face, concealing volatility, that the traumatised returning from war often have. His children can still, fifty-five years after his death, summon up an adoring father, relaxed and devoted. John recalls a family game of rugby at Christmas in the University Parks in Oxford which his father had arranged and which only ended when 'he gave the ball a great boot up and it landed on my head with a great bonk'. They built sandcastles together on the beach, although his father felt he had been spoiled by his native Tasmanian shores. And there was the inevitable generational conflict: John had a (long-since renounced) passion for T. S. Eliot, while his father found *The Waste Land* pretentious.

Katherine is aware of the widespread perception of her father. 'He had a reputation for being very shy and unforthcoming in public, but with his family he was very good. With his children he could be very funny. He relaxed with us in a way he didn't with anyone else; he played practical jokes, he told the most appalling puns. I think of him as someone who made me laugh.' And she laughs as she says this.

Antony Beevor's book on Crete captures these contradictions – Tom's shyness and his fierceness, his relaxation and humour with his family yet his petrifaction before a lecture hall of students. Beevor calls him 'engagingly paradoxical' and Captain Hugh Fraser remarks that he was 'immensely brave and immensely modest'.

What for Katherine symbolises her father's love for his

family was that he would rather walk the mile back to their house in north Oxford every day for lunch than stay in college where the food was provided by servants and the company was august. There is another story, too: his colleagues in Crete had not known he was a husband or a father until they found him in tears one Christmas; he said it was the holiest day of the year and he was missing his wife and children. In Crete by necessity, he had privileged his work over his family; in England, he would not do the same.

A.12. AGENT MANAGEMENT: MOTIVES
4. *Likely Motives and How to Appeal to Them*
B. *Religious or Political Motives*
Also more suitable for recruiting agents than for obtaining isolated services. Possibility of influencing the activities of religious or political groups of individuals – but danger of disagreements over policy.

Crete faced a double difficulty during the war, for it, like mainland Greece, was fighting two battles at once. The one against the Nazis was not divisive, barring the 'bad Greeks' on Crete – few wanted the Germans to rule their island, and those who collaborated were more in search of immediate advantage by aiding the powerful than despisers of their own kin. The other was much more corrupting, more insidious, a true divider of families and a cause for bloodbaths – civil tensions between restive communists and resistant nationalists.

EAM (National Liberation Front) was the communist party on Crete; its military wing was ELAS (National Popular Liberation Army). EAM was originally an offshoot of the mainland communist party, and in 1941–2 it was so small that 'there was no point in taking it seriously'.[138] Its leader, General Mantakas, was not an acute man, his mind dulled by the Molotov–Ribbentrop Pact. 'It was only after Hitler's invasion of Russia, three weeks after the fall of Crete, that [he] realised that he was supposed to be antiGerman [*sic*].'[139] One of the dreams of the communists was *laocratia*, which etymologically means 'rule of the common people' (much more radical than representative democracy), but practically meant disarming the gendarmerie and seizing stores.[140]

Crete was not natural ground for communists. One of its greatest sons was the nationalist Eleftherios Venizelos, the architect of modern Greece, who led Crete out of the Ottoman Empire and into union with Greece, an economic and constitutional reformer and several times prime minister. Nevertheless, EAM had taken root and Tom, perhaps with the hatred for communism of most in the English-speaking world before the war, perhaps with the foresight that a strong communist party in Crete would mean its post-war betrayal to the Russians and untold Soviet atrocities, spent a lot of time trying to organise a counterbalance. It meant that he was at the centre of a very complex, and seemingly self-contradictory, matrix, fighting the Nazis, opposing anti-Nazi communists, and praying that the nationalists didn't see the Nazis as defenders against communism.

'In October 1942, after uphill work,' wrote SOE officer Jack Smith-Hughes, 'Major Dunbabin was able to announce the birth of EOK.'[141] EOK (National Organisation of Crete) was brought together by Tom's negotiations as a nationalist response to EAM, drawing in as founding principals Cretan doctors and a professor, two military commanders and the *kapetanoi* Bandouvas and Petrakageorgis – some semblance of a unity of the orders. Eventually EOK became the official resistance movement, acquiring a 'species of legality' with recognition by Emmanuel Tsouderos, Greek prime minister in exile.[142] There was a nationalist cell in every village: 'Something solid was taking shape, which survived rude shocks.'[143] But it took Tom's reorganisation to force EOK to operate 'on principles a little more in accordance with the rules of a secret society and a little less on the lines of a village women's institute', he wrote.[144] Tom did not judge the overall Cretan contribution to the war a success, but praised their 'corporate loyalty'.[145] Jack Smith-Hughes has perhaps too deterministic a view of such a fraught endeavour, believing that 'EOK never really looked back' after its recognition because it later became more powerful than the communists, whereas the energy Tom expended on meetings with both sides, trying to reconcile them and unite them against the Germans, is much more revealing of the tenuous balance of power – the communists could not be ignored.[146]

There were some anti-communist accommodations Tom was not willing to make. Nikolaos Plevres, a colonel in the Greek army and possibly a German collaborator, told Tom that he wanted to help the Germans against the communists, but in his own report Dunbabin says 'some plain-speaking by Major Dunbabin convinced him of the personal danger he would run by taking up this position'.[147] That Tom is using the euphemism 'plain-speaking' to describe his own behaviour is surely a wry joke.

The politics of this period were no less – and no more – complicated than any civil strife since Thucydides' *stasis*. The struggles within cities were bloody, opportunistic, instantly reversible. In between the Italian surrender in September 1943 and the arrival of a new military commander in summer 1944, the nationalist-held city of Heraklion was up for grabs and the communist EAM 'cashed in on its rival's misfortunes', having grown on Crete as on the mainland.[148] That Heraklion ultimately remained in the hands of the nationalists was Tom's responsibility, Jack Smith-Hughes says, in an admiring note handwritten in his *General Survey of Crete*: 'He kept the nationalists going in their hour of despair.'[149] On the same page he mentions how a breakaway faction of EOK was still-born because Tom would not touch it.

Tom was as much reconciler as partisan. In April 1944 he negotiated and oversaw an agreement between the nationalists, the communists, the Greek government in exile and Allied headquarters in the Middle East concerning a common supply system and control of the guerrillas. Naturally, politics intervened and the agreement was never acted upon, but that Tom could bring them together and get them to agree, temporarily calming private interests and making a compelling case for the Cretan good, is indicative of his power.

The same was evident at the liberation of Heraklion in October 1944. 'Liberation' is perhaps a little wishful: the Germans withdrew. Although the enemy was ostensibly the Germans, it did not take long for fights to break out between guerrillas of both sides who had entered the city; Tom and Jack Smith-Hughes exerted themselves in pacifying the situation.[150] The liberation had the added advantage of allowing the British officers to come down from the hills; they 'slept in beds again after months or years in caves'.[151] The Villa Ariadne, before the war Tom's home and during the war the seat of the German generals, once again became Tom's base following the liberation. He was not the governor of Crete, but he had held the sway of one.

EOK–EAM sniping continued after the German evacuation and Tom was pessimistic about the National Guard he had lately helped to create on Crete, believing that although he had brought both nationalists and communists into a force that would protect Crete, this had not led to reconciliation, just a closer collision of opposites.[152] Ultimately he was right about this fractiousness, but it was more important that he was right that in the short term the force would protect Crete. No communist insurgency occurred and Crete was spared the civil war that killed 160,000 people on the mainland.

Despite his expressions of frustration at time wasted – natural after the climax of a long and difficult period of service – his role on Crete was dynamic and pivotal, enduring until after the island's full liberation. There was the potential on Crete during the Second World War for two equally bloody conflicts – guerrillas against Germans, nationalists against communists – and Tom's ostensible task was to prepare one side for each of these wars. But neither ever reached that critical stage – and a great part of the credit for this must go to Tom Dunbabin, arbitrating, reconciling, reinforcing. He saved thousands of lives.

John Dunbabin: 'He died from cancer. It was very sudden. He had been in Greece over Christmas and the New Year and had climbed mountains. He went down, I suppose, in March, and it was all very sudden. It was towards the end of my Spring term – I was at boarding school – but when it was clear that he was going to die, my mother brought me back.'

Katherine Dunbabin: 'The first thing was my mother talking about his having lumbago and then suddenly he was in hospital. I still didn't realise how serious it was until just before he died. We had been sent home in quarantine for polio, as it happened, but I didn't really understand why I had to go and stay with a friend of my mother's; it was because otherwise she couldn't visit the hospital. The death of one's father when one is thirteen years old is simply shattering. Children are selfish, they have their world, and that world is supposed to go on existing. And it didn't.'

Tom's death on 31 March 1955, at the age of forty-three, devastated many. Someone saw Maurice Bowra, famous for his acid, intolerant tongue, in a state of severe depression; asked why, he said, 'Because Tom Dunbabin is dying.' Katherine Dunbabin says, 'There was a body of people at All Souls who thought the world of him.' Jack McManus, former chaplain at All Souls, saw Katherine in Oxford in 2001 and told her that although he had been a very young man, he had admired her father enormously.

To mention Tom's name to any of the few people alive today who knew him is to receive an instant radiant smile. At a reunion of Magdalen classicists in March 2010, Sinclair Hood, who had been one of the chief excavators of Knossos and was director of the British School at Athens in the fifties, was guest at High Table. Asked about Tom, Hood, his head crooked forward, replied straightaway that 'he was the warmest person I ever knew'. In a later letter Hood recalled meeting Tom when he returned to the British School at Athens after the war. 'I don't remember him ever saying anything unpleasant or hurtful about anyone,' he wrote.

Definitively and succinctly, the ancient historian Robin Lane Fox says: 'He was the most brave scholar we have ever seen in this university.'

It is clear to both of his children that this widespread

admiration for their father came from a combination of his service in the Second World War and the exercise of his duties in the university afterwards. John comments on his 'great strength of character', and Katherine on his personal integrity: 'In a world of academic sleaze, he was one everybody knew to be completely incorruptible. He had a sufficient reputation from his war years that he could refuse to go along with something and get away with it. He had the moral authority.'

Epilogue

When going through his papers in the Beazley Archive, among the countless drawings of vases and paper packets of photos I found a sheet of paper torn from a lined notebook of the standard school exercise-book size. On one side, in Tom's tight, slightly slanting hand, is a list of graves at Argos in Greece, recording their dates and their pottery contents: 'Skyphoi, imitating Attic', 'Conventionalizing pyxides', 'Black cup with impressed flower'.

On the other is writing the neatness of which reveals the concentration of a young hand. The first words are the end of a description of fireworks seen from a ship sailing across the Channel: they had 'silver arms of fire, and silver fountains of light'. It continues: 'As we could see the fireworks quite well from about 10 miles away they must have been enormous close…Daddy and I had quite good bunks by the side of the ship. I went to sleep fairly soon, and slept quite well, though I woke up several times. Daddy was always asleep when I woke up, but says that he did not sleep well.' From a reference to Katherine further down the page, it is clear that this is a holiday diary of John Dunbabin from the late forties or early fifties.

This piece of torn-out paper seems to grasp and describe exactly the Tom Dunbabin I have pictured in my excavations of his life – simultaneously the father, and the academic whose knowledge took him into the Cretan mountains to fight the Nazis. In many ways, it seems the sort of memorial token he would appreciate, fit for his modesty and emphasising the more conventional contours of his life, only by exigency taken to extremes. A hero – how he would have hated that word but how he deserves it – perhaps warrants more in memory, something in steel or marble, letters carved three inches high, his name gilt. But I think Tom would be satisfied with this scrap.

The hero Tom Dunbabin

MINISTERO DELLA EDUCAZIONE NAZIONALE

DIREZIONE GENERALE DELLE ANTICHITÀ E BELLE ARTI

ITINERARI DEI MUSEI E MONUMENTI D'ITALIA

CORRADO RICCI
ANTONIO M. COLINI - VALERIO MARIANI

VIA DELL'IMPERO

(147 ILLUSTRAZIONI)

LA LIBRERIA DELLO STATO - ROMA - A. XI E. F.

MINISTERO DELLA EDUCAZIONE NAZIONALE

DIREZIONE GENERALE DELLE ANTICHITÀ E BELLE ARTI

ITINERARI DEI MUSEI E MONUMENTI D'ITALIA

CORRADO RICCI
ANTONIO M. COLINI – VALERIO MARIANI

VIA DELL'IMPERO

(147 ILLUSTRAZIONI)

LA LIBRERIA DELLO STATO – ROMA – A. XI E. F.

TUTORING
(2006–12)

At the age of twenty-two, I started having opinions. This may surprise anyone who had previously been on the receiving end of a blast of What I Think Today, but – in a classical sense anyway – it wasn't until my final year at Oxford that I thought I knew what I thought about things.

During the twelve-hour days of Finals revision in the library, breaks regulated by the hours college had appointed for consuming whichever variety of stolid carbohydrate was on the menu, I had rediscovered my love for classics, already reinvigorated by my trip around Europe, and had begun to put together piecemeal views into coherent opinions, underpinned by broader knowledge and theory. Before this, I never felt I had anything more than a transitory, superficial reaction to what I studied, largely formed by the combative style of Oxford education – tutorials where you read out your weekly essay, your tutor eruditely attacked and you less eruditely defended, mostly ceding ground to arrive at a ceasefire on their terms. The style, if adversarial in nature, was never hostile, but its lesson tended to be how to win discrete victories and concede discrete losses, tactical charges or retreats, rather than strategic intellectual position-taking. Now I write this, however, I feel sure that I took the wrong approach and that I often wasted this opportunity. I should have seen these tutorials, my hours with the experts, as something more collaborative. I suppose that's a lesson of one sort.

I was very admiring and envious of one of my fellow students, Ian, who had been a partner at law firm Clifford Chance and had quit, a quarter of a century after his first degree, to do a BA in classics. The jealousy was not because he was much better at everything than I was – his age was a disadvantage for the rote-learning required for grammar and vocabulary and remembering the extensive tracts of text we had to read – but because he definitely had opinions. He had spent twenty-five years reading classical works and thinking about classical ideas in preparation for his eventual return, and had reached views on them. Wasn't Cicero rather *jejune* in his political philosophy? Aren't Caesar's *Commentaries on the Gallic War* an avatar of Blairite spin? He was my tutorial partner for several courses, and his views were assured. Whether he was right or not, I respected this short, sometimes strident man, with his well-considered opinions.

By my fourth year, I had views. And as soon as I did, Finals were over and I was done with classics. Or so I thought.

My classics books were ripe for acquiring a layer of dust on my shelves, my folders of notes and essays and articles for being stashed above my cupboards. I wanted to get on with my postgraduate journalism course at City University in London. Come December 2006, I was on my winter break, having done a term of news-writing and shorthand and a couple of weeks' work experience on the *Enfield Times* and the *Ham & High*, Hampstead's local paper, which had been enervating, when I got a call from my friend Raj, who lived nearby and had read classics at St Hugh's in Oxford. He had, in fact, applied to Magdalen in my year and had witnessed my first encounter with Ian-of-the-opinions. We were all having dinner in hall and I was chatting to Raj, whom I liked because he came from a similar background and understood my deracinated experiences at a posh private school, when Ian, whom I had barely spoken to, volunteered, 'Don't mind Josh – he always shows off when he's nervous.' (I do show off, but rarely from nerves.)

Raj called and asked me if I was interested in tutoring a girl who lived not too far from me for her Latin GCSE. It wasn't something I had thought about and I figured that between a full-time journalism course and my Saturday job at Daunt Books, one of London's smartest independent bookstores, where all the books were arranged by country (so Italy would have the *Rough Guide to Rome*, Dante, *The Leopard* and a book on the Cosa Nostra), I probably had enough on my plate. Nevertheless, I said yes and made an appointment to see the girl. The ability to charge £25 an hour may have played a part, too.

I think I learned more in that first lesson than Sonali did. She was very rusty with her noun tables, taking standard examples through their cases only haltingly, even though these are among the very first things you learn and are fundamental to translation. Nouns in Latin change their ending depending on their function in their sentence: the nominative case is for the subject (*the dog* trapped the cat), the accusative for the object (the cat evaded *the dog*), the genitive for possession (the owner *of the dog* put it in a cage), the dative for the recipient (the owner gave the dog *to the vet*), the ablative for the deprived (the vet took the testicles *from the dog*), and the vocative for the addressed ('*O testicles*, how I miss you!' cried the dog). You can't understand a Latin sentence without knowing what the different case endings look like.

My instinct with Sonali was to be rigorous and perhaps

stern, modelling myself on Andrew Hobson, the round, shiny, high-handed yet oddly grounded ex-Westminster master who took us for translation classes at Magdalen. At the height of the Laura Spence affair, when Magdalen rejected a state school student with straight A grades and then-Shadow Chancellor Gordon Brown stirred up a row about elitism, Hobson was photographed by a newspaper wearing his Newcastle shirt, determined to disprove Oxford's social isolation. In his classes he made us examine each word as we went: what did its endings tell us? what function was it performing in the sentence? why had it been placed here and not there? If you couldn't tell the first declension ablative plural from the third declension genitive singular, there was a disapproving pursing of the lips or perhaps a sharp remark masked with a smile, so you soon became quick on your feet.

I thought this would work with Sonali. It didn't. A sixteen-year-old girl who is unsure about her endings will not respond like a hyper-trained public-school-and-Oxbridge boy, so I rapidly found myself moving from disapproval to encouragement, making the rigour palatable and profitable. The funny thing was, I actually *felt* more encouraging – it wasn't simply a mask.

Soon after I started seeing Sonali, I stopped working at Daunt, for reasons that still aren't entirely clear to me. They were expanding, therefore needed fewer people, I was told. Suddenly tutoring became my income while I studied and lived at home. I put a couple of adverts on websites and quickly garnered enough pupils to make up for my lost income in a quarter of the time, without the annoying interaction with a finicky public and the longueurs leaning over the counter, surreptitiously reading the stock. Over the next six years I taught dozens of pupils and the encouraging smile accompanying the rigorous approach always served well. But in my lessons I forsook all drama – unlike Belinda Dennis in hers.

BELINDA DENNIS
(1915–2003)

As I interviewed friends, colleagues and pupils of F. B. K. Dennis, known as Belinda, she was compared to various figures from classical mythology, drama and history, and so I intended to begin this chapter with a quotation spoken by or relating to one of those figures. A former Latin teacher would like that, surely – something pithy or eloquent drawn from her life's work, touching on her character. I rifled through some books in search of something illuminating, but I knew even before I started that this would be a fruitless task. The figures in connection with which Belinda had been mentioned were wicked women, some of the worst the Greeks imagined or the Romans endured.

A fellow Latin teacher, Lynda Goss, knew Belinda from the summer schools held by the Association for the Reform of Latin Teaching (ARLT). On the last evening of each summer school, which was held in a school or college around Britain, there would be an 'entertainment', usually a play in Latin. Lynda recalls that Belinda 'took the part of Agrippina in a hammed-up version of Tacitus, *Annals* XIV' with 'masses of enthusiasm'. Agrippina was the devious final wife of the Emperor Claudius, who murdered him with a poisoned vomiting-feather, according to Tacitus, and guaranteed the succession of her son, Nero, whom she tempted incestuously in order to retain his favour. In Tacitus' desperate portrayal, even at the moment of her death she used her femininity as a defiant weapon, or at least a shield: *in mortem centurioni ferrum destringenti protendens uterum 'ventrem feri' exclamavit* ('As the centurion drew his sword for the death-blow, she pointed to her womb and cried, "Strike me in the belly!"').[153]

Her style was evocative, too. Lynda relates how she used to wear 'lots of those Greek dresses, cotton ones' at the ARLT summer schools, where, for a week or two, Latin teachers from across the country would make and remake their friendships. Belinda's dress summoned up the *peplos* robe carved so lightly in the Parthenon frieze or draped over mythological maidens in paintings from the Renaissance onwards, although Lynda compared Belinda not to a priestess or a maiden: 'She looked like Clytemnestra – in the nicest possible way! She looked regal.' Clytemnestra is not the obvious choice for a compliment. Perhaps the most reviled of clever classical women, she murdered Agamemnon and his concubine Cassandra in their bath after he had returned from his decade at Troy. The shock of Clytemnestra, bloody, panting, looming over the body in the bath, sword still in hand, was bequeathed to us by the tragedian Aeschylus, who took advantage of a new piece of stage technology, the *ekkyklema*, to roll out the entire scene on a low platform from backstage; it soon became the dominant image of the queen. Although there are arguments about Clytemnestra's character and motives – she killed Agamemnon to avenge their daughter Iphigenia, whom he had sacrificed to calm the winds for the journey to Troy – her name is not normally the first to one's lips in praise of a woman.

Even Belinda's name has suggested a fierceness. Her birth name was Freda Blanche Kathleen Hulme-Hewitt. One version has it that her husband, Philip Dennis, thought she was more of a 'Belinda', and thus she was known for the rest of her life. Another suggests that she refused to tell him what the 'B' stood for. John Hazel, a classics teacher and friend, says that for him 'Belinda' always evoked 'Bellona', the Roman goddess of war. He certainly agrees that she was 'actressy', one among many adjectives used of her – 'theatrical' and 'dramatic' recur, too. The reason these words recur is a key to Belinda's career: she was a pioneer of a controversial mode of instruction in Latin, which had dialogue, the essence of the dramatic form, as its cornerstone.

I t is hard to imagine ructions in the world of classics teaching. One would think that its type of pedagogy had been ordained since time immemorial, perhaps inherited from the Romans themselves, or their monkish successors, or even the tutors to Renaissance princes. Certainly, you would think that by the nineteenth century it had all been settled, just in time for its decline into unpopular obsolescence.

How untrue this is. According to James Morwood, former head of classics at Harrow and emeritus fellow of Wadham College, Oxford, even the establishment in the mid-nineteenth century of a standard Latin grammar, written by Benjamin Hall Kennedy, was cause for an erudite fuss: 'His primer came in for severe criticism, raising a storm of correspondence in *The Times*. Thirty-six letters on (and somewhat off) the subject appeared there between 29 August and 9 November [1866].'[154] The chief complaints included difficulty, unfamiliar terminology and a belief that 'the authoritative imposition of a uniform standard would be a serious blow to individual freedom'. Little changes.

But this was a *tempestas* in a teacup, surely? In fact, the battle over how to teach Latin soon extended beyond the order of the cases of nouns, and what exactly a factitive verb is, into how you imparted knowledge of the classics at all. Rival movements sprang up and an educational experiment emerged which flourished for a few decades before withering, leaving some converts in safe-haven schools to continue with their new manner of teaching. Belinda Dennis was one of those converts.

Dr Christopher Stray, an honorary research fellow at Swansea University and an expert in the history of classical scholarship and teaching, met Belinda one summer in the sixties. 'I graduated from Cambridge in 1966 and then did a year's teacher training in London. In the summer in between I went up on a scooter to Keele, to a summer school run by the Association for the Reform of Latin Teaching, of which she was a leading light.' Indeed, Belinda was elected president in 1982. He didn't know her well, but remembered her as 'smiling, but potentially quite ferocious. I was told that she could be a pretty hard nut.'

The ARLT's name no longer makes people think of agitating classicists, but a century ago the 'Reform' part was significant. It was set up in 1911 by Dr W. H. D. Rouse, says Dr Stray, 'to promote Latin and Greek by conversations in those languages', an immersive technique he called the 'Direct Method', which was modelled on the experience of missionaries in India. (Belinda, interestingly, was born in India, to a British military father.) Demonstration lessons were important for teachers to propagate the Direct Method, and reading contests for pupils to prove that they had learned the sounds, rhythms and cadences of Latin speech. Latin and Greek literature, evolving before writing, was originally oral, and when later written down was meant to be read out loud, so an oral approach is in fact highly faithful.

Dr Rouse founded the ARLT in opposition to the staid Classical Association. He bullishly wanted the CA to concede that his system was superior to the CA's reading-based grammar–syntax–text progression, which had acquired the patina of authority through long use. There was also an element of professionalisation. Public schools at that time felt that a first was sufficient to make a good teacher, but Dr Rouse thought that teacher training was vital. Although the two camps had become reconciled by the Second World War (Latinists united against Hitler!), there were still teachers out there who preferred the Direct Method.

Dr Gillian Spraggs, who was a pupil at Harrow County Girls' School when Belinda was head of classics there (out of a department of two) and is now a poet, translator and historian, has acute memories of Belinda, who taught her for a few weeks of Latin in 1965 using the Direct Method, and then for O-level Greek from 1967. She is another witness to her dramatic tendencies: 'We were trained to greet her in Latin at the start of the lesson, "*Salve, O magistra!*" to which she would reply, "*Salvete, O puellae!*" We were given Latin names, which were always used in the classroom. If we answered a question incorrectly she would say "*Minime!*" If we were right it was "*Ita*" or "*Ita vero*", or "*Bene*". She had a strong theatrical streak: I remember her crying "*Eheu!*" in mock distress if someone made a silly mistake. When we were all really hopeless it was "*O me miserrimam!*"' Claire Carr remembers the Latin names, too, which were their surnames translated (Cox was *Gubernatrix*, the feminine form of 'helmsman') – they had to wear them round their necks on pieces of cardboard until Belinda had learned them all. Belinda also regularly attended a society where only Latin was spoken, says Diana Veale, her niece by marriage.

Belinda and the Direct Method seemed suited for one another: it gave her formidable, 'actressy' side an academic yet performative outlet. Of course, one can ask which came first, the actressy side or the Direct Method, but whichever did, they certainly fed into one another. Despite its increasing unpopularity in the face of the *Cambridge Latin Course*, there is evidence of her continued passionate belief in the Direct Method in newspaper clippings from 1980 when she was the director of the ARLT's summer school – in York that year – for pupils who needed to work on their Latin. An article in the *Yorkshire Evening Press* says that boys from St Olave's School would have their first lesson during the summer school using what sounded a lot like a demonstration of the Direct Method . 'The days are gone,' says Belinda in another press cutting, 'when you could throw a book of Caesar's "Gallic Wars" at a boy and tell him to learn it. The language may be dead but there are many different ways of making it more interesting, and we are always exploring different ways of teaching the subject.' In a third article she says that 'we believe in the value of bringing the languages to life by speaking them again'. (As these articles were in three different county-wide newspapers, her quotes are not just evidence for her support of the Direct Method in Latin but also for a thriving local newspaper industry inconceivable today.)

The problem with the Direct Method, says Dr Stray, was that 'unless you were a very good classicist it was very hard'. Anyone who has experienced classes where no English is spoken – such as the ones that put me off Japanese when I was thirteen – knows that they are unforgiving. 'It was a separate world in which you didn't speak English at all. It was all or nothing. A lot of people followed [Rouse] for a short time, particularly women, who were more receptive to a totalising vision.' (Whether you accept this view of the female mind or not, it sounds, not wholly coincidentally, like the theory of how early Christianity was spread through Rome's wealthy women.) There was even a Pre-Raphaelite-cum-Marxist ideology to go with it – for Dr Rouse, if not for all of his followers. He saw the Direct Method as part of 'a cosy, rural, cheerful time, which he supposed had existed before then' – that is, before the Industrial Revolution and class division. He believed, in fact, that you could go all the way back to the ancients, learning how to think as they thought, by speaking their languages.

By the time Christopher Stray was learning to be a teacher, the binary debate had died down and the proliferation of state schools had led to a greater variety of teaching methods, the most successful of which, emerging in the early seventies, was embodied by the still-popular *Cambridge Latin Course*. The *CLC* and its ilk, as suggested in a previous chapter, featured recurring characters and continuous stories which developed chapter by chapter, with linguistic points taught through the stories. The grammars and piecemeal translation books of earlier eras, which had extracts from ancient authors adapted for various degrees of difficulty, disappeared, and as schools ceased doing Latin they flooded the second-hand market, so that you can now pick up titles for fifty pence or a pound.

'Very little [of the Direct Method] has survived,' Dr Stray says. 'If I regretted anything, it would be the lack of practice in reading out aloud, the ultimate test of whether you can shape and produce a sentence to show you understand it.' Oxford still has an annual declamation competition, with four contests: reading from a prepared text (first prize £50) and recitation of verse from memory (first prize £25), in both languages. One of my Magdalen contemporaries was very successful in this, being a stickler for faint stresses and syllabic quantity, which seemed a rather fey discipline even by classical standards. At school level, a few evangelists remained as headmasters or heads of classics departments who would allow their staff to use the Direct Method, but with fellow teachers unsympathetic and parents suspicious, the sect has largely died out.

Even though her pedagogy of choice was in eclipse, Belinda believed that Latin itself was thriving, as she dryly says in the first of those newspaper articles: 'Seventy-four people will attend, which may be surprising for a conference devoted to the teaching of dead languages.'

Although Belinda Dennis started her career in the 1930s after reading classics at University College London, there are still many of her pupils about, accessible through Facebook and Friends Reunited, from Harrow County Girls' School and St Mary's Grammar School for Girls in Northwood. Most were very willing to talk about her and they confirm the influence of the Direct Method on her teaching style. They also, of course, evoke her character, albeit as perceived from a wooden school desk rather than over a coffee in the staff room.

Words like 'enthusiastic' and 'compelling' crop up in her pupils' descriptions, but so do 'eccentric' and 'scary'. Her appearance certainly made her remarkable. Claire Carr told me that 'she used to dye her hair very black and everybody used to think she modelled it on a Roman matron' – another stiff, unsmiling figure in the tradition of Agrippina (a *matrona* herself). Elisabeth Hallam says her persistent jet-black hair, which they always assumed was dyed, seemed out of keeping with the age her face suggested. The internet is not short of evidence of this. The ARLT maintains an in-depth website with photos from previous summer schools, including the one at York in 1980 of which Belinda was the director. One photo shows a large black bouffant above a lined face and wry semi-smile, another a broad smile as she stands next to a Canadian delegate.

There are some recollections of unalloyed joy, such as Catherine Percival's: 'Mrs Dennis was the greatest teacher in the history of the universe, a thoroughly wonderful person. She's one of those teachers you remember as being the one that made going to school worthwhile when nothing else did!' But these are rare among the more nuanced, equivocal memories, which are balanced between her schoolmarmish authority and the strong support she gave her pupils.

An important part of the Direct Method, as mentioned above, was the reading contest to show how the sounds of Latin and Greek had been absorbed, and Belinda passionately pushed her pupils to succeed. Elisabeth Hallam, who was at St Mary's Grammar School for Girls, recalls how she enthusiastically, theatrically organised a team: 'When I was about fifteen she took a group of us to a Greek speaking competition. We were the only girls there, and from the only state school, so the posh boys were a little startled at our performance as wild women of Bacchus. I can actually still remember some of it, we were so well drilled. We had garden canes with ivy wrapped around them, which we had to strike the floor with rhythmically, while spitting out the words. It was something

I'll never forget! I don't know if we won or not but we certainly came first or second. That was all Mrs Dennis's hard work; she chose the piece, drilled us, organised the props and drove the minibus.' Claire Carr recalls that Belinda urged them not to feel inferior because they were from a state school: 'She gave us a bit of a pep talk about not being ashamed of our roots and holding our heads high. She was a bit like Miss Jean Brodie, talking us up.' Afterwards, she took them out for tea.

Dr Gillian Spraggs has memories of Belinda that bear profound significance for her. 'The reading list she gave us at the start of the course included Mary Renault's historical novel *The Mask of Apollo*. She was insistent that we should read it as background to the Greek drama. This was the first book I ever read in which homosexual relationships were treated as a normal, taken-for-granted part of life, and it made a profound impression on me. This, of course, was only a few weeks after the passing of the Sexual Offences Act. "Queers" or "homos" were seldom mentioned in polite society, and when they were the required tone was cold distaste or tittering nervousness. For a teacher to recommend a novel with a homosexual theme, even a novel set in ancient Greece, to fourteen-year-old schoolgirls required unusual open-mindedness and some spine.'

This meant more to Gillian than to most of her peers. Gillian's first forays into Sappho – who wrote lyric poetry in the Lesbian dialect of Greek about lesbian attraction – also received help from Belinda. 'In spring '69 a school friend lent me Paul Roche's translation of Sappho, in an imported US paperback edition. I do not now like that translation much, but then it fired me to tackle the original; so I started on the only texts I could find, the selection included in *The Oxford Book of Greek Verse*. I quickly realised that Lesbian Greek was a different dialect to the Attic Greek we'd been studying; however, I worked my way through most of the shorter fragments without much trouble. But of course, I started to run into variant forms I wasn't sure about, and passages where the grammar was a bit puzzling; also, I wanted my work checked. So I showed the project to Mrs Dennis. I formed the impression she was mildly amused, and really rather pleased. She kindly forbore to point out what we both knew, that I had not been putting anything like the same amount of work into preparing the O-level set texts.'

Whether Belinda was severe by nature or had chosen that mask for her classes, her pupils remember her as a formidable woman. When she left Harrow County in 1969, however, her pupils saw a different Mrs Dennis. Marilyn Macey says, 'My only really strong memory of Mrs Dennis is her leaving speech. She chose to sing "Stay Sweet as You Are" to us, which she did very well despite being a little tearful. It was very moving because I had seen her as rather an authoritarian figure and it was a surprisingly motherly song to choose.'

> Stay as sweet as you are,
> Don't let a thing
> Ever change you.
> Stay as sweet as you are,
> Don't let a soul
> Rearrange you.

Her peers found her formidable, too. Brian Sparkes attended a talk she gave in Southampton about the pronunciation of Latin (the influence of the Direct Method again): 'Belinda was a great advocate of spoken Latin and was an excellent judge in competitions. On this occasion we remember that she had sent out passages for us to prepare in advance and treated us like a class of her pupils for whom she had set homework. Some had been assiduous in their preparation; others had been very lax and consequently were unenthusiastic about speaking out loud and revealing their shortcomings to others.' For those unprepared, she flourished a Latin dictionary that had markings to show you how to pronounce each word. 'By this she was letting us know that there was no excuse for mispronunciation, as the answer was in the cheapest Latin dictionary available. For some it was a salutary lesson.'

A peer with a strong memory of Belinda is John Hazel, who was head of classics at City of London Boys' School until he retired in 1996, although he had first met her in a far less salubrious neighbourhood, at Hackney Downs School in east London. She was giving a demonstration lesson to some Latin-less pupils and John says that 'it was quite clear that she was an extremely successful teacher'. Lynda Goss recalls a demonstration class Belinda gave in 1963 that left the pupils 'entranced' – 'and this was fifty years ago more or less, so it was pretty dynamic stuff.'

The obituary of Belinda that was published in the *JACT Bulletin* laid much emphasis on her role in propagating the Direct Method and on her own style: 'Belinda used "eggs, lollipops, crocodiles and considerable acting ability" to make pupils aware of the importance of endings! She was almost ahead of her time in her strong focus on skilful teaching techniques and ensuring that pupils really enjoyed lessons and had fun.' (It is unclear who is being quoted in the first sentence.)

One aspect upon which some commented was Belinda's skill as a peacemaker. John Hazel says, 'She was very good at bringing people together again.' Lynda Goss gives a concrete example. At one summer school, the Latinists were staying in the same place as a group of travellers from Saga, the organisation for the over-fifties, led by 'a rather grim type of woman'. On the final night of the school, after the Latin entertainment, the Saga people were displeased with the level of noise coming from the demobbed academics at midnight, which Lynda says was just 'singing and chatting', and there was a knock on the door from the 'obviously incensed' leader. 'What did we think we were doing? Were we fit people to teach a younger generation?' Belinda, who was 'charming and gracious', apologised. The irony, says Lynda, was that Belinda was much older than most of the Saga travellers.

One of her oldest surviving peers is Joan Newey (née Silverwood), who graduated from the University of London in 1945, shortly before Belinda, and was also the director of an ARLT summer school. Joan's teacher-training course was run by Francis Kinchin-Smith, who liked his 'high-fliers' to look after one another, and so when he called Joan it was to ask her to take an interest in Belinda. Joan took her on at Harrow County and Belinda took over Joan's job when she left to have children. They knew each other very well, says Joan, although she adds that, at eighty-seven, she can no longer remember much of Belinda. Nevertheless, she recalls that she was amusing and that they often shared suppers together.

Despite the keen value these teachers put on the intensive time spent together at the summer schools, Lynda Goss points out that they only met for five days once a year and at a teachers' refresher day at the beginning of March, but 'you think you could get to know a person desperately well.'

Between her professional and personal lives there was a gaping disconnect, as two of her nieces by marriage testify. 'I think she was one of those people who keep their friends and family in separate boxes, without wishing to mix them together at any time,' says Diana Veale – which is exactly the sort of skill a teacher needs to prevent their job seeping into the rest of their life.

What this meant, however, is that the stern facade Belinda presented to her pupils and colleagues – as well respected as she was – was at odds with the warmth her family saw in her. Diana, who was Belinda's executor, says her family were very fond of her, and they kept up their relationship for forty years after Belinda's husband, Philip, who had been her connection to Diana, died suddenly in the mid-sixties. Belinda would stay with Diana, who says that 'she sort of adopted us', and Juliet Scott at Christmas and occasional weekends.

The experiences of Belinda's early life in India are lost, but the bare facts remain. She was born on 29 August 1915 in Allahabad, in Uttar Pradesh, to Sergeant Major Frederick Hewitt and Blanche Hulme. She had two brothers, Wilson Stachey Hulme-Hewitt and Hilaire Louis Terence Theodore Hulme-Hewitt. British rule in India at this point was by no means moribund. Indian independence was thirty years away, over a million Indians worked for the British as soldiers and labourers, and the local potentates sent money and ammunition. Yet plots for freedom were active, and in 1912 certain revolutionaries tried to secure arms from Germany for use against the British. When the First World War broke out, Germany supported the Ghadar Party, an expatriate organisation set on a military uprising to seize power. In February 1915, there were a number of failed or aborted mutinies within the British Indian Army, stoked by Ghadarite infiltrators. Indeed, so worried was the British government in India that they passed the Defence of India Act in March 1915, giving the governor general the right to use punishments up to and including the death penalty, 'for the purpose of securing the public safety and the defence of British India and as to the powers and duties of public servants and other persons in furtherance of that purpose'. Of far less immediate concern to the Indian government was the return to India in January 1915 of Mahatma Gandhi after his civil rights work in South Africa. The role of Belinda's father in any of this is unclear, especially since the hotbeds were in Bengal and the Punjab, not Uttar Pradesh.

The family returned to England, although Diana, when she got to know Belinda after her marriage, had the impression that she had no family. It was, in fact, the marriage itself, in February 1942 at Cockermouth Register Office, that made this seem so. 'She never really spoke about her family to us,' Diana says, 'because her family disapproved of her marrying my uncle. I think it was religion – they were Roman Catholic,' while Diana's family were Anglican. 'She really was an outcast from then on.' While some fences were later mended, there was never a full reconciliation.

Any impression of severity her pupils received would have been banished if they had seen Belinda arriving on Juliet's family's Wiltshire farm for summer and Christmas holidays on the back of Philip's motorbike, as was their habit. 'Belinda and Philip were never fortunate enough to have children of their own,' says Juliet, 'but Belinda enquired and was interested about every member of the family and was always up to date with what everyone was doing: my brother, sister and myself;

my cousin and her family.' After Philip died of a heart attack in December 1967, Belinda never remarried.

She never lost her joy, though, says Juliet. 'She loved to travel, especially with her students, and she continued to travel well into her seventies when she managed to climb the Pyramids shortly before an operation for a second or third hip replacement, only to be "run over" by a donkey later that day!' Belinda also supported the construction of the revived Globe Theatre and lived to see its completion. 'She was one of the most interesting and warm people I have known in my life and I miss her.'

One pupil, Veronica Kotziamani (then Lemon), mentioned in an email that she had been on a trip to Italy with Belinda and Philip when she was at Harrow County Girls' School, aged seventeen. Diana Veale says that Belinda 'adored' going to Italy annually. This is no shock – classicists often make that pilgrimage, especially in the company of schoolchildren – but it provides at least one excursion when she might have used the book of hers I now have, *Via dell'Impero*, by Corrado Ricci, Antonia M. Colini and Valerio Mariani, a volume with a troubling origin.

The book is a slim, small paperback tourist guide to Rome in Italian – specifically, the monuments of the Via dell'Impero, the straight road that runs from the Piazza Venezia to the Colosseum alongside (and over) the ruins of the grand public squares commissioned by various emperors. It has a duck-egg blue cover, faded to grey three quarters of an inch from the spine – the ghost of another, smaller book placed in front of it on a sun-exposed shelf – and to dirty grey-brown on the spine itself. It looks as if, were you to drop it, the delicate threaded binding would snap and the pages sluice out of the covers. On the cover is written 'FBK Dennis' in red biro, although the 'F' seems reversed, like a seven, and in pencil Belinda (it looks like her hand) has put some page references – Curia 54, Tullianum 52, p. 49. (The Curia is the Senate house in the Roman Forum, the Tullianum part of the Forum's prison, which was really more of a holding cell.) The only other handwriting is the second-hand bookseller's, a quick '1.00' at the top right of the title page.

Anyone familiar with Rome may well have picked out something odd in the previous paragraph. The road that runs from the Piazza Venezia to the Colosseum is not called the Via dell'Impero – it's the Via dei Fori Imperiali, named for the imperial fora beside and underneath it. I remember it well because I was fascinated on my first visit to Rome by these spaces, which are hardly ever spoken about in comparison with the Colosseum itself, the main Forum and the Circus Maximus. These massive imperial squares include Caesar's Forum, with the remains of his temple to Venus the Mother, on whose steps he refused to rise for a group of senators, intensifying the anger that led to his subsequent assassination (one historian pleads an attack of diarrhoea for the failure); Augustus' Forum, with the base of the temple of Mars the Avenger, which he vowed to build in 42 BC after defeating Caesar's murderers at Philippi, but which took forty years to complete; Vespasian's Forum, with a temple to Peace after the conquest of Jerusalem; Nerva's Forum, which was in fact started by the despotic Domitian in order to connect all the other fora; and Trajan's vast Forum, 120 metres by 200, with a large basilica for the empire's administration, a Greek library, a Latin library, a multi-storeyed curved market and a temple to Trajan, who was posthumously deified, all overlooked by Trajan's Column. Seeing these fora from the road is to enlarge your conception of Rome beyond the touristic, to begin to understand that there was a whole civic and political city here, rather than just isolated monuments – which is not easy when most of it is buried.

The clue to the book's history is in the naming, and the renaming. The road was Mussolini's project, finally laid down after decades of plans that predate him, and its original name conveys blunt dictatorial force: 'Power Road'. It was renamed after Mussolini's fall to the more neutral 'Road of Imperial Squares'. The first thing the cover tells you, therefore, is that this book dates from the fascist period.

The cover is prickly with these disconcerting details. At the top is the commissioning power, *Ministero della Educazione Nazionale*, and at the bottom the publisher, *La Libreria dello Stato*. It is number 24 in the series *Itinerari dei Musei e Monumenti d'Italia* (Guidebooks to Italy's Museums and Monuments). Previous volumes, listed on the final page, include guides to Ostia, Pompeii and the museums of Bologna, Parma, Florence, Naples and Milan. This is a comprehensive programme to document and glorify Italy's history and culture – no less than you would expect from any government, but especially from a fascist one that painted itself as the resurrection of the Roman Empire. The picture on the cover is of a Roman coin with the profile of the Emperor Augustus, with whom Mussolini liked to identify in propaganda, not least because Augustus had extended the Roman Empire far across Europe and Africa. The legend encircling Augustus' head says that he is 'the Divine Augustus, Father', referring both to his deification and to the title *pater patriae*, 'Father of the Country', which he was granted by the Senate, as if he were a new founder of Rome, a new Romulus. The heredity Mussolini considered his own is clear.

The smallest thing is the most disturbing. The very last letters on the cover are 'A. XI E. F.', which is a date: 1933. The letters stand for *Anno XI nell' Età Fascista* – the eleventh year of the fascist era, which began in 1922, when Mussolini became prime minister. Like other madmen of the twentieth century, Mussolini thought that history started with him.

I was going to write that 'Mussolini's propagandistic tropes filtered down even on to the cover of a book', but the 'even' struck me as wrong. Why should it be 'even'? Why should books, especially books on Roman history, be exempt? Mussolini's propagandistic tropes filtered down on to the cover of a book, which is *exactly* what you might expect from a fascist government with its hand on every lever of power, a fascist government that wanted its symbols everywhere, from the tarmac of a new road to the books on your desk to the coins in your pocket. This was inescapable, all-penetrating propaganda, and for one instant, just glancing at the cover of this book, I thought I understood just a fraction of how oppressive it must have been to live under the gaze of the ubiquitous Mussolini and his metonyms.

The introduction on page three is a blithe acknowledgement of all that the cover encodes:

> The plan for the excavation of the rest of the Imperial Fora, prepared in 1911 by Corrado Ricci and converted into a design by Lodovico Pogliaghi, only began to be put into effect in March 1924 by the will of HE Benito Mussolini, Head of the Government. The first stage was

up to the Forum of Augustus, then to the House of the Knights of Rhodes, then to the Forum and the Market of Trajan, finally to the Fora of Nerva and Caesar.

The extensive complex of the Imperial Fora assumed greater importance when, to investigate certain exposed discoveries and give Rome an artery worthy of its size and its new development, Prince Francisco Boncompagni Ludovisi suggested to the Head of the Government the plan of a road leading from the Piazza Venezia to the Colosseum, having at its sides the incomparable formation of the monuments that are described in this guide.

Such an outstanding road…was inaugurated by HE Mussolini on 28 October 1932. [my translation]

(Note how the road is portrayed as an afterthought to a worthy archaeological excavation.)

On page four is a large photo of men in uniform, medals drooping over sashes, white feathers, traditional symbols of cowardice now aggressively repurposed as a fascist emblem, standing erect on black hats, riding in a cavalry procession in front of the Colosseum. The caption, needing no translation, reads: *Il Duce inaugura la Via dell'Impero (28 Ottobre 1932 – XI)*.

It is tempting to see a motoring megalomania in the construction of the Via dell'Impero under Mussolini, but Dr Robert Coates-Stephens, a fellow of the British School at Rome, says the road has a longer, more pragmatic history. Rome in the mid-nineteenth century did not have major arteries fit for a modern city, let alone one that many dreamed would become the capital of a unified Italy, and so popes and politicians tried to give it the roads it needed. One pope began the Via Nazionale before the culmination of the Risorgimento took away the papacy's power, while after unification the Via Cavour was built. 'These were two big east–west roads,' Dr Coates-Stephens says. 'There was no north–south road that went down to the Colosseum and the south-east of the city. The Piazza Venezia came to a dead end in a network of tiny medieval houses.' For *viabilità*, 'they definitely needed a north–south road'.

All kinds of plans were discussed, including one taking a road right through the beautiful curved Market of Trajan. It is impossible to avoid one archaeological treasure in Rome without damaging another, although Dr Coates-Stephens asserts that Corrado Ricci, author of *Via dell'Impero* and excavator of the imperial fora, persuaded the engineers of the final road to run it through the open spaces of the fora rather than where the buildings were, thus preserving as much material as possible. As it was, when they built the Via dell'Impero they had to cut down the entire Velian Hill, apparently uncovering mammoth tusks in the process, which sets Rome's antiquity in its proper place.

By finally constructing the road, Mussolini was thus not solely summoning up a project for his own glorification, but responding to a civic need, even if he was 'much more strident' about its value, says Dr Coates-Stephens. Nevertheless, it had plenty of propaganda value. Opponents could be labelled Bolsheviks, and Mussolini was perceptive about the nationalistic and imperial benefits it could bring. 'It was milked for all it was worth from a fascist point of view, but it wasn't dreamed up for all of that.' It could, naturally, be used for parades and transporting military equipment – or prisoners – too.

Ricci is in an intriguing, compromising position here. He managed to direct the road where it would do least damage to his archaeological work, but some damage was inevitable.

How happy would he have been to be the author of a book celebrating this civic good, this fascist triumph, this destroyer of the historical record? He had overseen the excavation of the Roman Forum and the Baths of Diocletian before the imperial fora, and then he had to write a book to commemorate a road that wrecked some of his work. It is as if a doctor had been turned into a torturer, or a policeman into an inquisitor – neither an unusual path under fascist regimes, where compulsion and survival are two sides of the same coin. Ricci died the year after the book came out.

Mussolini took on other *grands projets* within the city to bolster his image and reinforce his ideology. As one academic writes, Mussolini excavated and relocated the Emperor Augustus' Ara Pacis – the ironic 'Altar of Peace', which honoured the peace Augustus had won through war – to demonstrate 'the rebirth of the Roman spirit (*romanità*) in fascism and the capacity of Mussolini's "New" Italy to reclaim and regenerate the classical heritage of the Eternal City'. His 'massive Augustan *mise-en-scène*' also included restoring the Mausoleum of Augustus within the new Piazza Augusto Imperatore, for which countless houses were razed, and building the Foro Mussolini (now the Foro Italico), a public sports complex with its unforgettable obelisk still marked 'Mussolini Dux'. All was propaganda. 'Through an aggressive programme of urban renewal, new construction and archaeological excavation, [the regime] sought to negate old stereotypes of Italian backwardness and indolence, and present a dynamic and youthful nation to the rest of the world.' [155]

In ploughing a wide new road through the centre of Rome, Mussolini was perhaps proving himself an appropriate heir to the emperors – not least Augustus, in whose mantle of potency and success he wanted to cloak himself. All of the fora had involved destruction as well as construction; they were not empty fields on which they were built. Trajan tore down sides of the Quirinal and Capitoline Hills for his Forum. The imperial biographer Suetonius records Augustus boasting that he refused to expropriate local residents for more land to build his Forum, but the fact that he said it at all shows how unusual such restraint was. Mussolini, whose plan was simultaneously to enhance opportunities to see the fora and to destroy them with intensive construction on top of them, clearly knew his Roman history. Of course, whereas the Caesars wanted to build spaces for justice and administration, Mussolini wanted to build a road for motor vehicles and the military. How much of this did Belinda know when she bought her guidebook?

As she grew older, Belinda still tried to attend the summer schools, although mobility issues slowed her down. She eventually suffered from serious dementia and then caught MRSA in hospital, which hastened her death in February 2003. When they last met in 1996, staying near Hook in Hampshire, Lynda Goss says Belinda had had five operations on each hip – but she still joined in. 'There was a kind of lift from one floor to another. She got into this lift and came up through the hatch like an upside-down *dea ex machina*,' the god that usually descended from a crane at the end of Greek tragedies. Even in her old age, Belinda was always the actress.

Belinda in Italy

PREZZO L. 6,75

Plato

Euthyphro
Apology of Socrates
Crito

Edited with notes by
JOHN BURNET

J.E.M. Naylor
Easter 2004

PLATO'S EUTHYPHRO

APOLOGY OF SOCRATES
AND CRITO

JAMES NAYLOR
(1985–2009)

O liver Taplin, who resembled Paddington Bear with a
PhD, was holding his annual party to welcome the fresh-
ers. It was Michaelmas term 2003, a few weeks in, and a crowd
of classicists was unshelling pistachios Oliver had brought
back from Greece the day before and drinking dry white
wine. Oliver, who had by then been Magdalen's classics tutor
for thirty years, had a room in the Palladian New Buildings,
one of the finer of Magdalen's failed architectural projects. His
was a small ground-floor study looking out across some grass
which, depending on the time of year, had the college's deer in
it, chomping the greenery and tangling antlers and avoiding
becoming a ceremonial dinner. From floor to ceiling, fourteen
feet away, every wall was a rainbow barcode of book spines, and
on his desk between the windows an ancient iMac wheezed.

The company of the intake of 2003 being welcomed that
evening would prove much more amenable to me than my
own year's – perhaps because of certain passive-aggressive
friendships I had developed with people in my group, perhaps
because of my competitiveness with, and powerful jealousy
of, my intellectual superiors in my year, and my consequent
insecurity. Despite this, I was being uproariously funny and
bitingly *bon mot*-ish, I kid myself, still in that stage where I
took it for granted that being a classicist at Magdalen meant
I could automatically drape myself in Oscar Wilde's spangled

mantle. As it happened, that evening I met another Magdalen classicist who had no ambition to be Oscar – his heart was set on Cole Porter.

James Naylor – Jem to his friends at university – was a sweet-faced, curious boy, with a mouth that disclosed gentle mischief even when the rest of his face was trying to hide it. His cheekbones jutted forward, his hair was thick and light brown, his eyes blue. There was a hesitancy about him in this large group, and he seemed to be engineering a discreet process of fading into the background. He could be as boisterous as anyone among his intimates, but in Taplin's study he quietly picked at the pistachios. We arranged to meet for lunch the next day.

As I got to know him better, it became clear that Jem's tendency to disappear into crowds, as he had tried to do at Taplin's, derived partly from a natural awkwardness, but equally it allowed a measure of disinterested observation, like a naturalist who had his binoculars trained on Oxford's jungle. This led some people to underestimate him and there could be a rare sharp remark pricking a pretentiousness that thought it had got away scot-free – probably, on occasion, at my, deserved, expense. Whether Jem looked wide-eyed with surprise or even innocently interested, you could be fairly sure he knew what was going on. This is not to say his expression was fraudulent, but he liked to let other people talk – and I liked to be let talk. It was a form of politeness – he was divinely well mannered and considerate – and reserve and self-deprecation. This meekness was unwarranted and he never quite realised that people talk because they are given the time to do so, not because they have something to say. He, of course, had plenty worth listening to, if it could be coaxed out.

We became close friends for a couple of months, a flare in winter's darkness before the shadows gathered again. I remember watching Woody Allen films with him, me failing to laugh because I had exhausted my laughter on them already, but rejoicing in his fresh joy. We went to a club night at the Old Fire Station pub where I had to convince Jem that dancing with your hands clasping the back of your head was not a good look.

At the end of his first term, there was Hall Bop, the party held in Magdalen's dining hall, until the fire brigade went on strike and the college realised the hall's wood panels and por-traits were flammable. It was fancy dress, but then most things at Oxford were, whether subfusc for exams or costumes to suit the themes for the fortnightly bops in the college bar – things beginning with the letter T, costumes made from bin bags, evil Christmas. (Two of my friends' cling-film dresses were unsurpassable.) I went as Groucho Marx, cracking someone else's wise, wearing an all-in-one structure with thick black eyebrows over thick black glasses (hanging on over my own thick glasses), a bulbous nose and a thick black moustache which tickled my lip. I exuberantly flapped a cigar about and made sly, nasal remarks about elephants and pyjamas. Jem, not one for costumes, had to be persuaded to come along and he borrowed my cowboy shirt, which had never been further west than Oxford. He danced awkwardly and I remember his pleas-ure when it was over.

We saw each other a couple of times over the Christmas vac, including when he and another friend stayed over for my birthday. He bought me the *Penguin Dictionary of Modern Humorous Quotations* ('a little something to make your Groucho impression even more convincing than before') and

A Handful of Dust ('to introduce you to the delights of "getting tight"', a phrase he had taught Waugh-less me). The quotations I loved, but I found *Dust* bleak and sterile, and I suspect it suited Jem's sober worldview more than mine. We also spent a very happy New Year's Eve at our friend Maya's, listening to Amy Winehouse before anyone had heard of her and relaxing with his year's classicists.

We did stay friends, but our friendship suffered from an embarrassment of closeness – when an intense period of intimacy ends, it always pushes apart. I attended his twenty-first birthday party dinner in Oxford, at the smart Cherwell Boathouse, and afterwards we all went out for cocktails and then back to his room for chocolate cake. (I was quite ill that evening after combining a rich meal, wine, whisky sours with egg white and birthday cake.) His room in college summed up the elegance he loved and wanted to live, art deco posters of continental holiday destinations and trains shooting at you from the vanishing point. As I said before, it was the era of Cole Porter that he loved, the snappy style and shooting from the wit, an era of slick musicals and sharp songs. He loved 'Anything Goes', yet seemed quite immune to its lascivious charm, taking only its delicate poise and generous humour. I bought him the terrible Porter biopic *De-Lovely* on DVD for his birthday once, and it crossed my mind that he would have been happier in the Oxford of the Roaring Twenties, or a little earlier, when Ivor Novello had been at Magdalen. He liked other musicals, too. In his final year at college, I went up to stay with him so we could see a production of Sondheim's *Company* and he spent the entire walk back to his room trying to recall the various groups of ladies who lunch.

It became easier, however, to see him in his group. I grew closer to his friends Mohan and Becky, also classicists, who were as animated and outgoing as I was. Although Jem was always quick to laugh, he could never be persuaded to stay later of an evening than some time he had set in his mind. This was a mysterious inflexibility, as if to prove something to himself, or to avoid some irremediable action, seeing submitting to the call of a little more pleasure as a defeat. In retrospect, it was the same discipline he would exercise to its ultimate measure. As Becky said in his eulogy, in a gentle phrase I do not forget, he excused himself too early from parties as he did from life.

After university, Jem became unsettled and made some odd choices, which I glimpsed through sporadic contact and his friends' reports. He had fallen out of love with classics in his second year and dallied with changing course, and the bitter way in which he had chewed up his final two years meant further study was not an option, even though he had brilliance to spare for it. His father, Dan, got him a job at Lloyd's of London, where he had worked for decades, but Jem did not take to it. He decided to study medicine at Newcastle, starting in autumn 2008, and worked stacking the dairy aisle in Tesco to fund himself as he studied for his science A-levels, despite his parents' ability and willingness to support him. He stuck out a term in Newcastle but then quit; he would not let the university hold his place for a year, his parents say, because he wanted to give it to someone he felt was more deserving. Dan and Ann say that working at Tesco, a job that demanded no interiority, was Jem's happiest time towards the end of his life.

Chris Chalk never usually called me. He was a good friend from Magdalen, who had been in the year below me – as an archaeologist and anthropologist, an associate of the classicists. A very tall Etonian, Chalk had the dry, derisive-but-sweet sense of humour and the emotional suit of armour common to those who have spent five years there. We had probably drifted apart as friends since Oxford, but I still saw him at parties and he, the nicer of his year's classicists and I would get together for drinks or meals. We were not close enough and he wasn't the type, anyway, to call me out of the blue.

It was a bright Saturday in early January 2009 and I was in my second lesson of the day, in the basement kitchen of a pupil in Hampstead, teaching her nothing I can now remember. My iPhone rang and over the *Orange Marilyn* screensaver Chalk's name appeared in white. I never believed in the presentiment of ill news carried in the ring of a telephone but I felt something was wrong. When I answered, he told me that Jem had killed himself. I put the phone down and found that I was grasping my pupil's shoulder for support. She looked cheerfully bewildered.

The internet had given him instructions, his doctor the means – Jem claimed he was having trouble sleeping. My cheerful memories of that evening, chewing my way through a large steak drowning in garlic butter at my brother's birthday dinner, are now rapidly intercut with, or run parallel to, imagined scenes of Jem's bedroom, like watching two films of irreconcilable tone at once. The last time I had – attempted – contact with him was in late December. I had the perverse habit of going Christmas shopping, or rather spectating on the frenzied Christmas shopping of others, on my birthday, two days before Christmas, and while walking down Oxford Street with my friends Will and Tristram, who was another classicist in Jem's year, I had the urge to call him. He didn't pick up, so we all yelled a festive greeting into his voicemail.

All of Jem's friends went down to Kent to see his parents a week after his death. I had spent that week ritually letting his tutors know what had happened, and I paced around outside the Naylors' house on the phone to another soon after we arrived. A ceiling-high wall unit in the kitchen was covered with photos of James, including one I had taken of him, Becky and Mohan, his best friends, after they had finished Mods, crowned with confetti. His black jacket rested over the back of a chair. His mother Ann looked utterly empty and Dan was red-faced, raw. A dozen of us sat around the kitchen table and ate and drank and bequeathed Ann and Dan our memories of Jem, and I hoped it was slightly comforting, though since then I have realised they can never be comforted.

In Greek texts, people customarily have their fill of weeping, as if once you have wept a dribble or a cup or a pint of tears you can be satisfied, but what I learned over the following weeks was that there is no such thing as a fill of weeping – there is just more. I went out to lunch with an old friend and soon after she started asking me about Jem, I hid my face behind my menu and sobbed. I was punch-drunk with grief and in private moments insensible, and all the time what made it worse was that I knew my grief was only a fraction of others'. I wept for Jem and for myself and for his friends and for his parents and for his family and for every other friend, lover, parent and relation of a suicide. I became a monster of empathy; there was no one's suffering I did not feel. I became religious, but not even my own – I thought I knew what was meant by God's love for Christ and Christ's love for mankind, something that had never even occurred to me before, because I understood that this love was suffering. And I cried, I cried when I carried Jem's coffin on my shoulder into the chapel at Tonbridge, his old school, and I cried by his graveside as if my heart had turned to a handful of dust, watching his coffin disappear into the hard cold ground and his mother collapse – knowing that what I had once felt for him had never been completely extinguished, only hidden away deep inside me, and never could be.

O n that first evening in Kent, Ann and Dan insisted that we should not leave without taking some memento of James from his attic study, and as much as we protested, they insisted. We finally went upstairs and browsed his bookshelves, and I felt like some grotesque trophy-hunter, wanting to take something meaningful and hating myself for the inappropriate momentary satisfaction that came from seeing something I might like. In any case, for me it turned out to be an obvious book, as well as his copy of Forster's *Maurice*.

As part of Mods, you have to do a philosophy paper and mine was on Plato's *Euthyphro* and *Meno*, the former a dialogue on holiness as an aspect of virtue, the latter on the broader topic of virtue itself. The paper was an accessible introduction to Plato's moral philosophy and epistemology, although you had to read both dialogues in Greek. Platonic Greek is largely simple, albeit with plenty of conversational gambits, tones and interjections you are not used to, and you have to consider all of this in your translation, even as you try to understand the substance of his argument. I had photocopied the text of the *Meno* but bought a second-hand copy of John Burnet's annotated edition of the *Euthyphro*, and after I had finished Mods I knew Jem was studying the same paper, so I gave him my book.

I was listlessly scanning Jem's shelves when I saw its sludge-green spine. He had put 'J.E.M. Naylor, Easter 2004' on the top left of the inside front cover and had pencilled in some thoughtful notes on syntax and translation. It seems in some awful way the perfect book for him, containing Socrates' relentless search for virtue, just as Jem had sought virtue all his life without mercy to himself. By the end of his life, however, Jem had finally, mistakenly, concluded that he was wanting in it. I was pleased he had had use of the book, but I would gladly have never had it back. I wish that I never could have had it back.

James Naylor

(1985–2009)

When the book was first published in 1924 *The Times* forecast that it was "likely to be the standard edition of these dialogues for some time to come". In the present edition the hard binding has been replaced by a soft cover, but the contents are unchanged.

Companion Volume

Plato's *Phaedo*
Edited with introduction and notes by John Burnet

OXFORD UNIVERSITY PRESS

£3.50 net in UK   ISBN 0 19 814015 0

ACKNOWLEDGEMENTS

I am grateful, first of all, to everyone who spoke to me: both the people who used to own my books, and the family, friends, colleagues and pupils of those who did. This book would, quite obviously, not have been possible without them.

Many people provided me with papers and photos or access to papers and photos, including Deirdre Levi, Sister Mary Anthony, Cressida Connolly, Matthew Levi, Professor Katherine Dunbabin, John Dunbabin, Professor Donna Kurtz of the Beazley Archive, University of Oxford, and the staff of the Liddell Hart Centre for Military Archives, King's College London.

I was lucky to have three wonderful friends who were also astute, sympathetic and honest readers of this book at various stages, and their comments were invaluable: Philip Abraham, Noor Rassam and Claudia Rothermere.

Dr Al Moreno and James Morwood pointed me in the right direction when I needed it.

Thank you to everyone at Unbound, especially Isobel, Emily, Georgia, Mark and Jimmy, who believed in this book and have helped make it happen.

Finally, thank you most of all to everyone who has funded this book: with your support, the stories carried in my books can finally be told. I hope this book now becomes part of your story.

NOTES ON RESEARCH

Finding my subjects was the first hurdle in a rather long course of hurdles (anonymity, secrecy, lack of email, death). Some of them I knew because they had given me the book, such as Donald Russell, who had let me have Sidgwick and Morice's *Introduction to Greek Verse Composition*. A mature student from my tutoring days had bought us both a school edition of Ovid's *Heroides* so we could read in Latin these melodramatic letters from abandoned heroines (imagine a mythological *Sex and the City* without the brunch), but she did not wish to be written about. Other inscribed names I had heard of before, like Fernandez-Armesto in North and Hillard's *Latin Prose Composition*.

Several readers had been kind enough to put their college, university or school after their name. 'TJ Dunbabin, CCC, Oxford' meant a call to the archivist at Corpus Christi College, and 'W Clark, Sidney Sussex, Cambridge' one to his counterpart in the Fens. 'D Rundle, Coll Magd, Oxon', with its dignified and antique Latin formulation – *Collegium Magdalenense, [Universitas] Oxoniensis* – signified a return to my old college. Although those three gentlemen were at university in the first half of the twentieth century, the tradition of adding your college persisted. In the eighties Mark Richards of Keble did it, and in the noughties Emilie Vleminckx of Wadham, too; their alumni associations put us in contact. Leo Stevens had written on a Highgate School bookplate, beneath the school's crest, a horizontal sword beneath a helmet of armour and above what looks like a dragon's head.

Oxford and Cambridge have been meticulous about keeping tabs on their alumni for some while now, and even during the years when they didn't realise alumni could be tapped for donations they still kept extensive records, in the manner of places that always live in hope of posterity. Not all universities had been as diligent. Despite one inscription quite clearly reading 'Dave Warren, Classics Dept, Man University', no one at Manchester could find any mention of Dave Warren, nor was the University of London much better with 'Josephine Miller, Queen Mary College, U of London'.

Schools are even worse than universities. I took to trawling Friends Reunited, searching for people first by school then by approximate year, messaging people I thought might be their classmates and asking if they knew Kate Allen or Claire Fraser of Bedford High School, as I had two books from the same school. Perhaps I could find anyone from the County High School for Girls in Macclesfield who had used North and Hillard's *Greek Prose Composition* some time from the fifties onwards. There were several books with only school names in – the salty *Satires of Juvenal* came from Enfield Grammar School, the *Res Gestae Divi Augusti*, a self-penned record of the Emperor Augustus' achievements, from Mill Hill. One book just said 'class copy'.

Women presented a rather significant problem – in a research sense only, of course. If their school or university has not kept tabs on them and the book dated from even ten years ago, there was a chance they would have got married and their name would have changed. Without any further details and with books that date from the sixties or seventies, it is almost impossible to trace Jane J. S. Barr or Tamsen Atkinson or Mary Scott.

The internet was an unimprovable if hard-to-navigate enabler for some people, tracking down by fits and starts and hook and crook Michael Brown – or MBMcC Brown as he was known to me from his inscription – and another accumulation of initials, FBK Dennis. With both MBMcC Brown and FBK, the searches were several, ambitious, unrefined and finally considered.

My first attempt at finding MBMcC Brown brought me to an online PDF from *Injury: The British Journal of Accident Surgery*, which was a parodic piece on the physiological problems bell-ringing can cause, called 'Coping with Crises in Campanology'. It warns of the dangers posed to old men running up the bell tower after 'nubile women in their early twenties', who are apparently now a significant constituency in the bell-ringing community. Rudimentary cartoons of the accidents likely to befall such bell-ringers are accompanied by Latin translations – a man, cheerful for the moment, holds the rope between his legs, above a caption that reads '*castratio praesens* – perhaps the most painful of accidents'. The translations were credited to MBMcC Brown, but there was no greater clarification.

I tried putting the name into Google with spaces this time, 'M B McC Brown', and the fourth result was a page about uncontested elections in 2008 from the administrative section of Oxford's website: 'PGMcC Brown, Trinity, Fellow of Classics...' I remembered Peter Brown as a lecturer from my time at Oxford, and I figured there couldn't be too many unrelated Browns with elaborate forenames one of which was McC, so I emailed him and he told me about his brother, Michael, who now lived in Australia and had translated the captions for his father-in-law.

A google for 'FBK Dennis', written in maroon biro on the cover of *Via dell'Impero*, turned up a note in an article called 'On Teaching Classics' from *Didaskalos*, a journal of classical pedagogy, and so I emailed James Morwood, an old tutor from Oxford who was particularly involved in thinking about teaching: 'One of my books has the name "FBK Dennis" written in it; all I've been able to find out about him is that he wrote an article in *Didaskalos* about teaching Latin, which made me think you could know who he was. If you did, or if you knew anything at all about him, I'd be really grateful to learn it.'

I had presumptuously got the pronoun wrong, but my tutor did know who Belinda Dennis was and set me on the right path towards her. In retrospect, it has become clear that had I tried a little variety of spacing in my searching for FBK Dennis, it would have pulled up Belinda's name in a much less roundabout way, but nevertheless, what this chase reinforced to me was that even the internet, with its exabytes of data, cannot always outdo human memory.

NOTES

Abbreviations

Dunbabin MS = Tom Dunbabin, manuscript of memoir

Final Report = Tom Dunbabin, *Final Report on SOE Missions in Crete: 1941–1945*

Flutes of Autumn = Peter Levi, *The Flutes of Autumn* (London, 1983)

Hill of Kronos = Peter Levi, *The Hill of Kronos* (London, 1980)

Light Garden = Peter Levi, *The Light Garden of the Angel King: Journeys in Afghanistan* (Newton Abbot, 1973, original edition Collins, 1972)

Smith-Hughes = Jack Smith-Hughes, *General Survey of Crete 1940–45*

Western Greeks = T. J. Dunbabin, *The Western Greeks* (Oxford, 1948)

1 Following quotations from Christopher Stray, ed., *Oxford Classics: Teaching and Learning, 1800–2000*, p.228.
2 'Classics and Intelligence I', *Classics Ireland*, 8 (2001), and 'Classics and Intelligence II', *Classics Ireland*, 9 (2002).
3 F. H. Hinsley and Alan Stripp, eds, *Codebreakers: The Inside Story of Bletchley Park* (Oxford, 1993), p.265.
4 Hinsley and Stripp, p.265.
5 Hinsley and Stripp, p.284.
6 Michael Smith, *The Emperor's Codes: Bletchley Park and the Breaking of Japan's Secret Ciphers* (London, 2000), pp.196–7.
7 Hinsley and Stripp, p.283.
8 Smith, p.199.
9 Hinsley and Stripp, pp.268 ff.
10 Smith, p.251.
11 Hinsley and Stripp, p.285.
12 Hinsley and Stripp, p.286.
13 Hinsley and Stripp, p.262.
14 Smith, p.335.
15 *Flutes of Autumn*, p.24.

16 *Flutes of Autumn*, p.15.

17 *Flutes of Autumn*, p.36.

18 'The Art of Poetry no. 14', *Paris Review* (1979), p.11.

19 *Flutes of Autumn*, p.65.

20 *Flutes of Autumn*, p.70.

21 Edward Lucie-Smith, ed., *British Poetry since 1945* (Harmondsworth, 1970), p.251.

22 *Flutes of Autumn*, p.52.

23 *Flutes of Autumn*, p.65.

24 *Flutes of Autumn*, p.65.

25 'The Art of Poetry no. 14', p.2.

26 *Flutes of Autumn*, p.60.

27 *Flutes of Autumn*, p.60.

28 *Hill of Kronos*, p.115.

29 *Hill of Kronos*, p.115.

30 'The Art of Poetry no. 14', p.33. Other quotations in this paragraph from the same article.

31 *Flutes of Autumn*, p.135.

32 *Light Garden*, p.110.

33 *Light Garden*, p.25.

34 *Light Garden*, pp.29 (script), 49 (*stupas*).

35 *Light Garden*, p.221.

36 Nicholas Shakespeare, *Bruce Chatwin* (London, 1999), p.227.

37 Shakespeare, p.222.

38 Shakespeare, p.227.

39 *Light Garden*, p.59.

40 *Light Garden*, p.68.

41 *Light Garden*, p.166.

42 *Light Garden*, p.171.

43 *Light Garden*, p.204.

44 *Light Garden*, p.188.

45 *Flutes of Autumn*, p.149.

46 *Hill of Kronos*, pp.202–3.

47 *Hill of Kronos*, p.14.

48 *Hill of Kronos*, p.7.

49 *Hill of Kronos*, p.203.

50 *Hill of Kronos*, p.50.

51 *Hill of Kronos*, p.19.

52 *Hill of Kronos*, p.116.

53 *Hill of Kronos*, pp.22, 49.

54 *Flutes of Autumn*, p.126.

55 *Flutes of Autumn*, p.132.

56 *Flutes of Autumn*, p.139.

57 Peter Levi, *Pausanias* (Penguin, 1971, revised 1979), p.3.

58 *Hill of Kronos*, p.31.

59 *Hill of Kronos*, p.8.

60 *Hill of Kronos*, p.181.

61 *Hill of Kronos*, p.152.

62 *Hill of Kronos*, p.186.

63 *Flutes of Autumn*, p.98.

64 *Flutes of Autumn*, p.152.

65 *Flutes of Autumn*, p.151.

66 *Flutes of Autumn*, p.142.

67 *Flutes of Autumn*, p.40.

68 *Flutes of Autumn*, p.93.

69 *Flutes of Autumn*, p.159.

70 'The Art of Poetry no. 14', p.23.

71 *Evening Standard*, 25 April 1988.

72 *London Review of Books*, vol. 10, no. 11 (2 June 1988).

73 'The Art of Poetry no. 14', p.25

74 *Flutes of Autumn*, p.128.

75 *Flutes of Autumn*, p.128.

76 'The Art of Poetry no. 14', p.7.

77 Peter Levi, *Viriditas* (London, 2001), p.49.

78 Peter Levi, *The Echoing Green* (London, 1983), p.28.

79 Translations from the Penguin Classics edition of Thucydides, by Rex Warner.

80 Dilys Powell, *The Villa Ariadne* (London, 1973), p.12.

81 Antony Beevor, *Crete: The Battle and the Resistance* (London, 1991), p.12.

82 Smith-Hughes, p.1.

83 Beevor, p.12.

84 Beevor, p.11.

85 'Lit. Hum.' is short for *Literae Humaniores*, 'more refined studies', and is the proper name for the second part of Oxford's classics degree.

86 Details from Harry Mount's article 'A Few Things Pointy-Heads Should Know', *New Statesman*, 4 October 1999.

87 Powell, p.113.
88 Beevor, p.3.
89 Powell, p.130 ('obstinate romantic'); Beevor, p.26 (bandit leaders).
90 *Final Report*, p.3; Powell, p.104.
91 Public Record Office, *SOE Syllabus: Lessons in Ungentlemanly Warfare, World War II.*
92 Powell, p.113.
93 *Final Report*, p.12.
94 *Final Report*, p.13 (Tom's mission), p.18 (DSO).
95 Powell, p.165.
96 Dunbabin MS.
97 Dunbabin MS.
98 George Psychoundakis, *The Cretan Runner: His Story of the German Occupation* (London, 1955), p.101.
99 Dunbabin MS.
100 Dunbabin MS.
101 Powell, p.165.
102 Dunbabin MS.
103 Psychoundakis, p.185.
104 Powell, p.162.
105 Powell, pp.166 ff.
106 Dunbabin MS.
107 *Final Report*, p.39.
108 Dunbabin MS.
109 *Final Report*, p.20.
110 *Final Report*, p.14.
111 Powell, p.165.
112 Beevor, p.97; Smith-Hughes, p.3.
113 *Final Report*, p.32.
114 *Final Report*, p.30.
115 Smith-Hughes, p.6.
116 Psychoundakis, p.173.
117 Psychoundakis, p.114.
118 *Final Report*, pp.46, 49.
119 Powell, p.171.
120 *Final Report*, p.41.
121 Powell, p.175; in *Ill Met by Moonlight*, p.130, Lindsay Moss writes, 'Still no news of Tom Dunbabin. I wonder what's happened to him?'

122 Psychoundakis, p.88.

123 *Final Report*, p.14.

124 *Final Report*, p.33 (*Nikê*), p.59 (*Deltion*).

125 Beevor, pp.320 ff.

126 Psychoundakis, p.216.

127 Beevor, p.273.

128 Beevor, p.273.

129 Beevor, p.321.

130 *Western Greeks*, p.ix.

131 *Western Greeks*, vi.

132 *Western Greeks*, vi.

133 *Western Greeks*, vii.

134 Public Record Office, *SOE Syllabus: Lessons in Ungentlemanly Warfare, World War II*, p.366.

135 Beevor, p.324.

136 Beevor, p.325.

137 Beevor, p.316.

138 Smith-Hughes, p.5.

139 Smith-Hughes, p.5.

140 *Final Report*, p.50.

141 Smith-Hughes, p.5; *Final Report*, p.18.

142 Smith-Hughes, p.7.

143 *Final Report*, p.31.

144 *Final Report*, p.33.

145 *Final Report*, p.66.

146 Smith-Hughes, p.7.

147 *Final Report*, pp.36 ff.

148 Smith-Hughes, p.7.

149 Smith-Hughes, p.7.

150 Beevor, p.324.

151 *Final Report*, p.52.

152 *Final Report*, p.65.

153 Tacitus, *Annals* XIV.8.

154 Morwood, *A Latin Grammar* (Oxford, 1999).

155 Joshua Arthurs, 'Fascism as "Heritage" in Contemporary Italy', in Andrea Mammone and Giuseppe A. Veltri, eds, *Italy Today: The Sick Man of Europe* (London, 2010).

SUPPORTERS

Unbound is a new kind of publishing house. Our books are funded directly by readers. This was a very popular idea during the late eighteenth and early nineteenth centuries. Now we have revived it for the internet age. It allows authors to write the books they really want to write and readers to support the writing they would most like to see published.
The names listed below are of readers who have pledged their support and made this book happen. If you'd like to join them, visit: www.unbound.co.uk.

Georgina Adam
Beatrice Aidin
Silja Nyboe Andersen
Peter Andrew
Tom Atkins
Clare Axton
Nick Baker
Emma Bal
Ann Ballinger
Jason Ballinger
Peri Batliwala
Adam Bedford
Diana Ben-Aaron
Michelangelo Bendandi
Margot Bennett-Mathieson
Shyam Bhatt
Raphaelle Bischoff

Richard J. Blake
David Blanc
Robin Block
Claire Bodanis
Jaime Martínez Bowness
Susie Boyt
Jon Bradfield
Joely Brammer
Rosalyn Breedy
Martin Brookes
Francesca Brooks
Close Brothers
Ismene Brown
Julia Buckley
Joseph Burne
Katrina Burroughs
Aslan Byrne

Collette Call
Giulia Cambieri
Robert & Claire Cambray
Sebastian Cameron
Xander Cansell
Simon Carroll
Alvin Caudwell
Lord Chadlington
Sandra Cheetham
David Child
Ana Victoria Chiu
Luuk Christiaens
Clare Christian
Julian Christopher
Nick Clark
Phil Clarke
Sharon Anne Clayton
Martin Clist
Philip Coakley
Philip Connor
Fidelma Cook
Holly Cook
Marta Cooper
Joseph Cotterill
Laura Cowen
John Crawford
Alan Crease
Judith Crichton
Alison Crutchley
Adam Dant
Harriet Fear Davies
Joshua Davis
Miranda Dechazal
Alex Delaney

Sean Derbyshire
Joy Lo Dico
Catherine Dixon
Wendalynn Donnan
Ned Donovan
Adam D'Souza
David Dunbabin
John Dunbabin
Vivienne Dunstan
David Easton
Thomas Eccleshare
Simon Edmond
Patricia Elliott
Mark Ellwood
Brian English
Sinéad Esler
Mark Evans
Paul Fahey
Gillian Fenner
David Field
Debbie Fine
Charlie Finnegan
Neil Fisher
Molly Flatt
Frank Fletcher
Jo Foley
Genevieve Ford-Saville
Isobel Frankish
Felicity Frith
Lauren Fulbright
Sam Gallivan
Rahul Gandhi
Amro Gebreel
Melanie Gerlis

Jo Gibson
David Gillespie
Penelope Girardet
Susan Godfrey
Ariel Sergio Goekmen
Ben Goldsmith
Andrew Gonsalves
Thomas Goodhead
Chris Gostick
Charles Gothard
Charlie Gould
Niven Govinden
James Grant-Morris
Amy Gray
Rachel Grigg
Daniel Hahn
Sophie Hall
Celia Hallpike
Mark Hammond
Alex Hanrahan
Sharron & Stephen Harris
Louise Harvey-Miller
Simon Haslam
Sophie Hay
Lisa Hayter
Claire Henley
Linda Hepper
Joshi Herrmann
Rachael Herron
Paula Higgleton
Dorothy Hill
Alexander S Hoare
Trevor Hudson
Melinda Hughes

Owen Hutchins
Rivka Isaacson
Harriet Israel
Paul Jabore
Mike Jakeman
Mike and Paula Jeffers
Tiffany Jenkins
Marjorie Johns
Max Johnson
Katie Jones
Marina Jones
Joseph Kennedy
Sara Ketteley
Anna Khay
Patrick Kidd
David Kilshaw
Daniela Laatz
Bharti Lalwani
David Learner
Rich Lennon
Ella Lister
Úna Ní Loingsigh
Dan Loose
Chris Lord
Jelle van Lottum
Penny Lovell
Anna Lundberg
Nick Maclean
Kate Maltby
Barbara Mann
Dan Marks
Norka Martinez Luque
Tom Masters
Louise Matthews

Michelle Matthews

Richard Mawdsley

Richard Jacob Mayne

Karen McAleer

Sophie McBain

Louisa McCarthy

Anne McElvoy

Philip McEvansoneya

John McLeod

Aven McMaster

Bob McQuillen

Vanella Mead

Anouschka Menzies

Paul Mesquitta

Carly-Jay Metcalfe

Mark Meynell

Anna Mikhailova

Coline Milliard

Stuart Mitchell

John Mitchinson

Llewelyn Morgan

Nigel Moore

Alfonso Moreno

Stephen Morrall

Kenneth Morrison

Michael Mosbacher

Daryl Moughanni

Hannah Musgrave

Ash Nagesh

Carlos Navato

David Nolan

Kevin O'Connor

Georgia Odd

James Olley

Alan Ong

Chris Owen

Thomas Oxenham

Dominic Parker

Giovanna Paternó

Guy Paterson

Sarah Patmore

Matthew Paton

Alex Peake-Tomkinson

Pauline Pearson

Frances Platt

Justin Pollard

Alex Preston

David Quentin

Faisel Rahman

Sean Rainey

Matthew Railton

Noor Rassam

Mandana Ruane

Ellen Richardson

Naomi Richmond-Swift

Oliver Rivers

Laura Roberts

Pamela Rockwood

Viscount and Viscountess
Rothermere

Rick Roxburgh

Ian Runacres

John Ryan

Theo Rycroft

David Scott

Emma Scutt

Andrew Seto

Nur El Shami

Andy Shaw
Melanie Shaw
John Sheehan
Arsim Shillova
Robert Shrimsley
Rachael Simmons
Eric Sinclair
Keith Sleight
Elaine Smith
Deborah Smithies
A S H Smyth
Philip Spedding
Natalie & Graham Spero
Ollie Spero
Randi Spray
Karen Squire
Serena Stallard
Beverly Stark
Henriette Stavis
Alastair Stewart
Candida Stevens
Tom Stevens
James Strachan
James Suenson-Taylor
Calum Sutton
Susan Swabey
SyKhalid SyKhalid
Oliver Taplin
Stephanie Theodore

Ken Thomson
Philippa Thomson
Amanda Thurman
Michelle Tupy
Justin Tunstall
Mike and Lesley Thurman
Simon Tyler
Katherine Usher
Mark Vent
Olivia Vinden
Katharine Vine
Jo W
Clementine Wallop
Sophie Welch
Emma Wheeler
Anne Wheelhouse
Robert Whelan
Hilary Whitney
Matthias Williams
Elly Williamson
Keeley Wilson
Iwan Wirth
Gretchen Woelfle
Alice Woods
Stacey Woods
Steve Woodward
Dr Kenneth Wright
Milo Yiannopoulos